First Published in 2001 by Authentic
USA   1820 Jet Stream Dr., Colorado Springs, CO
80921 authentic@us.ibs-stl.org or www.authenticbooks.com
UK   9 Holdom Avenue, Bletchley, Milton Keynes,
Bucks, MK1 1QR www.authenticmedia.co.uk
India   Logos Bhavan, Medchal Road, Jeedimetla
Village, Secunderabad 500 055, A.P.

ISBN-13: 978-1-932805-91-8
ISBN-10: 1-932805-91-5

Worldwide co-edition organised and produced by
Lion Hudson plc
WILKINSON HOUSE, JORDAN HILL ROAD,
OXFORD, OX2 8DR, England
Tel: +44 (0) 1865 302750
Fax: +44 (0) 1865 302757

Printed in Singapore

Window on the World

When we pray
God works

**Daphne Spraggett with
Jill Johnstone**

Authentic

COLORADO SPRINGS · MILTON KEYNES · HYDERABAD

Contents

Introduction

Muskaan and I slipped off our shoes outside a simple village church in India. We joined the sari-clad ladies sitting together on the floor on one side of the church and chatted with them until the service began.

The pastor began by thanking God for his great love and for sending his Son Jesus to die on the cross so that we might be forgiven our sins and have our hearts made clean. He thanked God that Jesus is our special friend who is always ready to help everyone who trusts in him. I was excited because wherever we go in the world we meet people who love Jesus and belong to his great family.

The pastor then prayed for the people in the village and the millions of others in India who know nothing about God's love. And I was reminded that although there are more than 2,015,743,000 Christians in the world, there are many more people who have never heard about God's love or that he sent Jesus to be their Savior. How will they hear about him? I don't know, but I do know that God wants us – you and me – to pray for them.

About this book

There are about 230 countries in our world, and the people who live in them belong to thousands of smaller groups that speak different languages and have different customs. These are all called people groups. In India alone there are at least 4,635 people groups and 1,652 different languages.

In this book you will read about some of these countries and people groups. There are chapters, too, about special groups like missionaries' children, street children and refugees. Each chapter has stories, information and pictures to help you learn a little about them. When you have read a chapter, find out more about the country or people group by reading books and magazines, watching news and educational programs on TV, looking on the Internet and asking questions. The more you know and understand, the better you can pray!

God has answered lots of prayers since the first edition of this book was written, so I have included some things to thank God for. As you pray, keep your eyes and ears open for the answers. Your prayers are helping to change countries, people groups, situations and individuals. That's exciting! And remember to thank God for answering your prayers.

Why should we pray?

People often say that God could work without our prayers because he is the King of kings and Lord of lords. So why should we pray? In Luke 10:2 Jesus told his disciples, "Ask the Lord of the harvest to send out workers into his harvest field." God wants us to pray because he wants us to share in his work in the world.

Some of the countries in this book have been changed, or are being changed, because people prayed and went on praying – sometimes for years and years. Albania, China, Mongolia and Russia are just a few of them.

To help you pray

Prayer is simply talking with God. We can pray anywhere, at any time and about anything. We don't have to use special words, close our eyes or put our hands together. I often pray when I'm walking or working or when I wake up in the middle of the night.

Remember, the more we pray and learn to listen to God, the more we get to know and love him. He wants us to pray because, when we do, we are working with him to change the world.

There are times when we pray but God doesn't seem to answer our prayers. Sometimes it's because we've done things that haven't pleased him. If we've said or done things to hurt others or been selfish or forgotten to help others, we have to make these things right and ask God to forgive us. Then he hears and answers our prayers (Psalm 66:18).

We have to remember, too, that Satan wants people and countries to belong to him and not to God. He even tempted Jesus to do things his way, not God's way (Matthew 4:1–11). So don't give up, but keep praying!

When nothing seems to happen, remember that prayer is like planting a seed in the ground. For weeks and months you may see nothing, but a lot is happening underground. Keep on trusting God, because one day you will see the answer to your prayers (Matthew 21:22) just as one day you'll see the plant begin to grow.

So … let's pray and work with God to change the world!

To Help You

■ On pages 198 to 209 there are short chapters telling you a little about animism, Buddhism, Christianity, Hinduism, Islam and Judaism.

■ You will find the meanings of difficult words in this book in the Word List on pages 214 to 217.

■ There is a map of the world on pages 112 and 113.

■ On page 210 you will find some ideas to help you, your family and Sunday school get involved in missionary work now.

■ If you want to learn more about the countries and people groups you are praying for, turn to pages 212 and 213 where there is a list of Christian agencies who might be able to help you. This is what to do:

● If you want to ask about a people group, find out first what country or countries they're in. Then look at the list on page 212 to see which agencies may be able to help you.

● If it is listed, look on their web site.

● If you write a letter, don't ask about more than one or two people groups or countries at a time. Say what you want to know, and why. Ask what materials they have and tell them how you will use it (for example, at home, Sunday school or club).

● Make sure that you write at least a month before you need materials or information. (This is important because they could have lots of requests at the same time, or they might need to send your letter to someone else to answer.) Remember that it costs money to help you, so be ready to pay for what they send you.

A Country at War with Itself

Mountains and deserts

Afghanistan, a land of great mountains and scorching desert, is in the heart of Central Asia. The climate is harsh with hot, dry summers and bitterly cold winters.

Invasions and war

Fierce battles have been fought in Afghanistan for hundreds of years. The Persians, ancient Greeks, Mongols, Turks and, much later, the British and the Soviets, have all invaded Afghanistan. To make matters worse, there has always been fighting between the many different tribes in the country.

Afghan Freedom Fighters

Fact file

Area: 251,825 sq. mi. (a little more than twice the size of the British Isles)

Population: 22,720,416

Capital: Kabul

Religion: Islam

Languages: Pushto; Dari

Chief exports: Carpets; fruit; cotton; gemstones; opium

In 1978, the Soviet Union invaded Afghanistan and millions of Afghans fled to Iran and Pakistan. In 1988, the Soviets withdrew their forces.

No peace

"Why don't we have peace? What's it like to live without fighting?" Saud asked his father.

"Unfortunately, I don't know what that's like either," his father replied. "The most recent fighting started when the Communists came. We fought a *jihad* against them."

"What's a *jihad*?" asked Saud.

"It's a holy war that we as Muslims fight to defend our country against people who don't worship Allah. Many of us became *mujahidin* guerrillas to get rid of the Communists. A guerrilla fights for a special cause against the government, and a *mujahidin* guerrilla fights for the cause of Islam," his father told him. "Our *jihad* was successful, and the Communists left in 1989. But each group of *mujahidin* wanted to have all the power. So the fighting went on.

Then, in 1996, a group called the Taliban took over the country. Their name means 'seekers after truth,' and there's much less fighting now, but we have to follow lots of very strict Islamic rules."

"That's why girls aren't allowed to go to school, isn't it?" Saud asked. "Someone said that in the boys' school we have to spend a lot more time studying the Koran than they used to. I can't go up to the next class unless I pass my Islamic exams."

Pakistan is now home to these Uzbek refugee boys from Afghanistan

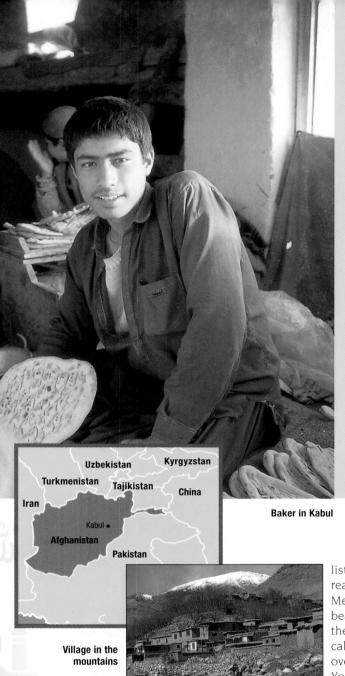

Baker in Kabul

To help you pray for Afghanistan

You can thank God for:

- the secret believers in Afghanistan.
- the New Testaments translated into Pushto and Dari.
- the aid workers caring for those who are injured, blind, poor, sick and needy.

You can ask God:

- to bring peace to this war-torn land.
- to help and protect those who are translating the Scriptures into other languages spoken in Afghanistan.
- to give understanding to people who listen to Christian radio broadcasts, often in secret, so that they can know Jesus and the peace he brings.
- that the different groups who are fighting for power will realize that they are destroying both their country and their people.

Village in the mountains

You can read more about the Hazara and Uzbek people on pages 76 and 174

"Yes, the Taliban have changed what you have to study and they closed all the girls' schools in Kabul. And it's because of the Taliban that your mother can't work or go out without covering herself with a *chaderi*. She also has to have one of the men from our family with her wherever she goes. Women whose husbands and sons have died in the fighting often don't have enough money to buy food for their children," Saud's father explained. "If we kept strictly to all the rules we wouldn't watch television, listen to music or read foreign books. Men have to grow beards and wear these long shirts, called *shalwar kamiz*, over baggy trousers. Your little sister isn't even supposed to play with dolls or teddies because they look like living beings."

Help for victims of war

Six-year-old Ramazan saw a truck loaded with sacks of wheat coming down the street. He ran to gather a few grains that had trickled out from a hole in one of the sacks. He was all alone. His parents and brother had been killed when a mortar shell destroyed their house.

There are many children like Ramazan. Aid workers from around the world are working in Afghanistan to help the poor, orphans and sick and hungry children, as well as those who have been blinded or badly injured during the 20 years of war.

God answers prayer

Ten days after being burnt in an accident, Hyerloh's feet were blistered and infected, and they felt like they were still on fire. An aid worker stopped when she heard him cry out from his father's shop, "Please help me!" She didn't have any medicine, but she prayed that God would heal his feet.

Three weeks later, she saw Hyerloh again. "Look! look!" he exclaimed. "My feet are all better!" There was no sign that they had been so badly burned.

"That's wonderful! Let's thank God for answering our prayers and healing you," the lady said to Hyerloh. She told him about Jesus, God's son, who loved him and had healed many people while he lived on earth.

God Answers Prayer

One of Europe's poorest countries

The Albanians call their country Shqiperi, "the land of the eagle," and they have a double-headed eagle on their flag. That's not surprising, because if you climbed the rugged mountains in Albania you would see many eagles circling overhead.

Albania has many natural resources, including chrome, oil, natural gas, copper and iron – so it could be a rich country. But it's actually one of Europe's poorest countries. How could this be?

Selling peppers in the market

Italy

Yugoslavia

Macedonia

• Tirane

Albania

Greece

Dark days

In 1944 Albania became a Communist country. For the next 41 years a man called Enver Hoxha ruled Albania. He didn't allow Albanians to travel abroad or have things like cars and fridges. He forced them to live with very little food and few supplies. People couldn't worship in mosques or churches, say prayers or own Muslim or Christian books. Parents were even forbidden to give their children Muslim or Christian names.

God's people all around the world heard about the sad situation there, but they weren't allowed to go to Albania, so they prayed. And, after many years of praying, in 1991 the Communist government was forced to resign. Immediately people from other countries were ready to take supplies into Albania. Christians were ready, too, to share Jesus' love with the

people of Albania.

They were shocked to discover the terrible conditions in which many Albanians were living. Hospitals were poorly equipped and had no medicines. The people often didn't have enough money to buy food for their families. Sad, starving children filled orphanages and children's homes, with very few people to care for them.

Sometimes aid workers felt like they were stepping back in time. Out in the countryside villages had no electricity or running water. In Tirana, the capital, there were more donkey carts and bicycles than cars.

God's light

The new government allowed Christians and Muslims to worship and speak about their beliefs. Before the Communists came to power, Albania

Fact file

Area: 11,100 sq. mi.

Population: 3,113,434

Capital: Tirana

Language: Modern Albanian

Religion: Islam

Chief exports: Iron ore; petroleum; fruit; vegetables

was the only Muslim country in Europe. Now Muslims from other countries are offering help to people in Albania and teaching them about Islam.

Christians from many countries have helped care for children in orphanages and shared the good news and hope of Jesus with many Albanians. Now there are several thousand Albanians, mainly young people, who follow Jesus.

 ## To help you pray for Albania

You can thank God for:

- each Albanian boy, girl and grownup who follows Jesus.

- the way that Albanian Christians, even though they are poor themselves, showed his kindness and love to the refugees from Kosovo by helping and caring for them.

You can ask God:

- to encourage all Christians to learn more about him and to share his love with everyone.

- to teach Christians that even though many of them are poor, he blesses all those who give to others.

- to help Christian workers get jobs for the refugees so that they will have enough money to care for their families.

- to give his strength to leaders in the churches as they teach people from the Bible and encourage them to follow Jesus.

- to bring peace and hope to the people of Albania and give them leaders who will rule the country wisely and fairly.

Street in Tirana, the capital of Albania

You can speak Albanian

Hello is "Tungjatjeta" (toon-jat-yeta)

How are you? is "Se jeni?" (see-yenee)

Where are you going? is "Ku po shkoni?" (koo-paw-shkawnee)

Goodbye is "Mirupafshim" (meer-oo-pafsheem)

Showing God's love

Although they were very poor themselves, the Albanian Christians wanted to help these refugees. In Tirana, the churches gave them food, water, clothing and love. Other Christians provided homes for mothers with young babies.

Niki and his family were refugees. Niki had been born with a hole in his heart and the journey from Kosovo had made him very weak. He had to be carried everywhere. Christians caring for Niki and his family prayed that God would work a miracle and send help for him. One day,

there was a fax from the International Red Cross. "Bring Niki to Tirana tomorrow," it said. "We've found a group who will pay for his medical treatment." Two days later Niki had a successful operation in Paris. God answered prayers for Niki's physical heart to be healed. With Jesus in their hearts, Niki and his family will live forever.

Collecting water with a donkey

More dark days

In 1997, thousands of Albanians lost all their money and blamed the government. People lost their homes and belongings. There was so much crime that thousands of people fled the country. Many Christian workers also had to leave Albania for a while.

A year later war broke out in Kosovo, a province of nearby Yugoslavia. Although the Serbs claimed Kosovo for themselves, most of the people living there are Albanians. The Serbs killed hundreds of Kosovar Albanians and destroyed their homes. Thousands of them fled into Albania to escape.

Azeri

The Fire Guardians

Farzali lives in the city of Baku, the capital of a country on the Caspian Sea called Azerbaijan. His people, the Azeri, are Muslims. A people called the Armenians, who have a Christian background, also live in Azerbaijan. During the 1990s there was fighting between the Azeri and the Armenians, and many Armenians left the country.

Are we Muslims?

Farzali was excited when his friend Babeli invited him to come to his house after school. "I'll ask my mother, but I'm sure I can come," he said. "I'm so glad there isn't any more fighting with the Armenians. I used to get so scared, and my mother never let me go anywhere without my big brother!"

📋 Fact file

Main countries:
Azerbaijan (the Azeri make up 83% of the total population)
Iran: 8,130,000 Azeri
Iraq: 38,000 Azeri

Population of Azerbaijan: 7,734,015

Capital of Azerbaijan: Baku

Religion: Islam

Language: Azeri

Main occupations: Oil and natural gas industries

Children from a Christian family

Do you know?

- Before oil was discovered in the Gulf States, more than half the world's oil supplies came from oil fields near Baku.

- The people of Azerbaijan built the first oil tanker in the world and the first oil pipeline (which was made of wood).

- Natural gas leaks from the earth in Azerbaijan, causing fires that burn spontaneously.

- Azerbaijan was once a republic of the old Soviet Union and is now a member of the Commonwealth of Independent States.

Babeli nodded. "My mother was the same. I loved going to Samweli's house to play, but she never wanted me to go because his family was Armenian. She said they would try to make me a Christian. Samweli and his family had to go to live in Armenia when the fighting got really bad. I miss him. Do you think it's so bad to be a Christian?"

Farzali frowned. "I think it would be terrible. My great-grandfather says it's unforgivable for an Azeri to become a Christian."

You can thank God for:

- the fact that the fighting has stopped between the Azeri and the Armenians.

- the few Azeri Christians.

- the New Testament and children's Bible in their language.

You can ask God:

- to send Christians to Azerbaijan to teach what the Bible says.

- to show the Azeri people that only Jesus can give them the holiness and purity they want so much.

- to help the Christians planning Azeri radio broadcasts to answer the questions Azeri people have about Jesus.

- to bring Azeri to believe in Jesus.

Workers on an oil field in Azerbaijan

Fire guardians

The ancient Greeks called the Azeri "fire guardians" because they worshipped fire. Farzali's cousin even wore a fire-red dress on her wedding day. Farzali was confused and wondered which was true – the old Azeri religion, Islam or the Christian religion? He knew they couldn't all be true.

Clean and pure

Azeri want to be made clean and pure, but only Jesus can do that for them. Few Azeri people have heard about Jesus, but now the New Testament and a children's Bible have been printed in their language, and they can listen to Christian radio. Now is the time to pray that Jesus will take away Farzali's confusion.

"Why do they make such a big fuss?" Babeli asked. "My family all say we're Muslims, but we never go to the mosque."

Farzali wasn't sure if his family were Muslims or not. His great-grandfather certainly was, and he read the Koran every evening. But his father never read it. He was more concerned about politics and money. He said that the government was rich because of all the oil, but most of the people were still poor.

The next day, Farzali went with his father and great-grandfather to visit his uncle's farm. Farzali loved his great-grandfather. He was over 100 years old, but he was still very strong.

Farzali's uncle told them, "Today is a special day when we speak with our ancestors and bathe in the river that flows from the mountains. Before the Azeri became Muslims we worshipped fire and our ancestors. A few of us still keep some of these ancient ceremonies."

Farzali bathed in the river. Even great-grandfather lowered himself into the cold water. Farzali wondered if he really was in touch with his ancestors.

Muslim schoolgirls in Azerbaijan

Balinese

From the Island of the Gods

A beautiful island

Anne thought Bali was the most beautiful place she'd ever seen. It had sandy beaches, brightly colored flowers, rice fields of green and gold and thousands of temples. She could see the mountains in the distance – some of them were volcanoes. She had even seen a performance of the graceful legong dances, which tell the stories of gods and demons, witches and kidnapped princesses. The dancers had worn dresses of gold, scarlet and green, with headdresses glittering with gold and bright, tropical flowers on their shiny black hair. And all the Balinese people she'd met had such gentle, smiling faces.

It's no wonder that more than 1,500,000 tourists visit Bali, a small island in the long necklace of Indonesian islands, each year. Visitors often call it "the island of the gods" or "the last paradise."

Traditional dancers

Invitation to the gods

There are thousands of temples on Bali, because the Balinese are Hindus and worship many gods. The Balinese had many gods long before they became Hindus, and they still worship these gods, too. Every day they give small offerings to the spirits of their ancestors who have died. They believe it's very important to be on their good side.

At the beginning of every year (the year in Bali is only 210 days long), the Balinese hold a special feast for the gods. At this feast they bring their gods out from their shrines and invite them to live in objects made of wood, stone and coins for a while. The people ask the gods to join them in feasting and dancing for ten days. At the end of that

time, the gods are put back in their shrines until the next ceremony.

Spirits of the ancestors

The Balinese believe that the spirits of their gods and ancestors live in the mountains. When they build their houses, they make sure that the room with the altar for the spirits faces the mountains.

The Balinese are very concerned about what happens to them when they die. Sometimes a family will save money for several years so they can build an elaborate funeral tower and hold a cremation ceremony.

They believe that the soul of the dead person can't take its place with the spirits of all the other ancestors in the mountains until after such a ceremony.

Jesus' power

There aren't many Balinese Christians yet. Sometimes their Hindu neighbors treat Christians badly because they're afraid that their gods will be angry if people follow Jesus.

Eight-year-old Nyoman was afraid. Some people in the village had done mean things to his family because

Do you know?

The Balinese have a legend that says that their beautiful island was once flat and nothing would grow there. When the island of Java became Muslim, the Hindu gods moved the short distance to Bali. They needed mountains where they could live, so they created some. Then water from these mountains made the island fertile.

they're Christians. "Why won't they let us have water for our fields? They don't want to have anything to do with us. What did we do wrong?" he asked his parents. "The other kids make fun of me and won't play with me. They even said that some night, when I'm asleep, the gods will come and punish me because I don't follow them."

"Don't be afraid, Nyoman," his father replied. "Jesus has promised that he'll always be with us. He's more powerful than anything or anyone who wants to harm us. People in the village think the gods are angry because we've become Christians. They want us to turn back to our old gods. But we know that with Jesus we don't have to fear their gods. Jesus will look after us even when we're asleep. Let's pray, Nyoman, and ask him to take away your fears."

Christians often try to show Jesus' love to their Hindu neighbors by helping them in practical ways. They want them to know that Christianity isn't a boring religion that belongs to white people, so Christians are beginning to tell Bible stories the Balinese way, through dance and mime.

One by one, Balinese are coming to know Jesus as the friend who is always with them. And those who follow Jesus are praying that many more Balinese will realize Jesus is far greater and more powerful than all the thousands of gods they keep in their shrines and bring out on special occasions.

Fact file

Country: Indonesia

Location: The island of Bali (three-quarters of a mile east of Java)

Numbers: About 2,000,000

Languages: Balinese; Indonesian

Religions: Hinduism; animism

Occupations: Mainly farmers growing rice, maize and coffee; weaving and wood carving

To help you pray for the Balinese

You can thank God for:

- the Balinese who are coming to know Jesus as their friend.

- the Bible translation in Balinese.

- the groups that are using Balinese-style dance and mime to tell the Christian story.

You can ask God:

- to help Christians show Jesus' love to their Hindu friends and neighbors.

- to show the Balinese that he is so much more powerful than all the gods they worship.

- to help Christians like Nyoman know that evil spirits can't harm them when they trust in Jesus.

- for whole families to come to know Jesus so that children can learn about Jesus when they're young.

Lake temple

Baloch

Carpet Weavers of Pakistan

Hard work

Abdullah tossed the freshly cut wheat onto the bullock cart. "Not a bad harvest this year," he thought. He looked over at his grandfather, with his wrinkled face and white beard, wearing his turban and long homespun shirt over baggy trousers. Abdullah knew his grandfather was glad he was there to help, because he couldn't manage the small farm on his own anymore.

Abdullah's father and his brother Ghaus had gone to the city of Karachi to find work. Even though Abdullah was only 12 years old, they left him in charge of doing most of the farm work. It was especially difficult because of the fierce heat in the summer and the bitter cold in the winter.

Warm quilts for sale in the bazaar

The old bullock plodded into the high-walled courtyard leading to the house Abdullah's father had built. The house was much better than the shack made out of reeds where they used to live, or the goat-hair tent that had

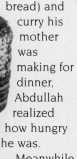

been his grandfather's home.

Abdullah's sisters were sitting at the carpet looms, where they worked most of the day. Their nimble fingers had to tie thousands of knots as they wove beautiful carpets. The pretty designs had been passed down through the family from one generation to the next. When he smelled the *nan* (wheat bread) and curry his mother was making for dinner, Abdullah realized how hungry he was.

Meanwhile, in Karachi, Abdullah's brother

Ghaus lay half-conscious in the gutter. His father hadn't seen him for months, but he didn't want the rest of the family to know. Every day, as soon as he finished work at his kebab stall on a busy street, he went looking for his son. Like thousands of other young people, Ghaus was taking drugs. His father was afraid that by the time he found him it might be too late to help him.

A rich province ... but a needy people

Abdullah's farm is in Balochistan, one of the four provinces in Pakistan. Balochistan has natural gas, copper, iron ore and coal, and there are lots of fish in the sea. But the Baloch people feel that the Pakistan government neglects them. They complain that Pakistan's other provinces use most of Balochistan's natural gas. They desperately need better roads and railways, clean water supplies and good health care and schools. Some Baloch people would like Balochistan to become an independent country.

Because they're poor and feel neglected, lots of Baloch have left the country areas to find work in Karachi or overseas. Since

 ## To help you pray for the Baloch

You can thank God for:

● the New Testament in Balochi.

You can ask God:

● for whole Baloch families – women and girls as well as men and boys – to follow Jesus.

● for Christians from other countries to teach reading and provide the Baloch with health care.

● to send caring Christians to reach out to the drug addicts in Karachi and show them that Jesus can help them.

● that the few Baloch Christians will tell others what Jesus has done for them.

● to help the team preparing radio broadcasts.

● that many Baloch will listen to the Christian radio broadcasts.

Do you know?

A Baloch proverb

"Strong water can flow uphill." (The powerful can do anything.)

Friendly Baloch boys

there aren't many schools in the mountainous countryside, very few Baloch learn to read.

The Baloch like to listen to programs in their own Baloch language from Radio Quetta (the capital of Balochistan). Some have started to tune in to Christian programs in Baloch and have written to the radio station to find out more about Jesus and what he taught.

The country of Pakistan is strongly Muslim. It's difficult for Christians to get into Balochistan to talk about Jesus, but about 15 young Baloch men have decided to follow Jesus. Christians find that their Baloch friends listen carefully when they explain the Bible to them. And the Baloch now have the New Testament in their own language.

How can Christians help the Baloch? They need jobs, health care and reading

lessons. Christians can show Jesus' love by trying to meet some of these needs. God recently healed some sick Baloch when Christians prayed for them. This miracle showed them that Jesus is all-powerful, and they decided to follow him.

21

One of the Poorest Countries on Earth

Fact file

Area: 55,600 sq. mi.

Population: 129,155,150

Capital: Dhaka

Language: Bengali

Religions: Islam; Hinduism

Chief exports: Jute; tea; clothes

Homeless

"What are going to do now?" Chandra cried. Scared to death, he sat close to his father on the pile of mud where their house used to be. He held a squawking chicken that was struggling to escape. Aziz, his father, gripped a small basket of rice. That was all they had managed to save when floodwaters from the huge Brahmaputra River, along with pounding rain and strong winds, had destroyed their home.

"We'll start again, somehow," Aziz sighed. *"The floods bring fresh soil so we can grow good crops, but the winds and heavy rains destroy everything. They kill people and take our homes and our cattle. Oh, if only I knew what's happened to your mother and little sister. We can only hope they're safe somewhere."* Aziz tried to reassure Chandra, fighting back his own tears.

Do you know?

Bangladesh grows the best jute in the world. It's used to make rope, mats and sacks. Jute is Bangladesh's most important export and its biggest source of income. Because other countries are now using more artificial fibers, like nylon, instead of jute, Bangladesh jute farmers are even poorer.

Floods and cyclones

Almost half of Bangladesh is made up of low-lying islands, most of them less than nine feet above sea level. It rains in Bangladesh for about six months every year – from May to October. Every year when the snows on the Himalayan Mountains melt, the water comes rushing down the mighty Ganges, Brahmaputra and Meghna rivers to the ocean. Every year the rivers burst their banks and flood the countryside, bringing fresh soil to the land. Every year homes and fields are washed away, and animals and people die. When a cyclone hits the country, the chaos and destruction are terrible.

It's no wonder that Bangladesh is one of the poorest countries in the world. There are so many rivers, so little land and so many people that it's also one of the most crowded countries on earth. Everyone, from the smallest child to the oldest grandfather, has to work hard just to live.

Despite the work of missionaries, there are still very few Christians in Bangladesh

A new nation

The country we call Bangladesh was once a part of India. In 1947, it became the eastern part of the new Muslim nation of Pakistan.

West Pakistan, a thousand miles away on the other side of India, governed this new country called East Pakistan. The people of East Pakistan felt the government wasn't fair to them, and civil war broke out in 1971. India fought on East Pakistan's side and helped it to become the new nation of Bangladesh.

Most Bangladeshis are Muslims, and some are Hindus. For more than 200 years, Christian missionaries have worked here. They've shown the people God's love by

To help you pray for Bangladesh

You can thank God for:

- the work of groups like Tearfund and Tearcraft.
- every Christian who is showing God's love to the people of Bangladesh.

You can ask God:

- to help the leaders of Bangladesh to be honest, wise and fair to both rich and poor people.
- to help Christians show God's love to the people of Bangladesh.
- that every young man and woman studying in Bible school will learn how to teach others about Jesus.
- to bring Christians to care for the many homeless children in Bangladesh.
- that men would have respect for women and stop violence against them.

Walking through flood water

Bangladesh
● Dhaka
● Chittagong
BAY OF BENGAL

Bangladesh
India
BAY OF BENGAL

(a part of Tearfund) helps many people there to earn a living. Maybe you've seen some of the beautiful jewelry or carvings from Third World countries like Bangladesh. You may even have bought a jute *sika* or a handmade card for your mother.

In Bangladeshi homes, *sikas* are used like shelves. It's quite easy to make a *sika*, but growing the jute and getting it ready for use is very hard work.

Shaheen and his family grow jute in one of their fields. "It grows in water, like rice," he explains, "but it's much taller than rice. A good crop will grow between nine and 12 feet high. The jute fibers are found inside each stalk.

"When it's time for harvest, the men and boys cut down the heavy stalks and bring them home by boat or ox-cart. The women arrange them in big, round stacks to dry. It smells terrible! When the jute is dry, everyone in the family has to help beat the stalks, until all the fibers come loose. Finally, it has to be spun.

teaching their children, caring for sick people and setting up hospitals and schools. They've done everything possible to help those suffering as a result of the many natural disasters, but there are still very few Bangladeshi Christians.

God uses many ways to help his people

About 25 years ago, a Christian visiting Bangladesh wanted to do something to help the poor people there. He realized that the Bangladeshis could use local materials to make items to sell in other countries. Now Tearcraft

"Christian groups often buy the jute and sell it to village women and girls who make *sikas*, bags and mats. My wife and daughters like making these things, and they're paid for everything they produce. Life has been so much easier since these groups started to help us. Sometimes, when they come to buy the things my family has made, they tell us about God's love and that he sent his Son Jesus to die on a cross for us and be our Savior. It's a wonderful story, and we'd like to know more about Jesus."

23

Beja

Frightened by the Evil Eye

What about the future?

Amna watched her grandmother carefully. Amna hoped she would be as wise as her grandmother someday. As they sat together on the palm matting outside their wooden house, her grandmother dropped five cowrie shells. She looked closely at the shape they made on the ground. Then she shook her head and scooped them up again.

"What's the matter?" Amna asked anxiously. "What do the shells say?" She knew that her family needed some good luck right now because her older sister, Khadija, was going to be married after the Idd (a Muslim festival). Khadija was worried. She was only 12 years old, and their parents had arranged her marriage to her cousin Ahmed.

Do you know?

To-Bedawiet is a very difficult language to learn and has not yet been written down. The group of Bejas and linguists who are working together to write it down will start by writing the Beja's ancient stories and poems.

"What's Ahmed like?" Amna asked Khadija, who was sitting behind her on the mat, patiently braiding Amna's frizzy hair. "Have you ever met him?"

"He's been here to talk about our marriage and drink *jabana* (Beja coffee) with our brothers, but I've never met him," Khadija replied. "He must be really old because he's been working for our uncle in Khartoum for a long time. It'll be so strange to go to live with his mother and sisters on the other side of town. I'll be very lonely without you, Amna." After the wedding Khadija had to stay with Ahmed's family, but because of their marriage customs she still wouldn't meet Ahmed face to face for another year.

Sometimes Khadija and Amna sit and listen to the conversation between their brothers. "I don't like it when they talk about the war between the north and south of the country," Amna said. "And I wish our eldest brother didn't have to go away to Eritrea just so he wouldn't get called into the army." Her brothers used a lot of Arabic words, and Amna wished they would just talk in their own language, To-Bedawiet, so she could understand what they were talking about.

Bound by fear

The Beja (*bay-juh*) are a group of tribes living in the eastern part of Africa that borders the Red Sea coast and stretches from southern Egypt through northern Sudan to

Map labels: Egypt, Saudi Arabia, BEJA, RED SEA, Sudan, AFRICA, Eritrea, Ethiopia

Beja nomad under a *howdah*

To help you pray for the Beja

You can thank God for:

- Sudanese Christians who want to tell others about Jesus.
- Christian radio broadcasts in Arabic and To-Bedawiet.
- the few Beja who decided to follow Jesus after reading the Bible in Arabic.
- the Beja man who hopes to translate the New Testament into To-Bedawiet.

You can ask God:

- to send help to the Beja, who often go hungry.
- that the Beja will accept help from Christians and understand God's love for them.
- to help those who are putting the To-Bedawiet language into writing.

Fact file

Countries: Northern Sudan; southern Egypt; Eritrea

Numbers: About 2,000,000

Occupations: Most are nomadic herdsmen, but many are settling in towns and villages.

Eritrea. There are about two million Beja. They have lived as nomads in this hot, dry, desert land and the windy Red Sea Hills for more than 4,000 years, looking for pasture for their herds of camels, cattle, sheep and goats. But it's a harsh place to live, and now some Beja are settling in the towns and villages. They keep to themselves and don't easily make friends with strangers.

The Beja are Muslims, but few of them really understand the Muslim faith or pray and fast according to the Muslim law. They're afraid of the evil eye and *jinns* (evil spirits) which, they believe, want to harm them. Life is very hard for the Beja because of their fear and superstition, as well as drought, famine and war.

Only a few Beja people have ever become Christians. In 1978, some Christian missionaries were given permission to bring medical care to the Beja. The Beja didn't want the missionaries to be there, and the local Beja leaders forced them to leave. The missionary team started to work in another area, but they were forced to leave again.

Grinding *dura* (sorghum)

A new friend

One day, as she was buying milk from the donkey man, Amna made a new friend. Nora came from a place hundreds of miles away, in the south of Sudan. Her father had been killed in the long war, and now she helped her mother selling tea by the roadside. They needed to earn money to buy food for the family and pay for her brothers to go to school.

Amna missed her sister so much that she was especially glad to have a new friend. "Nora," she asked, "what do the shells say about your future? Will you have to get married soon? Will our brothers be safe?"

Nora squeezed her hand. "Amna, please don't worry. God loves us all, and we can trust him to take care of us. We don't have to be worried and scared of the spirits all of the time. You're my friend, and I want you to know Jesus, who's my best friend."

Jesus died for the Beja as well as for you and me. Will the Beja listen to the message God wants them to hear? Will they ever know Jesus as their friend? Your prayers can help make this happen!

Land of the Thunder Dragon

The thunder dragon

Sangay had been looking forward to going to his first Buddhist festival, but now that he was finally there he was scared. Monks were dancing around wearing big ugly masks with bulging eyes and sharp teeth, and he didn't want them to get too close.

"Why is there a picture of a fire-breathing dragon on the flag and on the temple walls?" he asked.
Sangay's mother told him the story of the thunder dragon. "Have you heard the dragon roar when there's a storm?" she asked. "A very long time ago, there was a monk who wanted to build a monastery. When he found a good place to build this monastery, he heard thunder. He thought the thunder was a dragon roaring, so he named his monastery Druk, which means 'Thunder Dragon.' So our country is called Druk Yul, 'the Land of the Thunder Dragon,' and we are called Drukpas, 'the dragon people.'"

Sangay's parents are farmers. Because the land is covered with mountains and hills, they grow their rice and wheat in special terraced fields, which are flat areas built into the sides of the hills. Sangay helps his parents in the fields and with their goats. Sangay's big brother lives away from home in a town where he goes to school. Sangay would like to go to school with his brother, but it would cost too much money for them both to go. So Sangay stays home to help on the farm and is learning to read and write at a small school in the local monastery.

Snow leopards and festivals

Bhutan, the land of the Thunder Dragon, is a small country between China and India in the Himalaya mountains. The southern part of Bhutan is warm and humid, while in the northern part it's very cold. The Himalayas are the

Fact file

Area: 18,200 sq. mi.

Population: 2,123,970

Capital: Thimphu

Language: Dzongkha

Religion: Buddhism

Chief export: Timber

highest mountains in the world, and snow and ice always cover them. In the valleys between the mountains there are forests and mighty rivers. Black bears, tigers, red pandas and snow leopards are just a few of the rare animals found in Bhutan.

Dancers at a festival

Bhutan is a Buddhist kingdom, and the colorful temple festivals are important occasions

 ## To help you pray for Bhutan

You can thank God for:

- Christians from other countries who work in Bhutan.
- Christian parents and teachers who tell children about God's love and teach them how to be like Jesus.
- the people who are translating the New Testament into Dzongkha and other languages spoken in Bhutan.

You can ask God:

- to lead children who are sent to study in Christian schools in India to know Jesus.
- to bring Bhutanese students studying in other countries to meet Christians who will share the good news about Jesus with them.
- to give Christians in Bhutan the courage to share God's love with others.
- to help the people and leaders to be able to adjust to new ways.

Young Buddhist monks watching a festival performance

Prayer flags

Nepal · Thimphu · China · Bhutan · India · India · Bangladesh · Burma

Since Bhutan is a Buddhist kingdom, religion, culture and traditions play a big part in the peoples' lives. Buddhist religious ceremonies are held for every occasion.

Although it seems very strange to us, some men in Bhutan have several wives and some women have several husbands. The king of Bhutan, Jigme Singya Wangchuck, married four sisters on the same day. The

Bhutanese people can visit the king whenever they want to, to ask him a question or talk with him. About 30 people go to see him each day. The king wears a knee-length tunic called the *kho*. All Bhutanese men must also wear the *kho* whenever they leave the house. The women wear the *kira*, a dress made from one piece of cloth with a wide belt and fastened at the shoulders.

Talking about Jesus

When the king saw the crime and other bad things happening around

the world, he decided to try to protect his people from these things. So he let the people in Bhutan watch videos and listen to the radio, but no one was allowed to watch television until 1999. The king realized that what we watch and listen to affects the things we do, the way we treat other people and the way we think.

It's very expensive to travel in Bhutan, and only a few people are allowed to visit the country each year. Experts from other countries help Bhutan with medical care, farming and engineering. Some of these people that come to help are Christians, but they aren't allowed to talk to others about their faith in Jesus. No one knows how many Christians there are in Bhutan, but many people pray for Bhutan and we can see how God is answering those prayers. In the southern part of the country there are small groups of Christians. In Thimphu, the capital, there are house churches where people meet together secretly.

Bijago

Who Believe in a Great Spirit who Punishes Them

Temples and idols

The Bijagos Islands belong to Guinea-Bissau, a small West African country. The islands, with their white, sandy beaches, palm trees and brightly colored birds, are very beautiful. But the Bijago people are very poor. Many live in round houses made of mud with thatched roofs that are very dark inside. Since they can't grow good crops, they don't get enough to eat and they're sick most of the time, and their cattle are very weak.

Headgear worn by village men at carnival time

📋 **Fact file**

Population: About 24,500

Location: Bijagos Islands (Guinea-Bissau)

Religion: Animism

Occupations: Farming; fishing

The Bijago are animists. They believe in a Great Spirit who made them but who won't help them and sends punishment and disaster instead. They build temples of mud and thatch with altars in the middle surrounded by the fetishes and carved idols that the people worship. The Bijago are afraid of the *iran* (evil spirits) and hope that if they sacrifice animals and perform special ceremonies, these spirits won't harm them.

Moving house ... again!

"Why do we have to move to the island of Rubane every single rainy season?" Carlos complained. "Why can't we live here all the time? Why do we have to sacrifice an animal before we cut down the forest to make our fields? And why do we have to go there to plant our rice anyway?"

Carlos stood beside his father, asking question after question. His father had sharpened his *machete*, a big broad knife, and now he was catching the chickens and putting them into a woven palm-branch basket. Carlos glanced across at his mother. She was collecting all the pots and pans, the kerosene lamp, her grass skirts and everything else the family would need for the next six months. Everyone in the village was busy packing their belongings and gathering everything from their babies to their pigs and chickens.

"It's our custom, Carlos," his father said. "Rubane is a sacred place belonging to our village. The *iran* won't let us build our homes there, and they'll send trouble and sickness to our village if anyone dies there. That's why the witch doctor sacrifices an animal even before we start to cut down the forest. Don't you

Do you know?

A Bijago woman chooses the man she wants to be her husband and proposes to him by giving him food. She builds a house and then invites him to live with her there.

You can speak Bijago

Hello (a greeting that means "You have got up!") is "Mensuxuque" (men-soots-ook-e)

Hello (the reply, which means "Yes, I have got up!") is "Ee nhensuxuque" (ee nee-en-soots-ook-e)

Goodbye is "Tosoxa" (toe-soets-a)

To help you pray for the Bijago

You can thank God for:

- the Bijago Christians.
- the Bible translated into Bijago.
- the practical help that organizations like Tearfund have given to the Bijago.

You can ask God:

- to help the Bijago pastors and evangelists as they teach their people that he is far greater and stronger than the *iran*.
- to bring more pastors and evangelists to travel from island to island, teaching the people about Jesus.
- for Sunday school teachers to help children to know and follow Jesus.
- to help Bijago students at Bible school.

Africa

Guinea-Bissau

Bissau

BIJAGO

Telling people about Jesus

remember that he gave us a piece of the meat to cook in the part of the forest where we made our fields last year? We call that 'paying the ground.' The *iran* will definitely harm us if we don't do that."

The port was a very noisy place that day. People scrambled to find places for themselves and their belongings in the small dugout canoes that they would paddle across to Rubane Island. Before long, the village was deserted.

They wouldn't be back for another six months.

Jesus helps a whole village!
Forty years ago, the village of Ancarave, on the island of Uno, was just like any other Bijago village. People and animals were sick. They got their water for drinking, cooking and washing from a dirty, slimy pool.

The witch doctors made offerings to the *iran*, but nothing improved. One day some Christian visitors came to the island. "You don't have to be afraid of the *iran*," they told the people. "The priests and witch doctors make sacrifices, but you still get sick and don't have enough

to eat. Your children and animals still die. God is far more powerful than any of the *iran*. He loves you so much that he sent his only Son, Jesus, as a sacrifice for you – so that you never have to make sacrifices again. If you trust in Jesus, he'll help you." Some of the people began to follow Jesus, but the village chief was afraid, so he went on following the *iran*.

These Christians translated the Bible into the Bijago language and, in 1973, Tearfund helped them dig a well. The people could hardly believe what a difference having clean, fresh water made. The village chief began to understand that Christians dug the well, but it was really God who had helped them. He became a Christian and burned all his

idols. The Bijago Christians danced and sang for joy. Other villages saw what Jesus had done for the people of Ancarave and wanted to follow him, too. Now there are Christians on other islands as well.

When civil war broke out in Guinea-Bissau in 1998, many Bijago who lived on the mainland returned to the islands. Some were strong Christians who helped lead the churches, but the Bijago still need more evangelists and pastors who will live among them and teach them about God's love.

Bulgaria

Dreams, Miracles and Life-giving Water

Christians

If you looked at a map, you would find Bulgaria in the southeast corner of Europe – beside the Black Sea. If you looked in a history book, you would read that Bulgaria was a Communist country from 1944 until 1989. If you asked a pastor in Bulgaria, he would tell you what it was like during those years when the government tried to stop people from going to church. He might even tell you that he was put in prison.

"Then what happened?" you ask.

"Well," the pastor says, "when the Communists stopped controlling the government, we hoped we'd be free to worship God. But this didn't last long.

"Most Bulgarians belong to the Eastern Orthodox Church, and the new socialist government decided that this was the religion of Bulgaria. They said that all other Christian churches were sects.

"We've tried to help the poor and care for orphans and the sick and elderly. We run camps for children and give food to the hungry. But people have accused some of our workers of wrongdoing and vandalized our churches. We have to remind ourselves that we're doing this to show Jesus' love and not get discouraged."

Muslims

If you asked one of the million and a quarter Muslims living in Bulgaria about his country, he would tell about their suffering, too. "The Communist government closed most of our mosques. We weren't allowed to wear our traditional clothes or use Muslim names – which we'd been doing for a long time before

God has used dreams and miracles to teach the people about Jesus

the Communists ever arrived!

"Many Bulgarian Turks and Gypsies are also Muslims. They are often very poor and live in crowded slums. It's hard for them to find work. Many of the schools are closed now, but even before that lots of Muslim children had stopped going to school because their parents couldn't buy them clothes or books. They said it wasn't worth going because there wouldn't be jobs for them when they'd finished. It's sad to see children with no hope for the future."

To help you pray for Bulgaria

You can thank God for:

- each person in Bulgaria who follows Jesus.
- the dreams and miracles that help people understand who he is.
- Scripture Union, Child Evangelism Fellowship and other groups working with children.

You can ask God:

- to show Muslim Turks that they can follow Jesus and still be Turkish.
- to help the different people groups love, understand and respect each other.
- to show churches and Christian groups how to work together.
- for church leaders and pastors to have good Bible training.

Children in national costume

Do you know?

Bulgarian Turks now have a Turkish New Testament written in the Cyrillic (Russian-style) alphabet. For example, the Turkish word for child, which is "çocuk" (*chaw-juk*) in our alphabet, would be "уодужк" in Cyrillic. And the word for girl is "kiz" (*kerz*), or "къз."

Dreams

Ahmed is a Bulgarian Turk who was taught that it was important to serve Allah. So he learned to read Arabic and studied the Koran, where he read about Jesus. When he was about 11 years old, Ahmed had a dream about Jesus.

"God and Jesus came to my house," he remembers. "Jesus offered me a jar of water, but I wouldn't take it until he promised he would never leave me."

Then, when Ahmed was about 20, a man gave him an old Turkish Bible. Ahmed read it, but he didn't really understand it. So he wrote to the man who had given him the Bible. The man came to see Ahmed, but he wasn't a Christian so he couldn't explain what the Bible meant.

"I wanted to know about Jesus, but no one could help me," Ahmed said. "Then I prayed and opened my Bible. I read the story in John 4 about the Samaritan woman who met Jesus at the well. He offered her life-giving water. I finally understood my dream from all those years ago. From then

on, I knew what it was like not to be thirsty inside, and I followed Jesus."

Asking for water: A miracle!

Güngüler (*gyoon-gyoo-lezh*) is a Gypsy girl who lives with her family in a city slum in Bulgaria. Every day she has to clean and cook and look after her little brother and sister while her mother goes out to work. Güngüler was born dumb and couldn't speak a word for the first nine years of her life. Her Muslim family often prayed to Allah and took her to Muslim teachers to heal her, but Güngüler still couldn't talk.

When some Christians visited the slum where Güngüler lived, she squeezed into the crowded room and listened to their stories about Jesus healing the blind, the deaf and the dumb. She wondered if Jesus could

heal even her. The Christians prayed for Güngüler, and God worked a miracle. For the first time in her life, Güngüler spoke. "May I please have a drink of water?" she asked.

Her mother couldn't believe her ears when Güngüler ran up to her, calling, "I can talk! Jesus healed me!" Her whole family were amazed and filled with joy. They wanted to learn all about this God who had healed Güngüler, and they decided to follow Jesus as well.

Although God doesn't always perform miracles when we pray, miracles do show people who don't know God how powerful and loving he is. All around the country, Bulgarians, Turks and Gypsies are coming to know Jesus as their friend. But they don't always understand the Bible well enough to put what it says into practice in their lives.

Buryat

Buddhists in Siberia

Punishment for sin

"What a great film!" Bator exclaimed. "I've never seen anything like it. Do you think it's true that God loves everyone so much that he sent his only Son to earth? Imagine sending him as a baby!"

"I couldn't believe how good Jesus was. I wish I could be like that, never doing anything wrong," said Temudjin. "And he was so smart, too. I was really sad when they put him on that cross. What if he really did die to take the punishment for our sins so that we can be clean before God?"

Bator and Temudjin sat on a bench outside a Buddhist temple. Brightly-colored prayer flags fluttered over the monastery, and the boys could hear the sound of gongs and the monks chanting inside the temple.

Prayer flags

Temudjin let his prayer beads slip, one by one, through his fingers. Earlier that morning he and his uncle had gone to the temple and set the prayer wheels spinning. "It's so different from Buddhism," Temudjin said. "My uncle says if we do bad things we have to be punished for our own sins. And we have to go on suffering for them each time we're reborn."

"Well, I'm going to read the book about Jesus that the teacher gave me," said Bator. "I want to know more about him. Come on – I'll race you home!"

A page from history

Bator and Temudjin are Buryats (*boor-yahts'*). They live in Buryatia (*boor-yaht'-ee-yah*), in southeastern Siberia. For hundreds of years the Buryats were nomads, breeding horses and cattle in the wide valleys between the forest-covered mountains. Several centuries ago Buryats, particularly those living to the east of Lake Baikal, became Buddhists. But they kept many of their old animistic beliefs as well. Buryat boys went to school at the Buddhist monasteries, and many of them became monks.

All this changed after the Russian Revolution. By the end of the 1930s, the Communists had forced the Buryats to settle in villages and had set up government-run schools for the children. They closed the monasteries and the people were no longer allowed to be Buddhists. They even destroyed a lot of their shrines and religious books.

There were more changes in 1989, when the Communists lost power.

Buddhist monastery

Fact file

Countries: Southeastern Siberia (Buryatia); Mongolia; Inner Mongolia

Numbers: 423,500 (Buryatia) 40,000 (Mongolia) 10,000 (Inner Mongolia)

Religions: Buddhism; Russian Orthodox Christianity; Shamanism

Occupations: Once nomadic herders; now many work in industry

To help you pray for the Buryat

You can thank God for:

- Buryats in Buryatia and Mongolia who follow Jesus.
- the translation of the New Testament into Buryat.

You can ask God:

- to show Buryats that only Jesus can take away sin and give them eternal life.
- for Christians helping in schools, farming and health care to show the Buryats how much God loves them.
- to show the Buryats that the Dalai Lama is not God, but only a man.
- that many Buryats will choose to follow Jesus.
- that Christians will pray for the Buryats to know Jesus.

Poster for *Jesus* film in Ulan Ude

Then, in 1991, the Dalai Lama, the Buddhists' spiritual leader, was allowed to visit Ulan Ude, the capital of Buryatia. He told the people to put all the years of atheistic Communism behind them and return to their Buddhist beliefs. Many Buryats have done just that, and now a lot of Buddhist monks are trained there to take the message of Buddhism around the world.

Another page from history

In 1817, the tsar (king) of Russia gave three English missionaries permission to travel to Siberia. He even gave them land and money to help them in their work among the Buryats. "Why do you want to help the Buryats? We certainly don't think much of them!" said

the Russians living in the region. The Buryats also wondered why the missionaries had come, and only 20 of them ever became Christians. Those missionaries translated the whole Bible into the Buryat language. Since then the Buryat script has been changed several times, and now no one can read their translation.

Then, in 1841, the tsar said that the missionaries had to leave. The Russian Orthodox Church set up its own mission to the Buryats and built churches, but there were still very few Buryat Christians.

A presentation to guests

Today

Today a few more Buryats, in all the countries where they live, are following Jesus, who died to take away their sins. The *Jesus* film has been shown in a lot of places and some people have started work on a new translation of the Bible.

Do you know?

Lake Baikal contains as much water as all the Great Lakes of North America put together, which makes it the biggest freshwater lake in the world. It's also the deepest lake in the world, and experts think it's the oldest lake as well.

What's the future like for young Buryats like Bator and Temudjin? People from different cults, sects and other religions are all trying to get their attention. What will they choose? Who will they follow? Your prayers can help them to decide.

33

Chad

Where the Lake is Drying Up

Too little rain

It hardly ever rains in Chad, so when it does rain little children take off their clothes and run into the streets, laughing and splashing in the puddles. The frogs come out to catch termites and people catch the termites, too – fried termites make a delicious snack!

Lake Chad, in the southwest of the country, used to be much bigger and full of fish. Today, the lake is drying up because so many people and cattle are using the water and there isn't enough rain each year to fill it again.

Fact file

Area: 495,750 sq. mi.

Population: 7,650,980

Capital: N'Djamena

Languages: French (spoken by the educated); Chad Arabic (60%); and 124 other languages

Main religions: Islam; Christianity

Chad is in the middle of north Africa, hundreds of miles from the sea. There are so few roads and so much desert, that it's very hard to get things like food and clothes and farming supplies from other countries. Because of this, as well as civil wars, infertile soil and lack of rain, Chad is one of the poorest countries in the world.

Many tribes and languages

Jill, a missionary in Chad, tells us what it's like to live there. "I learned two different languages when I came here: French and Chad Arabic, which most people know.

But different tribes speak over 100 different languages. So I also learned one of these tribal languages so I could talk to even more people.

"Chad is divided into three parts, just like its flag. In the north there are the cold, windy Tibesti Mountains and the Sahara Desert. In the central part there's dry grassland, which provides food for the camels, goats and sheep of the nomads. The south gets more rain, and cotton and dates grow well there.

"The people in each area are different, too. In the south there are quite a lot of Christians, but in the north and central parts of Chad most people are Muslims or follow their own traditional religions. Many of them wear charms, or little bags with bits of bark, hair or other 'magic' things inside, to protect them from sickness and other troubles. Muslims also wear charms with verses from the Koran inside. When people become Christians, they burn their charms because Jesus is stronger than any other power and they don't need to be afraid any more."

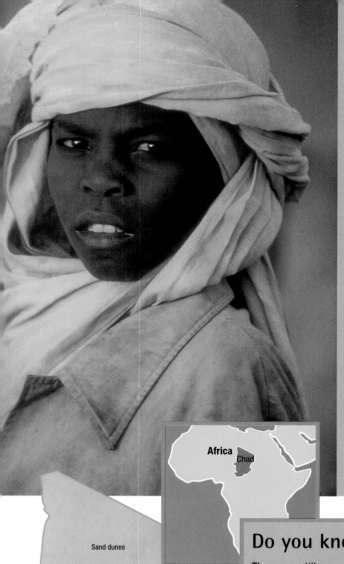

To help you pray for Chad

You can thank God for:

- every missionary who has gone to Chad to tell the people about Jesus' love.

- each Chadian who has decided to follow Jesus.

You can ask God:

- for more missionary doctors, nurses, teachers, Bible translators and farming specialists to go Chad to show people God's love.

- to help the missionaries' children in Chad who sometimes find it hard to live there.

- to remind people to read the Christian booklets and listen to the cassettes they are given and to help them understand who Jesus is.

- to show people in Chad that trusting in their charms will never really help them, but that Jesus promises to help everyone who trusts in him.

- to send enough rain each year so that crops will grow well and the people and their animals will have enough food to eat.

Africa Chad

Sand dunes

Chad

Dry grassland

Thick bush

Chad is divided into three different parts, just like its flag

Mission to Chad

Naomi and her sisters are Dutch and live in N'Djamena, the capital of Chad, with their missionary parents. "We do have a few Chadian friends,"

Do you know?

There are still more than 70 groups of people in Chad who don't have any part of the Bible in their own language and who don't have a Christian or missionary living among them. How would you have learned about Jesus if there were no Christians who spoke your language?

Naomi said, "but sometimes other children make fun of us. And we don't like mosquitoes, sandstorms or being sick. But it is fun living in such a different place. None of our Dutch friends can see camels, donkeys and men wearing turbans pass by their houses!

"Some of the missionaries here take care of children in orphanages or sick people. Others are translating the Bible into some of the different languages. There's a special school in N'Djamena where Chadians can learn English, and our parents teach some of them how to make sandals they

can sell in the market. We have lots of visitors, and our parents always tell them about God's love and give them Christian tapes and books.

"Brahim, who's about 12, comes to our house a lot. He'd like to go to school, but he has to work selling donuts so that he and his grandmother can buy food. He brings donuts to our house, and we always give him something to eat and talk to him about Jesus. One day he asked us to read him a story, so we told him the story of Jesus blessing the little children. He loved the story, but when we told him it was from the Bible he was really scared. His friends had told him that he'd get into trouble with the Muslim teachers if they found out he went into a Christian's house. He ran to the sink and washed his hands and ears because he'd touched a Bible and listened to the story. Then he left without even waiting to be paid for the donuts! We're all praying that someday Brahim will forget his fear and love and follow Jesus."

Children of the Streets

Homeless, Unwanted Children all around the World

Russia

"Get out!" Anton's mother screamed. "And don't come back until you have some money!" Anton ran out of the house, scared that his mother would beat him. He was hungry, cold and sick. His parents couldn't find jobs, and they spent what little money they had on alcohol. Anton is only nine years old. He's tired of trying to get food by begging and stealing. He'll probably get caught some day, and he's afraid. There are thousands of other children like Anton, living on the streets of St. Petersburg, Russia.

Street children in Delhi, India live in these pipes

Project Hope is a Christian organization reaching out to street children in St. Petersburg. Every day, workers invite children on the streets to their shelter. They give them food, showers and clothing. If they're sick, they can see a doctor. They can learn skills like carpentry and how to repair shoes and use computers. More than that, Project Hope teaches these children about God's love for them.

India

"Rupee! Rupee! Give me!" Little Ram stuck out a dirty, empty hand. His big brown eyes pleaded for just one of the hundreds of passengers to give him a coin so he could buy a *chapatti* to eat. He hadn't eaten all day, and he was so hungry. Ram's parents are both dead, and

Aid worker on the streets in South America

he has no one to take care of him. At night he huddles with other homeless boys on the street. Ram is just one of the two million children living on the streets in India.

Colombia

Señor Jaramillo, a rich businessman in Bogota, Colombia, saw a little homeless girl killed when she was running to pick up an empty box. It changed his life. He was shocked to find out that many homeless children live in the city sewers. Now he puts on scuba-diving gear and goes down into the

sewers every night, searching for these children. He gives food, clothes, education and jobs to as many of them as he can.

South Africa

There was a time when Johannes couldn't remember anything except being miserable. His

South American street children

What else can you do?

Find out if there is an organization in your area that helps the homeless. There are probably homeless people and families in the city nearest to where you live. How could you show the love of Jesus in a practical way to these people? Perhaps you could collect food, clothing, books or toys through your church or school to help those who do not have as much as you do. Or you could help to raise money to send to organizations helping street children in other parts of the world.

parents were always fighting and drinking. There was never enough food, and they beat him. He was sure they didn't want him, so he left home to live on the streets of Johannesburg. He started taking drugs, trying to escape from the pain of life. He stole or begged for food and drugs.

A few years later, he was invited to the Emmanuel shelter for street children.

"I never knew there were such kind people who wanted to help children like me," Johannes said with a smile. "I'm going to school and I've decided to follow Jesus, who loves all children. I thank God for protecting me and helping me."

Helping the homeless

In almost every country and major city in the world, millions of children are living on the streets. There may be as many as 200 million street children in the world today. That's almost as many as all the people living in the United States! Every one of these children feels lonely and unloved.

Some of these children are orphans, others live on the streets because they're afraid of drunken parents, abuse and hunger. Many of them sleep in cardboard boxes in railway stations and doorways, under bridges and even in sewers. It's often difficult to help them because they quickly learn to steal, fight, use drugs and even kill to survive. In some countries the police beat them and even shoot them.

These children need places of safety where people will take care of them and love them. Please pray that these hurt and lonely children will get help and feel Jesus' love. Many of these children are your age and even younger. As you pray for them, remember to thank God for your own home and family.

Young people at the Emmanuel shelter, South Africa.
Johannes holds the coke bottle.

Home on the street, Colombo, Sri Lanka

 To help you pray for homeless children

You can thank God for:

● the street children who have been shown love and kindness and who have begun to learn that they really do matter.

● the people who work with street children.

● Christians who give money to organizations to provide food and shelter for street children.

You can ask God:

● to bring these unwanted and unloved children to know Jesus as their friend who is always with them.

● to use each shelter, training project and camp to help street children learn that there can be more to life than living on the streets.

● to make governments realize that it's important to do all they can to protect children from the difficult – and often terrible – things so many of them have to face.

● to show boys and girls who have loving families, homes and toys, and who can go to school, how they can help children who have none of these good things.

God is at Work

So many people!

China is the third largest country in the world, after Russia and Canada, and it's almost the same size as Europe. About one-fifth of the world's people live in China, which means that more people live there than in any other country. There are at least 56 different people groups living in China. You can read more about some of these groups in this book – including the Hui, Dai Lu, and Tibetans.

About two-thirds of the people in China work as farmers. Rice is the most important crop, but they also grow fruit, vegetables, tea and cotton. China's towns and cities are big and bustling, and Shanghai is one of the biggest cities in the world.

Fact file

Area: 3,696,100 sq. mi.

Population: 1,262,556,787

Capital: Beijing

Main language: Mandarin Chinese

Religions: Buddhism; folk religions; Islam

Economy: China grows more rice and rears more pigs than any other country in the world. Industries include iron and steel manufacture, machinery, vehicles, ships, clothes and toys.

A fortune cookie

The door is slammed shut

In 1949, the Communist Party took control of China. They wanted to make China a country where everyone was equal, where nobody was either rich or poor. The Communists took land from wealthy landowners and set up big collective farms for the peasants to work on. They built big factories to produce iron, steel and heavy machinery and formed a huge army, but many people were still poor.

The Communists also wanted to get rid of all religions in China. Christian missionaries were forced to leave China in 1950. For 140 years, missionaries had shared the good news of Jesus with the people in China. Had all those years of work been for nothing? What would happen to the Christians they left behind? Would they remember all they had been taught and remain faithful? Would the pastors be allowed to teach and preach about Jesus?

The door into China slammed shut. For the next 30 years it was almost impossible for Christians outside to get news of their friends in China. All around the world Christians prayed for China. And God answered their prayers in an amazing way.

God opens the door

As they faced persecution, many of the Chinese Christians stood firm for Jesus. Their churches were closed down, and during the Cultural Revolution (1966–90) some of their leaders were killed. Others were put in prison or sent far away to work in prison camps. Life would have been much easier and safer for these Christians and their families if they had just said that they didn't believe in Jesus anymore. But they never turned their backs on Jesus.

The Chinese eat their food with chopsticks.

中华人民共和国万岁   世界人民大

To help you pray for China

You can thank God for:

- the millions of Chinese people who know Jesus as their friend, and all the Christians who shared God's love with others even when they were suffering themselves.

- Christians around the world who never gave up praying for the Chinese people.

You can ask God:

- that many children will hear about Jesus from their friends and families and that soon it will be possible for every church to have a Sunday school.

- to help Christians show Jesus' love by always being ready to give whatever they can to those who are in need.

- that soon there will be enough good seminaries, Bible schools and training courses where church pastors and leaders can study the Bible and learn how to teach and care for the people in their churches.

- that many young people and students at universities will come to know him.

- for leaders in China who will rule this huge country wisely and fairly.

Do you know?

China's population is growing so quickly that in 1979 the government introduced a law limiting each family to only one child. These children, especially the boys, soon became known as "Little Emperors" because they're often spoiled.

When the government tried to get rid of religion in China, the church grew instead

Russia
Kazahkstan
Mongolia
Beijing
China
Shanghai
India

Quietly, in their homes, they talked about Jesus and the help and strength he gave them. They also shared his love with other people, especially those who were poor or sick. Instead of disappearing, as the Communists planned, the church in China grew.

When the door into China began to open at last, Chinese people from other parts of the world visited their families there. Some were Christians who secretly carried Bibles with them. They brought back the great news that the church was growing.

Churches in China

No one really knows how many Christians there are in China today, but there are millions more than there were when the missionaries left.

There are all sorts of church groups in China. Some of the churches in the towns and cities have huge congregations, but in the countryside many churches meet in homes. Although the churches have a lot more freedom, there are still restrictions. Bibles are now being printed in China, but there are still not enough for everyone who wants one.

There are other restrictions, too. Yang is nine years old. His parents are Christians, and he likes to listen as they read the Bible and pray. Yang usually begs his father to read him another story from the Bible. "Can I have some of my friends over to hear the stories, too?" he pleads.

"You know we're not supposed to teach the Bible to young people," his father says with a smile. "But if one or two of your friends came sometimes, I could tell them Bible stories too. Go and get one of them now, but be quiet about it!"

Light shines in the darkness

Hope for the poor ...

Maria held her little brother's hand and dragged him through the crowd of children waiting for a sandwich and a cup of hot chocolate. Maria and Carlos hadn't eaten anything since the day before. That sandwich tasted so good, and the hot chocolate really warmed them up.

Maria and Carlos live with their mother in a small, dark room in a slum area of Bogotá, the capital of Colombia. Their mother is addicted to drugs and their father is in prison. Sometimes Maria earns a little money by washing cars or sorting through trash for bottles and papers that she can sell. Sometimes she steals food so that she and Carlos can eat.

Figure from San Augustin Archeological Park

There are lots of children like Maria and Carlos in Colombia's cities. Some have come from the countryside with their families, trying to escape from the violence of guerrilla activities and drug cartels. They usually don't have any money and can't find work, so they get poorer and poorer. It's easy to turn to crime when you're starving and have nothing.

A few Christian organizations run centers to help these people. They invite children to their centers, where

Family living in a slum, Bogotá

Fact file

Area: 439,735 sq. mi.

Population: 42,321,361

Capital: Bogotá

Language: Spanish. The Amerindian peoples also speak 65 different languages.

Religion: Christianity (Roman Catholic, but with a growing evangelical church)

Coffee

Chief exports: Oil; coal; emeralds; coffee; bananas

Colombians are learning that Jesus gives hope to the poor, the rich, and the prisoners

they can have a bath, clean clothes and food. Children can also play games and even learn to read there. But, best of all, children like Maria and Carlos are learning that God loves them.

Colombia is the fourth largest country in South America, and 100 years ago it was one of the poorest. A lot of people are still very poor, but others have made a lot of money from coffee, oil production and trade with other countries. Colombia is rich in gold, platinum and emeralds. There's a huge illegal trade in drugs as well, which is often the cause of terrible violence. "So many people think of Colombia as a place of begging, stealing, smuggling, killing, dying and drugs," a friend in Colombia said. "Although violence is unfortunately a part of life in Colombia, it's also a beautiful land. And most Colombians

 To help you pray for Colombia

You can thank God for:

● the people showing God's love and care to children in city slums.

● all of the prisoners who have asked Jesus to forgive them for the bad things they've done.

You can ask God:

● that people in Colombia who are hurt, afraid, poor, lonely and angry will discover Jesus' love, help and comfort.

● to stop the violence and drug trade in Colombia.

● to give Christian government leaders the wisdom and courage to speak out for what's right.

● to protect pastors as they talk about Jesus' love in areas where there's a lot of violence.

● that all Colombian Christians will work together to share Jesus' love with others.

Do you know?

Colombia is the largest producer of coal in South America. It also produces half the world's emeralds and is the world's second largest producer of coffee. It has 1,721 species of birds – the highest recorded number in any country in the world.

are warm and loving people. Evangelical Christians used to be persecuted for their faith, but now more people than ever are following Jesus."

... and hope for the rich

Juliana has everything she wants. She goes to a private school and plans to go to university. She spends most weekends with her grandparents in the country and every summer she visits her cousins in the United States. Her father is a wealthy lawyer. When her parents got divorced, Juliana was so sad ... but she didn't know who to talk to.

One of Juliana's friends at school saw how upset she was and invited her to go to church with her. "Whenever I'm sad," she told Juliana, "I talk to Jesus and he listens and answers my prayers." Juliana's parents are Catholics but, like many Colombians, they hardly ever go to church. Juliana went to church with her friend and found out that it was true that Jesus would always help her. She's praying that her parents will know Jesus someday, too.

... and hope for those in prison

Until recently, Medellin was one of the most violent cities in Colombia. It has a maximum security prison called Bellavista, or "Beautiful View," which is full of thieves, murderers and drug pushers. But something amazing is happening in the prison.

Several years ago, a man who had been a prisoner came to know Jesus. His life was changed so completely that he went back to tell the prisoners about Jesus. A lot of them have asked God to forgive their sins and to make them new people. Now they're studying in their own Bible school in prison, and every day they meet to sing and talk about what God has done for them. These services are broadcast on a radio program called "A Cry of Hope." People outside the prison listen to the programs and are coming to know Jesus, too. Once a month, the children of prisoners are allowed to visit their fathers. The prisoners who have come to know Jesus want their children to know about him, too. The children were very excited one visiting day when they were all given a book called "The Gospel for Kids."

Men and women, boys and girls – whether they are poor or rich – are discovering that God loves them. They're praying that, as God changes lives, their country will become a peaceful place where people can live without fear.

The Church is Growing

Sugar and slaves

In 1492, Christopher Columbus discovered the beautiful Caribbean island of Cuba and claimed it for Spain. Spaniards settled there and established sugar plantations. They shipped thousands of West Africans across the Atlantic Ocean to work as slaves on these plantations. Today, many Cubans are descendants of those slaves.

Sugar made a lot of people very wealthy, and by 1959 Cuba was one of the richest countries in Latin America. The beautiful beaches and the luxury of cities like Havana attracted many tourists from North America.

But not everyone was rich. Thousands of very poor people needed better homes and enough food and clothing for their families. They couldn't even afford to send their children to school.

Preparing the famous Havana cigars

There are still not enough Bibles in Cuba for all those who want one

Revolution and education

On 1 January 1959, Fidel Castro and his guerrillas overthrew the government. They wanted to make Cuba a better country. They made sure that every child went to school and

Fidel Castro (center) with Cuban church leaders

adults were taught to read, too.

Roberto was eight years old when the revolution took place. "We went to school in a small hut," he said. "My family was very poor. We didn't have shoes, our clothes were ragged and old, and I was very hungry most of the time. I was excited because they told me if I learned to read I'd get a good job. Then I could have more to eat and better clothes to wear."

He smiled sadly. "Everyone goes to school now, and there are more doctors and a lot of us have better houses than we used to have, but the revolution didn't really help us very much. The United States stopped trading with us because we were Communists. The Russians did help us, but they're not helping us any more. I'm still very poor. Medicine is

To help you pray for Cuba

You can thank God for:

- the public meetings that Christians were allowed to hold in 1998 and 1999.
- greater freedom for Bibles to be printed in Cuba and to be brought in from other countries.
- the many Cubans who are coming to know Jesus.

You can ask God:

- that people who have suffered because they follow Jesus will not be angry but will forgive those who hurt them.
- for more Bibles, books and teachers to train leaders and pastors to help all the new churches.
- to help the many people in Cuba who don't have enough food and other things we take for granted.
- that when Cuba is no longer a Communist country, the new government will lead the country wisely.

Do you know?

As in other Communist states, the Cuban government tried to get rid of Christianity but couldn't. Christians have been persecuted, arrested, imprisoned or forced to leave the country. Despite this, many Christians have stood firm for Jesus. Although persecution is still taking place, thousands of people, especially young people, are coming to know Jesus.

Young woman and child who have received the Scriptures

scarce, food is rationed and my children often go hungry and don't have good clothes.

"Right after the revolution, a lot of wealthy people left Cuba and went to live in the United States. Since then, thousands have tried to escape in small boats. Cuba is my home and it's very beautiful, but there are so many problems here it's hard to know where to start."

Cuba for Christ!

Although Cuba is now a secular country, almost half the people are Roman Catholics. After the revolution in 1959, police informers seemed to be everywhere. Because they wouldn't stop following Jesus, Christians were often persecuted and put in prison, where they were treated very badly.

Maria, a young Cuban woman, describes what it's like to be a Christian there. "In the 1980s, the evangelical churches started to grow – and they're still growing. A lot of Cubans, especially young people and children, have discovered the joy of knowing Jesus as their friend. Christians all over Cuba meet together in churches and homes. They're so excited to share the good news about Jesus. Everyone wants a Bible, but there aren't enough to go around. We're so grateful to people who bring them into the country and for organizations that send them. The government's allowing us to print some Bibles here now, but there still aren't enough! Christians have a little more freedom to meet together now. But there are still restrictions, and our pastors and leaders are still threatened and churches are closed down.

"In 1998, the Pope visited Cuba. Thousands of people joined him to worship God in an open-air service in Havana. A year later, the evangelical churches were allowed to hold 19 huge open-air meetings in cities all across Cuba. It was so exciting to hear thousands of people shouting, 'Cuba for Christ!' There were 100,000 people at the rally in Havana, and President Fidel Castro and several members of the government sat in the front row.

"We thank God for the Christians around the world who are praying for Cuba. Please keep praying that the people of Cuba will know and love Jesus."

Dai Lu

From the Land of Twelve Thousand Rice Fields

Xishuangbanna

In the Yunnan Province of southwest China, near the borders with Myanmar and Laos, there's a region called Xishuangbanna (Shish-wang-banna). This is the home of the Dai Lu people. Fifty years ago, monkeys, elephants, tigers, bears, deer and even peacocks lived in the thick green forests that covered the high mountains. Since then, they've cut down almost half the forest to make room for more people – especially for the Han Chinese, who have come to live in the area. Cutting down the forest has affected the climate. This means the rainfall has decreased and rivers have been drying up.

The Dai Lu people build their houses on stilts out of wood, bamboo and thatch. Pigs and hens make themselves at home under the houses.

Shrine at a Dai Buddhist temple

The Dai Lu grow coconut palms, banana, papaya and mango trees, pineapples and peppers all around their houses. And there are more paddy fields (fields where rice is grown) than you can count, because Xishuangbanna means "the land of twelve thousand rice fields."

Help for another life?

The Dai Lu people are Buddhists, and there's a temple in every village. Most children go to schools run by the government now, but seven-year-old Artuk's parents decided to send him to the temple for his schooling. Artuk tried to be brave as he waved goodbye to his parents and left with his big brother, who was taking him to the temple. He wondered what it would be like to live

A novice Buddhist monk

there for three whole years.

Forty other little boys were already there. "It's your turn to have your head shaved," a monk told Artuk. "And here's the robe you'll wear every day," he said, handing Artuk an orange robe.

"Will you teach us how to read?" Artuk asked. "Yes, we'll start tomorrow," replied the monk. "You'll learn to read the sacred Buddhist scriptures so you can earn merit for yourself and for your whole family. This will help you in your next life."

Artuk knew Buddhists believe that when they die they're reborn as another person or animal. This is called reincarnation. Artuk also knew that all the good things he did would help him in his next life. But he was frightened

 To help you pray for the Dai

You can thank God for:

- the few Dai Lu Christians.
- each person working on translating the Bible.

You can ask God:

- to help the Dai Lu understand that doing good things will never get them to heaven.
- to show them that the only way to stop worrying about sin and evil spirits is to follow Jesus.
- to show the Dai Lu that following Jesus will make them even happier than remembering their old stories.
- that Han Chinese Christians in Yunnan will show the Dai Lu how much God loves them.
- that some day there will be churches in every town where the Dai Lu live.

Paddy fields

sometimes – what if he ever did something wrong? What would happen to him in the next life?

The good guy wins again

"Tell us the story of the Water Throwing Festival! Please!" the children all begged their father after dinner one night. The Dai Lu

 Fact file

Numbers: About 614,300 in China

Locations: Yunnan Province of China; others in Myanmar, Thailand and Laos

Language: Dai

Religions: Buddhism; animism

Occupations: Farmers; traders

people love to tell stories and, like many of their stories, this one is about how the good guy wins and the bad guy loses.

"All right," their father said. "Once upon a time, a powerful demon-king ruled our people. He made life very hard for them. He had seven wives, but the youngest one, Yu Xiang (*yoo shang*), was a kind and gentle person. She didn't like to see anyone suffer. 'I wish the demon-king would die,' she thought, 'so the Dai Lu people can be free from his evil power.'

"The demon-king loved Yu Xiang very much, and one day he told her his biggest secret. 'My power is in the single white hair on my head,' he said, 'I can only be defeated if it is pulled out

and tied around my neck.' That night, when he was fast asleep, Yu Xiang pulled out that white hair, tied it tightly around his neck, and cut off his head.

"Everyone was so happy that the demon-king was dead! But as soon as his head touched the ground, it burst into flames and burned up everything it touched. At last, brave Yu Xiang was able to pick up the head. When she did, the fire stopped. But when she put it down, the fire started again. 'Quick, quick!' the people shouted as they threw water over Yu Xiang to put out the fire and wash away the blood. Now, when we celebrate the Water Throwing Festival and have fun throwing water at each other, we remember this

story. The water we throw makes us pure and clean and keeps us from harm."

There are only a few Dai Lu Christians. Most of the Dai Lu people don't know that doing good things or throwing water can never make their hearts clean or help them go to heaven. Who will tell them the best story of all, that God sent his only Son, Jesus, to defeat all of the evil powers? How will the Dai Lu know that the only way to have a pure, clean heart is to follow Jesus? Who will tell Artuk that he doesn't have to worry about the bad things he does if he tells Jesus he's sorry? How will he know that there's no other life after he dies, unless he knows Jesus and goes to heaven?

Dayak

From a Land of Jungles and Rivers

The omen bird

The villagers following Idjam along the jungle trail stopped when their leader cried out. "I can hear the omen bird. Look, there it is!" Idjam said. "It's warning us about something – let's go home. This must not be a good day to plant the rice fields. We'll come back tomorrow."

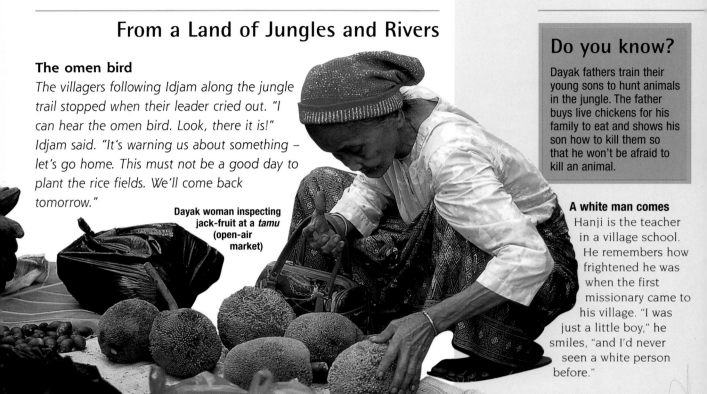

Dayak woman inspecting jack-fruit at a *tamu* (open-air market)

A white man comes

Hanji is the teacher in a village school. He remembers how frightened he was when the first missionary came to his village. "I was just a little boy," he smiles, "and I'd never seen a white person before."

Idjam wondered what was wrong as he hurried back to the village. They had offered a sacrifice to the spirits before cutting down the jungle for fields. They left some trees on the hilltop for visiting spirits to rest on. The ash left from burning the trees and undergrowth should guarantee a good harvest. But the appearance of the omen bird meant the spirits were angry.

Idjam and the villagers set out for their fields again the next day. They didn't hear the omen bird and were soon at work. Using sharp-pointed sticks, the men and boys made holes in the ground between the burnt-out tree stumps. The women and girls followed, dropping a few rice seeds into each hole. At harvest time the men cut down the rice with a knife, a few stalks at a time. The women gather the rice, put it in a square basket and then pound it to remove the husk.

Most Dayak live along the riverbanks and in the jungle areas of Kalimantan in central Borneo. While there are some Christians among them, most are still animists. They live in constant fear of evil spirits hiding in rocks, trees, rivers, caves and on the mountains, waiting to hurt them.

Dayak hunter with blowpipe

"Night after night he told us about Jesus, God's Son. He told us that Jesus had power over all the evil spirits. I was afraid of those spirits, so I decided to follow Jesus. Some of my friends did, too. At first the older men were afraid the spirits would be angry because we burned all our charms, but when nothing bad happened to us some of them became Christians too.

"The missionaries taught us to read, and it was great to be able to read stories about Jesus. Some of us went to Bible school and became evangelists to our own people. I opened the school here in this village."

Empty schools and churches

Hanji shook his head as he looked over at a group of boys playing in the river. "They should all be in school," he said, "but no one makes them go. Parents want their children to stay at home and help feed the chickens and pigs, look for food, or take care of their little brothers and sisters. Sometimes the children themselves decide they just don't want to come to school. That's too bad, because the Dayak way of life is changing and it's important to know how to read and write. Some children do come every day because they want to go to high school and even university.

Bajau Dayak horsemen at the weekly *tamu* (open-air market) in Sabah

"It's hard to help people understand that going to church is important, too – even though almost half the people in this village say they're Christians, some of them think they don't need to go to church. The girls like to come to Sunday school and sing and learn Bible stories, but usually the boys would rather play or go fishing. I keep praying that these children and their parents will want to learn more about Jesus and what it's really like to follow him."

 To help you pray for the Dayak

You can thank God for:

- Dayaks who are no longer afraid of the spirits because they trust Jesus.

- Dayaks who have studied at Bible school.

You can ask God:

- that church leaders will help others to know and follow Jesus.

- for more Christians to teach the Dayaks to read and write.

- for the Dayaks to want to read the Bible and learn more about God.

- to help young Dayak Christians who leave their villages to find good churches and Christian friends.

- to help Christians understand that it's important to go to church and Sunday school.

Fact file

Country: Indonesia

Location: Kalimantan, Borneo

Numbers: 2,500,000

Language: About 80 Dayak languages and dialects

Religions: Animism; Christianity

Occupations: Rice farming; hunting

A river in the jungle at the northern tip of Borneo. Many of Borneo's rivers are now muddy due to logging erosion.

One of the Hottest Places on Earth

Leaves or people?

"I'm not taking off," announced the pilot. *"The plane's overloaded and we'll never get over the mountain."* The passengers on board the flight to Djibouti were angry.

"How can we be overloaded?" someone asked a flight attendant. *"DC9s hold 72 passengers, and there are only 40 of us."*

"We're overloaded with eight and a half tons of khat, *but if we refuse to take it ..."* The flight attendant drew her finger across her throat. Khat *is a leaf that people use as a drug. People that chew it feel dreamy and don't want to eat.* Khat *is big business in Djibouti, and the airline makes a lot more money carrying* khat *than people.*

At last the plane took off, leaving behind two Somali ladies and a big pile of luggage. Even so, the plane just barely cleared the mountains near the end of the runway.

Lake Assal

Do you know?

Lake Assal, in the center of Djibouti, is 509 feet below sea level and is the lowest place in Africa. The water in the lake is even saltier than the Dead Sea in Israel and 10 times saltier than the water in the ocean. When the water dries up in the hot sun, islands of salt are formed which float on top of the water.

📋 Fact file

Area: 9,000 sq. mi.

Population: 637,634

Capital: Djibouti

Main languages: French; Arabic

Religion: Islam

Chief exports: Animal skins; livestock

When the plane landed at Djibouti's main airport, crowds of drug dealers pushed, pulled and yelled for their *khat*. As soon as they had it, they rushed into the city to their waiting customers. Soon there were thousands of people throughout the city with their cheeks bulging with *khat* leaves. Many of them sat chewing peacefully, forgetting how poor they were, or how hungry.

A really hot place

Peter lives in the city of Djibouti, the capital, with his missionary parents. "It's one of the hottest places on earth," he says. "It's usually much too hot to sleep at night, especially since we have to sleep under mosquito nets. There's almost never any rain,

Almost all Djiboutians are Muslims, but a few have decided to follow Jesus.

Cooking pancakes

and the ground is so rocky that it's hard for farmers to grow food. That means lots of people are very poor and don't have enough to eat.

"It's very noisy here, too," Peter continues. "The first thing I hear every morning is our neighbor, sweeping her yard, calling out to her friends and banging buckets and brushes as she washes the clothes. The children in the neighborhood make lots of noise, too, playing and arguing. And then there are the barking dogs, the braying donkeys, the roaring camels and the cars and trucks!

"Because Djibouti belonged to France for almost 100 years before it

48

To help you pray for Djibouti

You can thank God for:

- every missionary working in Djibouti.
- every Christian in Djibouti.

You can ask God:

- that missionaries teaching English will be able to tell their students about Jesus.
- that through their teaching, Bible translation, medical work, agriculture and youth work, missionaries can talk to those who want to know more about Jesus.
- to provide food for all the poor people in Djibouti.
- that Djiboutians will understand the message of the Bible.
- for missionaries' children to tell their Djiboutian school friends about Jesus.

Africa

Djibouti

Marketplace in the evening

Eritrea

Ethiopia

Gulf of Tadjoura

Djibouti
Djibouti town

Somalia

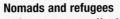

became an independent country in 1977, French is one of the main languages. Before we came to live in Djibouti, my parents had to learn French. I go to a French school and have lots of Djiboutian friends. Most of my friends want to learn English as well, and some of them study in the English language school where my father's a teacher. One of my favorite things to do is play soccer with my friends. They're all Muslims, but sometimes they ask me questions about who Jesus is."

Peter always loves going with his father to visit their Afar friends in Tadjoura. "We have to cross the Gulf of Tadjoura on the ferry to get there. It's lots of fun. There's only room for 12 cars, but most people are foot passengers. You wouldn't believe some of the things they take with them. There are always big boxes of groceries, crates of soft drinks, furniture and even huge bags of clothes to sell in the markets. The passengers usually include some sheep and goats, too. Everyone always seems to enjoy the trip."

Nomads and refugees

Djibouti is a small African country on the Gulf of Aden. On the map it looks a bit like a boomerang. It has a long coastline and borders with Eritrea, Ethiopia and Somalia. The two main groups of people living in Djibouti used to be enemies – the Afars in the north and the Issas in the south. Almost all the people were nomads, moving around the harsh desert and mountains with their herds of sheep, goats, cattle and camels. It's a hard way of life. Although many people still live as nomads, a lot of them have moved into the capital, which is a major seaport, hoping to find work. Refugees from civil wars in Ethiopia and Somalia have settled there, too, but a lot of people are poor and have no work.

Almost all Djiboutians are Muslims, but a few have heard about Jesus and decided to follow him. Some of the refugees from Ethiopia are also Christians. They pray (sometimes all night long!) for their own people and for the people of Djibouti. They ask God that these people will follow Jesus.

Dogon

Sharing the Good News

Cliff caves

If you gaze straight up the cliff face, you will see a tiny moving figure. That's Oumar, swinging dangerously on a rope. He doesn't dare look down! He climbs hundreds of feet to reach caves hollowed out of the cliff. He is collecting pigeon dung to sell as fertilizer at the market. Oumar's people are called the Dogon. They live in a part of Mali, western Africa that is very rocky. The fertilizer helps them to grow as much food as they can on the few fields they have. If you look directly behind you, you can see the Sahara Desert, where nothing grows. So every bit of soil is precious to the Dogon. The Dogon even bury their dead in caves high up in these cliffs.

The Dogon wear masks decorated with cowrie shells

When Oumar is safely down again, he'll tell you how he loves all of the ceremonies that are part of Dogon life. He can't wait until he is older to learn to dance on colorful stilts wearing a mask of cowrie shells and hibiscus.

Dogon dancers on stilts

How would you tell Oumar about Jesus?

Oumar has been learning about Dogon tribal beliefs since he can remember. He probably wouldn't understand at first if you told him about Jesus. But there are some truths in the Bible that would help Oumar understand.

If a Dogon person does something wrong, the elders (the leaders) may make that person leave the village. This is a terrible punishment, because it means they have to start

life again all by themselves. But if they admit that they were wrong and want to be forgiven, they have to bring a goat or sheep to the edge of the village. The elders kill or sacrifice the animal and make a trail of blood to the door of this person's home. Then the people of the village accept the person who did wrong.

So you could tell Oumar about how God teaches us in the Bible that sin makes us unfit to go to heaven, just as his people believe sin makes a person unfit to live in the village. But killing a goat or sheep

won't get us into heaven. God's own Son Jesus, who the Bible calls "the Lamb of God," sacrificed himself for us. Jesus died on the cross so that we can be forgiven for all the bad things we've done and be acceptable to God. All we need to do is believe in him and be truly sorry. Then God will accept us into heaven to live with him always.

Praying for rain

The land where the Dogon live is very dry, but they need rain for the crops. One year, despite all the sacrifices the spirit worshippers made and the chanting of Muslims, rain

Cliff village

Sahara Desert

Mali

Africa

Bamako **DOGON**

ATLANTIC OCEAN

MEDITERRANEAN SEA

Do you know?

The region of the Bandiagara cliffs in Mali where the Dogon live is a world heritage site. These cliffs protect many ancient archeological structures (houses, altars and *toguna*, or meeting places). People have lived in these cliffs for at least 1,000 years.

didn't come. A visitor told the elders in one village, "When Christians pray, their God answers their prayers. Why don't you ask them to pray for you? I'm sure their God will send rain." The elders weren't too sure, but they talked with some Christians.

"Yes, we'll pray," the Christians told them, "but only if you stop all your sacrifices. Then when the rain comes everybody will know that our God sent it." The leaders agreed, the Christians prayed and the rain came.

The spirit worshippers immediately ran out to make sacrifices. The rain stopped. The elders realized they had broken their promise. "We're sorry," they said. "Please pray again. Our crops are dying, and we will be hungry." God sent plenty of rain so that Oumar and his people would know that God hears and answers our prayers.

It's hard to forgive others as God forgave us

There are about half a million Dogon, and more than 15,000 of them have come to know Jesus. The nomadic Fulani people live in the same part of Mali with the Dogon. The Dogon Christians don't always tell the Fulani about Jesus, though, because their cattle ruin the Dogon crops.

The Dogon know that God forgave them – and some have forgiven the Fulani. There is even a church among the Fulani now. Missionaries and Dogon pastors even hold a Bible school for Fulani Christians.

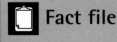 ## Fact file

Country: Mali

Numbers: About 500,000

Religions: Animism; Islam; Christianity

To help you pray for the Dogon

You can thank God for:

- the New Testament that has been translated into Dogon.

- the Dogon Christians who are sharing the good news about Jesus with the nomadic Fulani people.

You can ask God:

- to send enough rain for the crops to grow well so that the Dogon will have enough food for their families and some to sell in the market as well.

- to help the teams of Dogon Christians who are being trained to take the good news of Jesus' love to other Dogon people.

- to provide the resources for Dogon women to be trained, too, so that they can teach the Bible to other Dogon women and children.

- to help the team translating the Old Testament finish a translation that everyone will be able to understand easily.

- to provide plenty of books and teaching materials in Dogon for the new Doundou Ebon-Ezer Bible School.

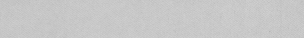

Druzes

Followers of a Secret Religion

The big secret

Do you find it hard to keep secrets? The Druzes have an important secret they've kept for almost a thousand years!

The Druzes live in the mountains of Lebanon, Syria, Israel and Jordan. Most of them are farmers who have olive groves and cherry and apple orchards on the hillsides and grow vegetables in their carefully tended gardens. Everyone has lots of work to do, but they still have plenty of time to visit with friends and family. Some Druzes live in the towns now as well. Wherever they are and whatever they do, the Druzes are known as hardworking people who can be trusted.

Their big secret is their religion. They keep what they believe to themselves and never share it with outsiders. Many people have tried to find out what they believe, but the Druzes often mislead them. Their religion has to be kept a secret.

Druze shrine where St Luke's tomb is claimed to be

No one can ever become a Druze – you must be born one. They believe that when they die, their souls immediately enter newborn Druze babies. That's the only way a person can become a Druze. A Druze should only marry another Druze, but if they marry someone of another faith their children will not be Druzes.

There are only a few people who know all the secrets about their religion. They are the 'Uqqal, the "Informed" or "Knowledgeable Ones." Both men and women can become 'Uqqal, but they must be at least 40 years old and have spent long periods of time studying the secrets of their religion. They are the only ones who are allowed to study the "Book of Wisdom," the Druze scriptures.

Knowledgeable Ones

On Thursday evenings, everyone in a Druze village meets in the *khilwa*, or meeting place. Let's talk to Samir and Salim as their parents join the other villagers. The women are all wearing long dresses, either dark blue or black, and white veils.

"Like most Druzes, our parents are 'Ignorant Ones', or Juhhal," Salim said quietly. "In the meeting room the women sit in one part of the room and the men sit in another."

"There's our uncle. He's an 'Uqqal," Samir whispered as a tall man walked by. "His white turban is a symbol of purity. He has to live by much stricter rules than our parents. He can't drink wine or smoke tobacco. He sometimes eats with us, but he always checks that we've bought everything or grown it ourselves. He wouldn't eat it if he thought the food had been stolen. They discuss all the village matters at the meeting,

Fact file

Estimated numbers: 300,000 – 450,000

Countries: Most live in Syria and Lebanon. There are smaller groups in Israel and Jordan.

then the Juhhal, including our parents, have to leave. But our uncle will stay with the 'Uqqal for secret meditation and to learn more about Druze beliefs."

Lessons to learn

"All the children in the village have to go to the meeting hall, too," added Samir. "We're taught many things, especially how we should live and how important it is to be honest and truthful, particularly to other Druzes. We must never tell anyone else about our Druze beliefs, or believe in anything else like Islam or Christianity. That's hard for

some of us, especially when we go to a Christian school."

The children are taught to always be ready to help each other and look after strangers, like Ali, who come to their village for help.

Bandits in Syria were hunting Ali, but he knew that he would find shelter in the chief's home in a Druze village. When the armed bandits came looking for Ali, the village chief walked out to greet them.

"Where's Ali? Give him up to us right now!" the bandits demanded. "We know

he's here. If he gives us money, he can live!"

"I am a Druze," the chief replied calmly. "This man has come to my home for shelter, and we will fight to the death to protect him!"

As the bandits raised their rifles, the Druze villagers fired shots at

them. The bandits ran away. The chief smiled. He had protected Ali.

The Druzes are waiting for Al-Hakim, the founder of their religion, to return to earth as their savior. But God wants the Druzes to trust in Jesus, the true Savior he has sent.

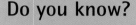

Do you know?

The Druze "Book of Wisdom" is written by hand and every copy is guarded carefully in a secret place. Only "Knowledgeable Ones" are allowed to study the "Book of Wisdom."

 ## To help you pray for the Druzes

You can thank God for:

● Christian schools and orphanages where Druze children are shown his love and can learn about Jesus.

● the many good things, such as being honest and truthful and caring for others, that Druze children learn.

You can ask God:

● to show children like Samir and Salim that studying the secret beliefs of the Druzes will never bring them eternal life.

● that Christians will make friends with Druze people and help them to understand that God wants the Druzes to be his friends, too.

● that many Druzes will be willing to read the Bible, and discover the truth about Jesus and his love.

● to send Christians to tell the Druzes that Jesus is the true Savior sent from God.

● to help the few Druze Christians to never doubt their faith in Jesus; to help them as their lives completely change – from keeping their religion a secret to sharing with everyone the great news about all that Jesus did when he died and rose again.

Mountains in Lebanon

Light Shines in the Darkness

"I wonder what we'll find today?" Dirty and ragged, Faud and Ramzi sit on top of the big pile of trash in their father's donkey-cart. As the tired old donkey plods along the busy Cairo street, cars, trucks and buses honk their horns as they pass. Every morning, Faud and Ramzi go with their father to collect trash from the city streets, offices and apartment blocks.

Faud and Ramzi's family lives in a crowded slum called "Garbage City" on the outskirts of Cairo, the capital of Egypt. When they get home, Faud and Ramzi carefully sort through the trash. They make piles of paper and cardboard, plastic and glass – they can make a little money selling these to factories for recycling. They leave the rest to the pigs, dogs and cats to paw through for food. Faud and Ramzi are used to the dirt and smell. After all, they've lived there all their lives.

Fact file

Area: 385,227 sq. mi. (96% of the country is desert)

Population: 68,469,695

Capital: Cairo (It is the largest city in the Middle East and Africa)

Language: Arabic

Religions: Islam (87.57%); Christianity (11.93%)

Chief export: Oil

MEDITERRANEAN SEA

Israel

● Cairo

Egypt

RED SEA

Sudan

A church in a cave near Cairo can seat 20,000 people

There are more than a million people in Cairo like Faud, Ramzi and their parents who scratch a living from the trash of the 15 million other people who live there. About half the people in Cairo are very poor, but there are also a lot of rich people, including at least 200,000 millionaires.

Teaching the poor

But some of the people in slum villages are finding hope through learning about Jesus. Farouk and Ali, two Coptic Christians (Coptic is an ancient name for Egyptian), go almost every day to the village where Faud and Ramzi live. "Why do you go there?" a friend asked them. "Aren't you afraid you'll get sick from all the trash?"

"The Bible says that God cares for the poor and needy," Farouk said, "and God wants us to care for them, too. That's why we go to the slums. The people there need all the help we can give them. Our church helps these people when they're sick, and we've set up a school where the children can learn to read. Come with us and meet some of the children."

Faud and Ramzi and the other children rushed over to Farouk and his friends as soon as they arrived. "It's time for our reading lesson," Farouk told them. "Go and get your books." Faud and Ramzi and some of the other children ran to their little

Do you know?

The Egyptians built the pyramids more than 4,000 years ago as tombs for the pharaohs. They are the only one of the seven wonders of the ancient world that still survives.

 ## To help you pray for Egypt

You can thank God for:

- Christians who go into the slums to help the poor.
- the *Jesus* film and Christian radio and television programs in Arabic.
- Christian bookshops and the work of the Bible Society.

You can ask God:

- that young people who learn about Jesus in Sunday schools, youth clubs and summer camps will decide to follow him.
- that as Christians study the Bible, their love for Jesus will grow.
- that Christians will always follow Jesus, even when they're persecuted.
- for those who don't know Jesus to see his love, joy and peace shine through Christians.

The pyramids, tombs built by ancient Egyptians

Garbage City, Cairo

huts and came back with their books. They were so excited to be learning to read. "Sometimes we bring Bible story books or tapes for them to listen to as well," Farouk told his friend.

There's a church in a cave on the mountainside beyond Garbage City. It can seat 20,000 people. "Many people from the slums are coming to know Jesus there," Farouk said. "They're discovering that even though they're so poor, they're important to God. In Psalm 113:7 it says that God 'raises the poor from the dust and lifts the needy from the ash heap,' and that's happening here."

An ancient church

A lot of stories in the Bible take place in Egypt. In Acts 2, in the New Testament, it says that there were Egyptians in the huge crowd in Jerusalem on the day of Pentecost. They heard Peter talk about God's love in sending Jesus, who would forgive their sins. Those Egyptians took the Christian faith back to their own country. The

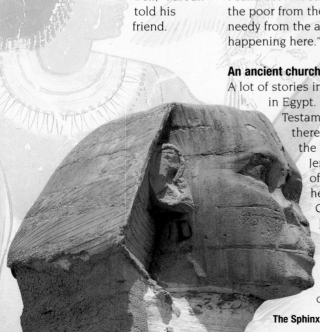

The Sphinx

Coptic church grew. It wasn't long before almost all Egyptians were Christians, and they were sending out missionaries to North Africa and Europe.

In AD 642, Arab Muslims invaded Egypt. Christians were forced to become Muslims, and thousands were persecuted and martyred. Egypt became a Muslim country. But the Coptic church never completely disappeared.

Today there are about nine million Coptic Christians living in Egypt. They have to have permission from the president himself to repair their churches or build new ones. They're often persecuted for their faith, but they're still finding ways to help people and share God's love.

Land of Refugees and Singing Christians

Ato is excited!

Seven-year-old Ato clapped his hands and jumped for joy. He had never been to school and he couldn't believe that some Christians had offered him a chance to go to the school they had started in his village. Ato's family used to be farmers in the highlands of Ethiopia, but they had moved to a slum in Addis Ababa, the capital city. Ato's mother had told him stories about life on the farm and about how hard it was to grow enough food for the family – especially when there were terrible droughts. His two sisters had become sick and died on the farm because there wasn't enough healthy food for them to eat. Ato also knew about the civil war that had been fought in his country and about how people from all over the world had sent food to help them. Life had been very difficult for his family on the farm, but life in the city was not much better and they were still very poor. For Ato, to go to school was a great opportunity for a better life.

The story so far

The first Christians came to Ethiopia about AD 300 and Orthodox Christianity became the state religion for the next 1,700 years. During the nineteenth and twentieth centuries, many Protestant missionaries worked in Ethiopia. They told people about Jesus, taught them to read and write and cared for the sick. But there are still people in some parts of Ethiopia who have never heard about Jesus.

A Communist government took over the country of Ethiopia in 1974. During the civil war that followed, many

Fact file

Area: 427,000 sq. mi.

Population: 62,564,875

Capital: Addis Ababa

Main language: Amharic, but 123 other languages are spoken

Main religions: Christianity; Islam

Chief exports: Coffee; animal skins; oil-seed

Do you know?

Ethiopia may hold the key to a great mystery! The ark of the covenant was the most holy object belonging to the ancient Israelites. The ark was a small box with a gold lid. Inside it were the stone tablets with the Ten Commandments that God gave to Moses on Mt. Sinai (you can read more about how the Israelites made the ark in Exodus 25). The ark was in the temple in Jerusalem until it disappeared in 587 BC when the Babylonians captured Jerusalem. Many Ethiopians believe that the ark of the covenant was smuggled out of the confusion and taken to Axum in Ethiopia. They claim that the ark is still there, in a small, closely guarded chapel.

Ethiopians fled to other countries to escape from the fighting. At the same time, refugees from nearby Sudan and Somalia came to Ethiopia, hoping to get away from the wars and starvation in their own countries. Instead, they only found more fighting and famine in Ethiopia. Aid agencies worked in the refugee camps to help the homeless, starving and dying people.

There have been Christians in Ethiopia for nearly 2,000 years

 ## To help you pray for Ethiopia

You can thank God for:

- the thousands of Ethiopians who are Christians.

- the Christians who are helping to show God's love as they bring food, medical care, education, clean water and new ways of farming to people in need.

- each small Bible school.

You can ask God:

- to protect Ethiopian Christians who are helping to translate the Bible into their own language, and to help them to write clearly and accurately.

- to help every pastor and evangelist to be faithful in the way they live as well as in the words they speak.

- to help Ethiopian Christians work together and show those who belong to different people groups that Jesus loves them all.

- to bring peace to Ethiopia and nearby countries so that refugees can return to their own homes.

Ethiopia has many needs and is one of the world's poorest countries

food for themselves and their families. These Christians are showing God's love in a very practical way to many people who are in need.

All over Ethiopia there are small Bible schools for training pastors and evangelists. There are lots of people becoming Christians, and they need people who can teach them about God in their own languages. This is especially important in Ethiopia, where 123 different languages are spoken!

Ethiopia continues to have many needs. There are still refugees who cannot go back to their own countries. The people still suffer from war and drought, and Ethiopia is one of the poorest countries in the world. Although some people are well educated and have good jobs and nice homes, many children never go to school and their families, like Ato's family, are very poor.

The Communist government imprisoned Christian leaders and closed churches, and many missionaries had to leave the country. In spite of this, the church grew larger and larger. When the Communist government was overthrown in 1991, it was discovered that thousands of Ethiopians had come to know Jesus as their friend. The Christians in Ethiopia love to sing. They often sing going along the road to market or washing their clothes by the river, and everywhere they go they tell others how Jesus died to give them eternal life.

Some Ethiopian Christians are working among people groups in their country who have never heard of the God who loves them. Some are helping missionaries with Bible translation and others are teaching children or working in health care projects. Some are trying to bring clean water to all the villages, and still others are starting agricultural projects to help people grow enough

Falashas

Black Jews from Ethiopia

"The House of Israel"

The Falashas (fah-lah-shuhz) are black Jews who have lived in Ethiopia for a very long time. The word falasha *means "stranger" in the Amharic language of Ethiopia, but they call themselves* Beta Israel, *or "the House of Israel."*

Some people think the Falashas may be descendants of Jews who returned to Ethiopia with Menelik, the legendary son of King Solomon and the Queen of Sheba – but no one really knows. The Falashas follow the Jewish faith, keep the Sabbath and obey the laws from the first five books of the Bible.

📋 Fact file

There may be as many as 100,000 Falashas, but no one really knows.

There are 20,000 in **Ethiopia** who still want to go to Israel.

There are about 60,000 in **Israel**.

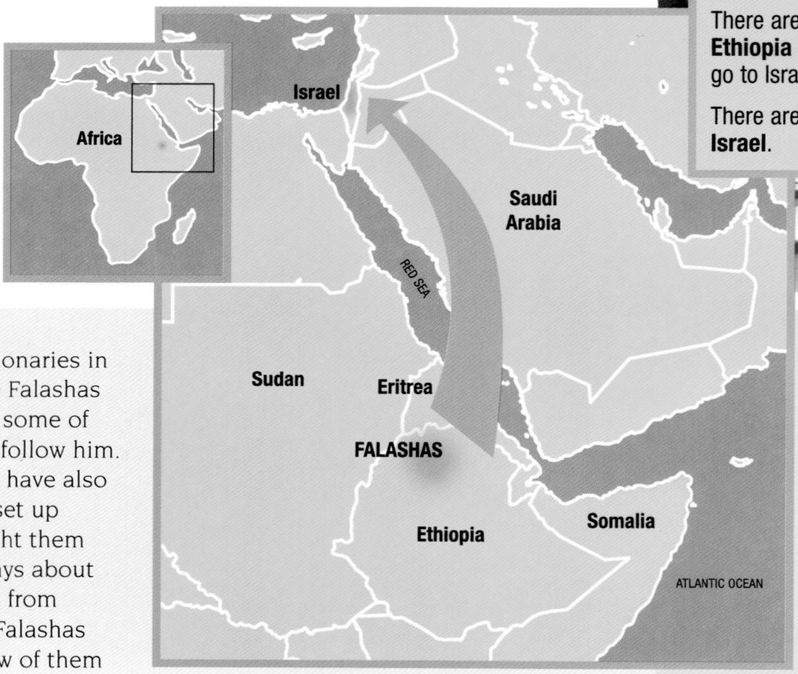

Christian missionaries in Ethiopia told the Falashas about Jesus, and some of them decided to follow him. The missionaries have also helped the sick, set up schools and taught them what the Bible says about Jesus. When Jews from Europe told the Falashas about Israel, a few of them decided to go there.

Map labels: Africa; Israel; Saudi Arabia; RED SEA; Sudan; Eritrea; FALASHAS; Ethiopia; Somalia; ATLANTIC OCEAN

Operation Moses

During the Communist revolution in Ethiopia in the 1970s and 1980s, the Falashas suffered a lot because they believed in God.

"It was terrible," Abraham remembers. "I was only a little boy. There was civil war in Ethiopia and, to make matters worse, we were starving because there was no rain to make our crops grow. Our animals died, too. My family joined thousands of others in the long walk to a refugee camp in Sudan. It took us ten days, and a lot of children and old people died on the way. We hoped that, once we reached the camps, we'd be able to go to Israel. The Bible says that the Jewish people will to return to Israel someday, and we thought maybe that day had come.

Falasha boys outside a school in Jerusalem

Falasha village in Ethiopia

 ## To help you pray for the Falashas

You can thank God for:

- every Ethiopian Jew who has come to know Jesus.
- the Israeli government, who rescued so many Ethiopian Jews and gave them a fresh start in Israel.

You can ask God:

- to show the Falashas that their journey to God does not end in Israel, but that he has a home in heaven for all who believe in Jesus.
- to help the Ethiopian Jews as they adjust to life in Israel.
- for the children to do well at school and for the older people to adjust to their new life.
- to give the Falashas good friends in Israel.
- for the Falashas to hear that Jesus loves them and wants them to follow him.

Falasha children on a school bus in Jerusalem, Israel

"We were very excited when we heard that the Israelis had arranged a secret rescue plan called 'Operation Moses.' They crammed us all onto planes, which was scary since most of us had never been on a plane before."

That was in 1984. About 13,000 Ethiopian Jews were flown to Israel, but the flights were stopped when the story leaked out.

Operation Solomon

For those left behind in Ethiopia, life became even more difficult. The civil war was even worse, and there was famine in the country again. Jews, along with everyone else, had to obey new laws. "These laws were hard for us," Hailu said, "especially since markets could only be held on Saturdays, the Jewish Sabbath. Like thousands of other Jews, my family moved from the countryside to Addis Ababa, the capital city. We registered with the Israeli Embassy there, hoping we could go to Israel. We had to wait a long time and sold everything we owned so that we could buy food. We were so glad that the Israelis and some Christians helped us.

"By 1991, the Communist government only controlled Addis Ababa and the area around the city. The rebel armies were getting closer to the city, and the Israelis were afraid that there would be a lot of killing and looting and the Ethiopian Jews would be blamed for it.

"The Israelis had secret talks with the Ethiopian government and the rebels. The government finally agreed to let Israeli planes fly in to get us, and the rebels promised not to attack the city for a few days.

"All the seats had been taken out of the planes," Hailu remembers, "and we weren't allowed to take any luggage so they could carry more people. In just 30 hours, 14,400 Ethiopian Jews were flown to Israel – and several babies were born on the way! 'Operation Solomon' was kept secret until we all landed in Israel."

"In Ethiopia," Hailu continued, "we lived in small villages and worked as farmers, potters, iron workers or weavers. Everything was so different in Israel. My family lived in a big apartment building with electricity, running water, flush toilets, elevators and new kinds of food. But we soon felt at home, especially once we learned to speak Hebrew."

Some of the Ethiopian Jews in Israel have been Christians for several generations, and a few others have come to know Jesus more recently. Please pray that many more Ethiopian Jews in Israel will meet Messianic Jews (followers of Jesus) who will tell them about Jesus.

Do you know?

The New Testament talks a lot about the Jews. They're the descendants of the Israelites of the Old Testament. Although the Jews in Jesus' day rejected him, God wants us to take the gospel to the Jews so that they can follow Jesus and live forever.

A Nation of Islands

The beautiful islands of Fiji, with their warm sunny beaches, are located in the South Pacific Ocean to the east of Australia. Although there are more than 300 islands, only 112 of them are inhabited. Vitu Levu and Vanua Levu, the two main islands, were formed from volcanoes and their steep mountain slopes are covered with forests. Suva, the capital of Fiji, is the biggest city in the whole of the South Pacific region.

Fiji is a fertile country. If you look carefully at the coat of arms on Fiji's flag you will see sugar cane, a coconut palm, a cocoa pod and bananas. Two of the country's main exports are sugar and copra (dried coconut). Coconut oil is extracted from the copra and used to make many different things – including soap, shampoo and margarine.

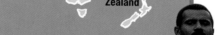

Fact file

Area: 7,050 sq. mi.

Population: 816,905

Capital: Suva

Main religions: Christianity; Hinduism; Islam

Official language: English

Chief exports: Sugar; copra; gold; fish

Sharing the good news

You will also see a dove of peace, a Christian symbol, on the coat of arms on Fiji's flag. Christians came to Fiji over 150 years ago to tell the people there about Jesus. Fijian Christians believed the good news of Jesus was too wonderful to keep to themselves, and many of them set out on dangerous journeys in deep-sea canoes to tell people on other Pacific islands about God's love. And so another symbol of Christianity in Fiji is a deep-sea canoe.

Many years ago, there was a missionary called Dr. Brown who wanted evangelists from Fiji to go with him to Papua New Guinea to tell people there about Jesus. Dr. Brown asked for volunteers at the pastors' training college, but he thought no one would be willing

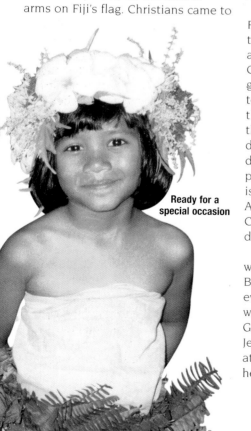

Ready for a special occasion

Presidential guard

to go because thousands of people in Fiji had just died from measles. He was very surprised when every one of the 84 students said they would go with him! One of their leaders stood up and said, "Our minds are made up. We have given ourselves to God's work. If we live, we live. If we die, we die." They were willing to risk everything to tell others that Jesus died on the cross so that we can be forgiven for the bad things we've done and have eternal life.

Indians of Fiji

About 100 years ago, people from India were brought to Fiji to work on the sugar plantations. Now there are almost as many Indians as Fijians in

 To help you pray for Fiji

You can thank God for:

- all the Christians in Fiji.

- the Indians who know Jesus.

- the friendships between Fijian Christians and Indians.

- the many Chinese people who come to work in Fiji for a few years and the young people from other islands who study there.

You can ask God:

- to resolve the political situation peacefully, restore democracy to the island and help the government leaders to always be fair.

- to help Fijians and Indians learn to live at peace with one another and to forgive each other.

- to bring many Indian boys and girls to know and love Jesus at Sunday school.

Do you know?

The International Date Line passes between the islands of Fiji. This means that Fiji is one of the first countries in the world to welcome each new day.

The fighting between Fijians and Indians makes it hard for them to see Jesus' love

Tuna packing factory

the country. Most of these Indians are Hindus, Muslims or Sikhs.

Fiji was a British colony for almost 100 years. After Fiji became a country with its own government in 1970, many ethnic Fijians were afraid that the Indians would take over their country. They were upset when the Fiji Labour Party, which tried to bring Indians and Fijians together, won the national elections in 1987. There were more Indians than Fijians in the

newly elected government, so the army tried to get rid of this government.

Some Fijians were angry with the Indians and did things that were very wrong. Some of them set fire to mosques and temples belonging to the Indians. But Christian leaders spoke out against these terrible actions. The Indian people felt angry and afraid, and many of them left Fiji. Because the Indians who still live in

Fiji have terrible memories of all of this, it is hard for many of them to believe that Jesus loves them.

Fiji was governed very differently for several years, with rules making sure that there would always be more Fijians elected to the government than Indians. But some Fijian rebels staged another coup in the year 2000 to try again to get rid of all Indians in government.

Many Fijian Christians have started to pray for people all over the world who haven't heard about Jesus, and some have become missionaries in other countries. Although they want to share the love of Jesus with those in their own country too, the uncertain political situation will probably make it even harder for Indians to accept Jesus. And it will also be harder for those Indians who have accepted Jesus already to live as Christians in Fiji.

Garifuna

Descendants of Slaves and Carib Indians

"Look what I've got!"

The man checking security at a small Caribbean airport rummaged through Roger's suitcase. He pulled out a book. "What's this? What language is it?" he demanded in Spanish. "It's not Spanish."

"It's a Garifuna (gah-ree-foo-na) New Testament," Roger replied. "Garifuna? That's my language!" the man exclaimed. "I've seen a Spanish Bible, but I've never seen a book in Garifuna. I'd love to learn how to read it. Where can I get a copy of this?"

"I'm afraid they're all sold out," Roger explained. "This is my only copy." "Please let me have it," the man pleaded. He was so excited when Roger gave it to him. He clutched the New Testament and showed it to everyone, shouting, "Look what I've got!"

Do you know?

Although most of them speak Spanish and some can read it, Garifuna is the "language that speaks to their hearts." One Garifuna minister was so delighted with his New Testament that he said, "May we chew God's word, swallow it and let it enter into our veins!"

The Garifuna New Testament has been reprinted since Roger gave his last copy to this man several years ago. Nearly all of the Garifuna speak Spanish, the language of the countries in which they live. But they speak their own language among themselves. Now they're learning to read in their own language and, as they read the New Testament and their teachers explain it to them, a lot of them are deciding to follow Jesus.

The Old Testament has now been translated into Garifuna as well.

Shipwrecked slaves

The Garifuna, or Black Caribs, are descendants of slaves that British and Spanish boats brought from Africa in the seventeenth century.

Sometimes these boats were shipwrecked and the slaves escaped. Their masters set other slaves free. Many of them settled on St. Vincent in the Windward Islands, where they married Carib Indians.

Because they caused some trouble, the British shipped them all off to the island of Roatan, far away across the Caribbean Sea, in 1797. Eventually they made their way to South America, where they settled in villages along the coasts of Belize, Honduras and Guatemala. A lot of them still make their living by fishing and farming.

![hand icon] To help you pray for the Garifuna

You can thank God for:

● the Garifuna Bible, both Old and New Testaments.

● each Garifuna who has come to know Jesus.

You can ask God:

● that the Garifuna will read and understand the whole Bible.

● to give patience to those teaching people to read the long and complicated words in Garifuna.

● to use the *Jesus* film to bring more Garifuna people to know him.

● to take away their fear of evil spirits as the Garifuna turn to Jesus.

● to send people to train Garifuna Christians to become pastors, leaders and evangelists.

![clipboard icon] Fact file

Countries: Honduras; Belize; Guatemala; Nicaragua

Numbers: About 100,000

Languages: Spanish; Garifuna

Religion: Animism

Occupations: Farming; fishing

They took their own African and Carib beliefs with them, and soon added Catholicism to the mixture. Nearly all Garifuna children are baptized into the Roman Catholic Church, but they also wear a ribbon tied around their wrist to protect them from evil spirits. They believe there are spirits living all around them and put a cross over the doorway of their houses to protect the family from harm. They believe dreams, crying chickens and howling dogs are all omens that foretell the future.

Jesus is alive!

Although many Garifuna knew a few stories about Jesus, very few of them understood who he really is and why God sent him to earth. There was great excitement when missionaries showed the *Jesus* film in Garifuna in a field outside one village. Two hundred people came to watch.

In the film, Jesus speaks to a small child in Garifuna, "Hello. What are you doing?" "Nothing," the child replies.

"He knows our greeting," the people cried in delight, clapping their hands. "He speaks Garifuna!" They watched the film with great excitement, talking with one another about what they saw and heard.

"Who wouldn't believe in Jesus?" one lady said to her friend. "Did you see how he healed the blind man?"

"Look!" some men exclaimed. "They fish like we do. We know what it's like to fish all night and catch nothing. When Jesus told them to put their nets back in the sea, they had a great catch! Amazing! And Jesus calmed that storm, too. Lots of people we know have died in storms like that. He must be more powerful than all the spirits of the sea if he can do that! He must be worth following."

As they watched Jesus dying on the cross, many of the people wept. At the end of the film, 35 people said they wanted to follow Jesus. More people came to watch the film the next night, and even more decided to follow him.

Many of the Garifuna want to hear God's word and learn how to follow him. The churches are growing. A missionary working with the Garifuna said, "It's great to know so many children are praying for the Garifuna." God is answering our prayers so let's keep praying that many more Garifuna will come to know Jesus.

Gonds

Forest-dwellers of Central India

"Who can help us?"

"What else can we do?" The people in Lion village were very worried. Lots of people were sick, and several had died. "What about the medicine man?" someone asked. "We've been to him," someone else said. "He prayed to the spirits and made sacrifices and offerings to them, but it only made things worse." "I don't know why the spirits are treating us like this," another person said sadly.

"Let's go talk to the Christians and their teacher," someone suggested. "They say their God is more powerful than all our spirits. Maybe he can stop this sickness."

Right: Dressed for a Gond wedding

Pakistan
• Delhi
India
GOND
• Nagpur
ARABIAN SEA
BAY OF BENGAL

So they went to the missionary. "Can you help us?" they asked.

"I'll pray for you, and so will all the Christians in the village," said the Indian missionary. "Our God is greater than any other god or spirit. He promises that he will hear and answer our prayers. He can heal this sickness."

As the missionary and the Christians prayed together, God healed ten people in Lion village! "It's true that the God of the Christians is greater than the spirits," the people said. "We want to follow him."

A forest village

Lion village is deep in the forests of central India, and the villagers belong to the Gond tribe. There are many different tribes in India, but the Gonds are one of the largest. Although the Indian government classifies them as Hindus, most of them are animists. They believe that evil spirits wait in the fields and forests, looking for ways to harm them. The Gonds make sacrifices to these spirits, hoping they will leave them alone.

Many of the Gonds work as farmers. They keep some cattle and grow millet, maize, wheat and beans. They make their simple homes from bamboo and timber with roofs of leaves. The houses have only one or two rooms. In one room there will be a few wooden stools and a hammock or two, and some cooking pots in the kitchen.

Many older Gonds can't read or write, and so other people often cheat them when they sell things in the towns. The Indian government wants to help them, and in some places it has set up schools where Gond children can study.

Gond herdboy

64

To help you pray for the Gonds

You can thank God for:

- every Gond who is following Jesus.
- Gond Christians who are studying the Bible and learning how to tell others about Jesus.

You can ask God:

- that lots of Gond boys and girls will decide to follow Jesus, who is always with them and helps them when they're afraid.
- to show the Gonds that he is far more powerful than all the gods and spirits they fear and worship.
- to keep the Indian missionaries safe as they travel to Gond villages.
- to help those who are translating the Bible into Gondi, which is a difficult language, so that everyone can understand it.
- that there will be a church in every Gond village.

Lion village

Because of the amazing miracle of healing, many of the people who live in Lion village are Christians. Let's go with an Indian missionary to visit them. Since there aren't any roads for cars or buses, we'll travel in a bullock cart. "It will take us all day to get there," the missionary warns us. "And the cart doesn't have springs or comfortable seats, so you'll probably feel a bit sore as we bump along the rough trails. It's a long way, but you might prefer to walk! Since we'll have to travel very slowly through the forest, you'll have plenty of time to see all the birds, and maybe even a bear or a tiger!"

Everyone in Lion village is excited to see us, and

Fact file

Country: Central India

Numbers: About 12,700,000 (they're the biggest tribal group in Central India)

Language: Gondi, but they often speak the language of other peoples who live in the same areas.

Religions: Animism; Hinduism

Occupations: Farmers; laborers; businessmen

they make us feel at home. "Since we started to follow Jesus," someone tells us, "he's changed our lives and made us into new people." "Yes," someone else says, "we used to be afraid of the spirits all the time, but now we know they don't have

any power over us. Jesus gives us joy and peace." Someone else is eager to tell us about the miracle. "We know Jesus cares for us," he said, "because when everyone in the village was sick, only Jesus had the power to make us well. Now we want to learn as much as we can about him. And we want others to know Jesus, too."

New life for the Gonds

Some of the Gond Christians are going to special training centers to learn what the Bible says and how to share the good news about Jesus with their own people. They're reaching out to more villages, but there are still a lot of villages where the people have never heard of Jesus. Please help change the world for the Gonds by praying for them.

Home of the First Olympic Games

Fact file

Area: 51,350 sq. mi.

Population: 10,644,744

Capital: Athens

Language: Greek

Religion: Orthodox Christianity

Chief exports: Clothes; olive oil

A visit to church

Like a lot of Greek boys, nine-year-old Dimitris had only been to church a few times. Every time he went with his grandmother, she bought him a candle, lit it and told him to bow down in front of a picture of a saint. These pictures, called icons, were everywhere in the church. Dimitris made the sign of the cross, kissed the picture and left the candle beside it. As they stood listening to the church service, Dimitris saw the joy on his grandmother's face.

Bulgaria

Albania

Greece

Turkey

Athens

MEDITERRANEAN SEA

Greek Orthodox priests

Another way of worship

Dimitris and his grandmother saw a group of young people singing and handing out booklets on the street one day. Dimitris wanted to listen, but suddenly a man started to shout at the group and some of the people who had taken the booklets dropped them.

"What's happening? Why is the man so angry?" Dimitris asked his grandmother. "The music was really good – and they were singing about Jesus. What's wrong with that?"

"They're evangelicals," she told him. "Almost all Greeks belong to the Greek Orthodox Church – even though most of them don't go to church very often. A lot of Greeks, like that man shouting, think the evangelicals are heretics because they don't belong to the Orthodox Church or follow our traditional way of worshipping God. Your uncle goes to an evangelical church. He says it's a very simple place with no icons, statues or candles to help them worship God. The people who go there talk about Jesus as their friend who is with them always. I just wish we could all get along as we worship the same God in different ways."

Sharing the good news

The evangelical church in Greece is small and not very popular. Some evangelicals have even been put in prison for talking about Jesus. As well as holding meetings in their churches, they preach on the streets, sing, put on plays, give out booklets and help those in need. Some groups publish and sell Christian books, and now there are two Bible schools.

Spinning yarn

c. 1400 BC
Earliest record of
Greek mythology

c. 776 BC
Race in Olympia

c. 450 BC
"Golden Age" of Greek

c. 400–300
Aristotle/Pla
Socrates

The Parthenon, an ancient temple, on the Acropolis in Athens

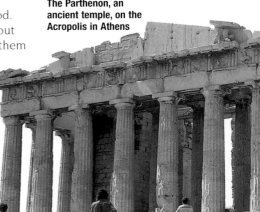

 ## To help you pray for Greece

You can thank God for:

- every Greek who knows and follows Jesus.

- Christian books, cassettes, papers and radio broadcasts that explain who Jesus is and what he has done to save us.

You can ask God:

- to help all who call themselves Christians to work together and be an example of Jesus' love.

- to encourage young people to be brave and not afraid as they talk to people on the streets about Jesus.

- that young people going to university will meet Christians who are filled with joy because they follow Jesus.

- to keep the "Morning Star" safe as it sails from island to island and to give the crew courage as they share the good news about Jesus.

- that Christian tourists visiting Greece will have opportunities to share Jesus' love with the people they meet.

Olympic gold medal

Birth of Christ

| C. AD 50 Paul preaches to the Greeks | 1054 The beginning of the Eastern Orthodox Church | 1829 Greece became independant | 2004 Olympic Games return to Greece |

C. AD 60
New Testament written in Greek

1896
First modern Olympic Games

There are hundreds of islands in the beautiful blue waters of the Ionian and Aegean Seas surrounding Greece. The boat "Morning Star" visits these islands with teams of evangelists. Angry protesters have tried to stop them from preaching on some of the islands, and sometimes the evangelists have been arrested. But people on other islands welcome the "Morning Star," and some have decided to follow Jesus because the evangelists have explained the truth of the Bible to them. Some of these people had always gone to church but never heard that Jesus is our friend and savior who is with us all the time.

Living history

Our world would be a very different place without the art, literature, theater, science and philosophy that came from Greece. A lot of ideas that people have today are based on what the great Greek philosophers said thousands of years ago. You may also know some of the myths about the Greek gods Zeus, Apollo, Athena and others.

Sports have always been important to the Greeks, too. The first Olympic game, a running race, was held in the Greek town of Olympia in the eighth century BC as part of a religious festival. The first modern Olympic Games were held in Athens in 1896, and again in 2004. They take place in a different country every four years.

Greece has beautiful beaches, ancient ruins, islands and mountain villages that haven't changed for centuries. More than nine million tourists visit Greece every year. But Greece still needs missionaries who will talk to people like Dimitris and his family about Jesus.

Do you know ?

Greece was the first country in Europe to hear the gospel, which was preached to them by the apostle Paul himself (about AD 50). The people are proud that the original New Testament was written in the Greek language. In Acts 16, 17 and 18 we read how God called Paul to take the good news about Jesus to Greece.

Greenland

The Largest Island in the World

An Eskimo boy

Eight-year-old Sigssuk snuggled into bed. He was tired, but much too excited to sleep. His father had taken him on his first ever seal-hunt today, and they'd caught two seals. He dreamed of becoming a great hunter someday!

Sigssuk is an Eskimo, or Inuit, and lives with his family on the northwest coast of Greenland. Hunting is a very important part of their lives. Almost as soon as he'd learned to walk, Sigssuk's father had given him a puppy and a toy whip so he could learn to train his own dog. His father also built him a special kayak (canoe), which he hung from a beam in the house so that it was just a few inches from the ground. Sigssuk had great fun sitting in it and learning how to control it with a small paddle.

Every summer, when it's daylight all the time, Sigssuk goes with his family on camping trips. He catches little auks (seabirds) in a net. They cook and eat some of the birds, but they put the rest in a special sealskin sack to save for food in the winter.

Fact file

Area: 840,020 sq. mi.; 85% of the land is a glacial ice cap

Population: 56,156

Capital: Nuuk

Languages: Greenlandic; Danish

Religion: Christianity

Chief exports: Fish and fish products

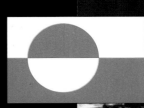

The sun never rises during the long, dark winter months in Greenland. During the winter Sigssuk goes to the village school, where he learns to read and write. School is much more exciting when some of the men teach them about hunting and show them how to build their own kayaks and sledges. It's usually too cold for Sigssuk and his friends to play outside in the winter. So they stay inside and play games, watch television and videos and listen to the grown-ups tell stories about hunting expeditions.

Greenland is the largest island in the world. It belongs to Denmark, but Greenland has governed itself since 1979. Most of the country lies inside the Arctic Circle, and an enormous ice sheet covers a lot of it. Some, like Sigssuk and his family, are Eskimos. But most Greenlanders are descendants of Eskimos who have married European settlers. Nearly all of them live in small towns on the south and west coasts, where they make a living from fishing and hunting.

Greenland may be a cold, dark place – but Jesus brings warmth and light

Greenland

Greenland

BAFFIN BAY

● Nuuk

ATLANTIC OCEAN

National costume is worn by Greenlandic children on special occasions

The first Christians

Erik the Red, a Norseman from Iceland, first discovered Greenland about 1,000 years ago. He called the country Greenland – even though it's covered in ice – to persuade his family and friends to join him there. A group of brave men, women and children set sail across the stormy seas. They took their horses, cows and sheep with them. Erik's son, Leif the

Lucky, became a Christian on a visit to Norway. When he returned to Greenland he told everyone about Jesus and a lot of people became Christians.

A missionary from Denmark went to Greenland in 1721, hoping to find that the descendants of those first settlers were Christians. But no one in Greenland followed Jesus anymore. Other settlers came from Denmark

To help you pray for Greenland

You can thank God for:

- the *Jesus* film in Greenlandic.

- camps where children can learn about Jesus.

- the new translation of the Bible in Greenlandic.

You can ask God:

- to show the people that being a Christian means far more than going to church once a year.

- to help Christians encourage one another to always follow Jesus.

- for Christians to go to the Discipleship Training School to study the Bible and learn to tell others about Jesus.

- that many in Greenland who are sad and lonely will discover that Jesus really is alive and ready to help them when life is difficult.

Boys enjoying themselves at the Christian camp run by the Ebenezer church in Nuuk

Do you know?

The ice sheet covering Greenland averages nearly 5,000 feet in depth. If the ice ever melted, all the oceans of the world would rise about 20 feet!

and Norway, and the Greenlanders started to follow Jesus again and were baptized. They built churches in almost every little town and village, and the Bible was translated into the Greenlandic language.

The *Jesus* film

Olaf and his family live in Nuuk, the capital of Greenland. Like many Greenlanders, they call themselves Christians and always go to church at Christmas time. But when Olaf fell and broke his arm, his mother stitched a charm inside his coat to keep him safe and asked the spirits of her ancestors to help him.

One day, Olaf heard that the first movie in Greenlandic, a film about Jesus, was going to be shown in Nuuk. Olaf and his family couldn't wait to see it. As Olaf watched the *Jesus* film, he realized that Jesus died on the cross to take away all the bad things he had done. He wanted Jesus to give him a clean new life.
Now Olaf and

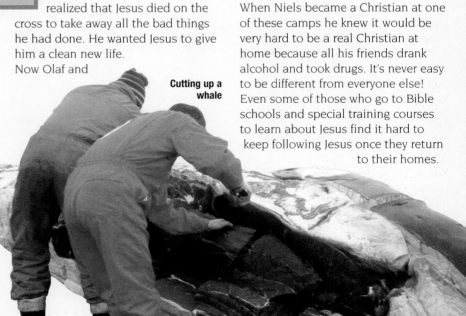

Cutting up a whale

his family really are following Jesus.

Several evangelical organizations in Greenland hold special meetings and camps for both children and adults. When Niels became a Christian at one of these camps he knew it would be very hard to be a real Christian at home because all his friends drank alcohol and took drugs. It's never easy to be different from everyone else! Even some of those who go to Bible schools and special training courses to learn about Jesus find it hard to keep following Jesus once they return to their homes.

Guinea-Bissau

A War-torn Country being Healed with God's Love

Escape!

"What's that noise?" Paulo cried. *"I'm so scared ... it sounds like lots of guns going off!"*

"Stay here with your mother and sister," his father said. *"I'll find out what's going on. Maybe the army's having an early morning firing practice."*

He came rushing back a few minutes later.

"Pack everything right now. We need to get out of Bissau," he told them. *"The army has revolted against the government!"*

Africa

Gambia

Senegal

Guinea-Bissau
• Bissau

Guinea

ATLANIC OCEAN

They grabbed what belongings they could and joined thousands of people trying to escape from the fighting in the city. Paulo's mother carried his little sister and Paulo ran beside his father, afraid that he might get lost on the way. Every taxi and truck that passed them was already filled with people, so they walked and walked until they reached safety.

Sharing God's love

"I'm tired and hungry," Paulo complained when they finally sat down to rest under a mango tree. "Where are we going to stay?" As they were sitting there wondering what to do, a man came by. "Come to my house," he said. "You can stay with me." The man was a Christian, and his house was already packed with other refugees. "You can stay here as long as there's enough rice in my house," he said.

When food supplies began to arrive in Bissau from other countries, pastors, Bible school students and other Christians helped give it out. As

they gave food to the people, they told them about the love of Jesus. Pastors talked about God's love and care over the radio. They also helped with peace talks between the two sides in the fighting.

This revolt on Sunday, June 7th, 1998 came as a surprise to Paulo and his family and most people in Bissau. The airport was closed down, along with the post office, schools and most of the stores. The civil war lasted for 11 months.

Paulo's family returned to Bissau

Many people learned about Jesus' love during the war when Christians helped those who were suffering

Do you know?

Many people in Guinea-Bissau are afraid of evil spirits. When twins are born, they're sometimes left outside to die because the witch doctor tells the parents that one of the babies is a spirit baby. That's changing now because Christians are explaining to parents that both twins are special and precious to God.

after the war. They, along with many others, found that their house had been destroyed and their belongings stolen. But they couldn't afford to fix or replace anything since they had scarcely enough money to buy food! Through the Christian love of the man

To help you pray for Guinea-Bissau

You can thank God for:

- the Christians who opened their homes to people fleeing from the fighting.
- Christian radio broadcasts and the *Jesus* film.

You can ask God:

- to help each new Christian to want to know Jesus more and more.
- to give patience to those helping adults learn to read.
- to provide enough money for those who want to go to Bible school to learn to teach others about God.
- that the tribes in Guinea-Bissau, who live in fear of evil spirits, will realize that Jesus is more powerful.
- that the leaders will rule the country fairly and wisely.

Fact file

Area: 14,000 sq. mi.

Population: 1,179,000

Capital: Bissau

Main languages: Portuguese; Creole

Main religions: Animism; Islam; Christianity

Main products: Peanuts; cashew nuts; cotton

Crushing cashew fruit. The juice is used to make a drink.

You can speak Creole

Good morning is "Bon dia" (bon dee-a)

How are you? is "Kuma di kurpu?" (Koo-ma dee koor-poo)

See you later is "Te logu" (Te log-oo)

who took them in when they were refugees, Paulo and his family learned that Jesus is their friend and helps them when life is really hard. Many other men and women, boys and girls also came to know Jesus. So now there are new groups of Christians in places where there were no Christians before the war. They have seen God's love at work. His love has filled their hearts, and they want to share that love with others.

A poor country

Guinea-Bissau is a small country in West Africa, between Senegal in the north and Guinea in the south. It's one of the poorest countries in the world. Portugal ruled Guinea-Bissau for many years, but in 1974, after a long war, the country became independent.

Most of the country is on the African mainland. Mangrove swamps and marshes cover the land along the coast, where rice grows. Further inland are rain forests and *savanna* where people grow peanuts, mangoes, beans and cotton. Offshore, out in the Atlantic Ocean, are the forest-covered Bijagos Islands.

Many languages

Although it's a small country, more than 25 people groups live in Guinea-Bissau. Each group has its own language, but most people speak Creole – a mixture of Portuguese and local African languages. The New Testament has been translated into the Balanta, Bijago, Mandingo and Papel languages, and the whole Bible has now been translated into Creole.

Cashew tree

Gypsies

Nomads of the World

Who are the Gypsies and where do they come from? About 1,200 years ago, large groups of people began moving out of the region that we call the Punjab in northwest India and northeast Pakistan. As they went, they earned their living as musicians and entertainers, horse traders, blacksmiths and craftsmen.

Today, there may be as many as 40 million Gypsies living all over the world – in more than 40 countries and on every continent. Many of them are still nomads, moving from place to place, often following their traditional work. Although most Gypsies speak the language of the people among whom they live, most of them also speak one of the 20 or more Romany dialects. There are many different groups of Gypsies, each with a slightly different dialect and lifestyle.

for the Gypsy people. But God has been answering prayers, and since 1950 thousands of Gypsies in many parts of the world have become Christians.

Inside a Gypsy caravan in the UK

Because Gypsies have kept their own way of life and have never become a part of the countries where they live, they are often despised, disliked and neglected. As they tend to move from one place to another, few of their children go to school long enough to learn to read or write.

Gypsy children are well loved. If your parents were Gypsies you would be sure to know to be respectful to older people and not to talk to strangers. You would also learn the many Gypsy rules about cleanliness. You would live in a caravan and help to keep it spotless. You would only be allowed to eat certain kinds of food. For example, Muslim Rom Gypsies eat chicken, but not pork. But Kaale Rom Gypsies from Finland think chickens are dirty. Some

Gypsies eat hedgehogs, while others think they're unclean. If you were a Gypsy you would learn many traditional dances and songs. If you were invited to a wedding, you might be there feasting and dancing for three whole days!

Are you a "Gorgio"? That is what Gypsies call those who aren't Gypsies. In 1901 there was a Gypsy called Rodney Smith who preached about Jesus to "Gorgios" in Britain and South Africa. Thousands of them became Christians. When people asked Rodney Smith why he wasn't preaching to his own people, he told them that the time had not yet come

Do you know?

In the parable of the great banquet (Luke 14:15–24), a man prepared a party for all his guests. But when those he had invited refused to come, the master told his servant to "Go out to the roads and country lanes and make them come in, so that my house will be full." Many leaders of the Gypsy Christians believe that they are these last guests, coming to Jesus now.

Gypsy site in London, UK

Clara's discovery

Clara was twenty years old. She lived with her parents in their Gypsy caravan. Sometimes as a child she had gone to school, but she had never learned to read. One night she was very upset after an argument with her parents.

Although she had heard about God's love for her, she didn't know very much about him. That night she asked God to help her read the Bible so that she would know the right way to live. She was very disappointed because nothing seemed to happen.

The next morning, when she was helping her mother clean the caravan, she found an old Bible. She opened it and was amazed to discover that she could read it! Excitedly she told her mother, who couldn't believe it until Clara read to her.

A few weeks later Clara began to understand what Jesus had done for her, and she put her trust in him. Ever since then, she has been telling people about God's special gift to her and, more importantly, about his gift of forgiveness and her new life in Jesus.

Gypsies worldwide

Life is often very difficult for Gypsies, but God's Holy Spirit is bringing many of them hope and peace. European Gypsies are sending money to help Gypsies in India and Madagascar, and going as missionaries to Gypsies in Argentina and Russia. Gypsy Christians from France have gone to many different countries to tell other Gypsies about God's love. Gypsy evangelist Tom Wilson has said, "We Gypsies are a nation of evangelists; we can't help gossiping the gospel."

Romanian Gypsies

Gypsy children baptized at the Great Dorset Steam Fair in the UK

To help you pray for Gypsies

You can thank God for:

- European Gypsies who are telling other Gypsies throughout the world about God's love and salvation.

- Gypsy Bible schools where Gypsies can learn more about Jesus and how to read the Bible.

- the Christian radio broadcasts that are made especially for Gypsies.

- the Gypsies who have started their own churches where they feel at home and can worship him in their own way.

You can ask God:

- to help Christians who are translating the Bible into the Romany languages to use the right words so that Gypsies will be able to understand God's word.

- to lead "Gorgio" Christians to be willing to help Gypsies when they are despised, to make friends with them and to help their children learn to read.

- to fill Gypsy Christians with love and joy and the readiness to always "gossip the gospel."

The Land Freed by Slaves

The country of Haiti occupies the western third of a beautiful island in the Caribbean Sea called Hispaniola. The other two thirds of the island form the Dominican Republic. More than 200 years ago, Haiti's French rulers brought people from West Africa and made them work as slaves in Haiti. These slaves rebelled against the French rulers and fought for their freedom for 13 years. On January 1st 1804, the whole country was declared independent. It was the first Black republic in the world.

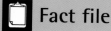

Fact file

Area: 10,580 sq. mi.

Population: 8,222,025

Capital: Port-au-Prince

Main languages: French (official); Haitian Creole

Main religions: Christianity; spiritism; voodoo

Chief exports: Coffee; sugar

Mexico · Haiti · South America · Cuba · Jamaica · Haiti Port-au-Prince · Dominican Republic · CARIBBEAN SEA

Poverty and voodoo

Sadly, Haiti has not really been a free country since 1804. One dictator after another has ruled Haiti. One was known as "Baby Doc" Duvalier. It is thought that while he was in power he stole millions of dollars from his poverty-stricken country.

Haiti is the poorest country in the western world. Although there are some very rich Haitians, the majority are poor farmers, descendants of those black slaves from Africa. Because they long for a better life with freedom from riots, fear and poverty, many have tried to make the dangerous journey to the United States in small boats.

Although most Haitians would say that they are Christians, not very many of them really know Jesus. Many Haitians practice voodoo, which involves worshipping spirits. This disobeys God's first commandment not to worship any other gods (Exodus 20:3). Because evil spirits can

People in Haiti have never really known peace or prosperity

take control of people who worship them and make them do strange and frightening things, these people are full of fear and sadness.

The witch doctor's son

Gerard, the son of a wealthy witch doctor, liked to listen to Christian radio broadcasts at boarding school. Some of Gerard's friends were surprised when they found him listening to a Christian radio station.

"Aren't you going to be a witch doctor some day?" they asked.

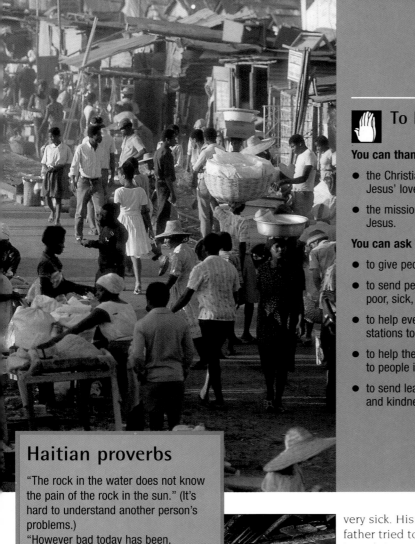

 To help you pray for Haiti

You can thank God for:

- the Christians in Haiti who are filled with joy and who share Jesus' love with others.

- the missionaries in Haiti who are teaching young people about Jesus.

You can ask God:

- to give people the strength to stop practicing voodoo.

- to send people to help the adults and children in Haiti who are poor, sick, hurt, afraid and hungry.

- to help everyone who hears about Jesus on the Christian radio stations to understand what is said.

- to help the missionaries know how to explain God's love clearly to people in Haiti.

- to send leaders who will rule the country wisely and with justice and kindness.

Haitian proverbs

"The rock in the water does not know the pain of the rock in the sun." (It's hard to understand another person's problems.)
"However bad today has been, tomorrow could be better."

Interior of a Haitian home

"Yes, just like my father," he answered, "but the music they play is really good and the Bible studies are so interesting. I've never heard anything like it before!"

His father was furious when he discovered Gerard and his sister listening to a Christian radio station at home. "Don't you ever listen to that station again!" he shouted. "If you become a Christian, I'll drive you out of the house with a whip!"

Not long after this, Gerard became very sick. His father tried to cure him with traditional medicine, chanting and drum-beating. But none of it did any good. Gerard's sister, listening to Christian radio when her father wasn't around, heard the story about Elijah. "Men who worshipped other gods shouted and danced around all day trying to get their gods to answer them. But nothing happened. Then God answered Elijah's prayer by sending fire down on his sacrifice, even though it was soaked with water!" she told Gerard. "Why don't you pray to the Christians' God and ask him to make you better?"

"I don't know how to pray to their God. I don't even know how to become a Christian," Gerard said sadly.

"Write to the missionaries and ask them," his sister insisted. "I'll get you some paper and a pen."

Gerard didn't quite understand the reply he received from the missionaries. He was still very sick, but he decided to go to the radio station. He had to walk part of the way and he had to sit down a lot to rest by the side of the road. When he arrived, they gave Gerard medicine and explained how to become a Christian. Gerard wanted to know Jesus so much that he wasn't afraid of his father anymore. He asked Jesus to forgive his sins and be his friend.

You can read more about Elijah in your Bible, in 1 Kings 18.

Although fighting and poverty are part of everyday life in Haiti, Haitian ministers, missionaries and radio stations are telling people about the love of Jesus. And some people, like Gerard, are finding that Jesus can forgive them for the bad things they've done and help them through their problems.

Hazara

Descendants of Genghis Khan's Army

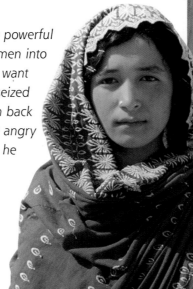

A story from history

Almost 800 years ago Genghis Khan, the powerful leader of the Mongols, sent some of his men into Central Asia. But the people really didn't want them there! So, the story says, the ruler seized them, burned their beards and sent them back to Genghis Khan. Genghis Khan was very angry that this ruler dared to insult his men, so he and his mighty Mongol army invaded Central Asia to punish him. The Hazara claim that they're descendants of that great Mongol army. With their slanted eyes and round, flat faces, they do look like Mongolians. Even their language, which is a Persian dialect, has many Mongol words.

Life in Hazarajat

In Afghanistan, the Hazara live in a region called Hazarajat. For most of the year they live in small village houses built of mud bricks. The houses have flat roofs, which are ideal for drying mulberries, grapes and peaches in the hot summer months. The Hazara then store the dried fruit for eating during the long, cold winters. Wealthier people live in large houses that look like walled fortresses. All the animals belonging to the family – dogs, donkeys, goats, sheep, hens, and even the cow – live in the courtyards of these big houses.

Abdul is a Hazara refugee living in Quetta, in Pakistan. Abdul smiles sadly when he remembers his country. "During the summer months we took our sheep and goats up to the high valleys in the mountains where there's plenty of grass for them to eat. The boys and young men had to watch the animals very carefully. I remember driving away many wolves and eagles who tried to snatch the smaller animals! While we were in the mountains we lived in *yurts* (tents) made from reed mats. The women and girls milked the animals. They churned some of the milk and used it to make balls of *crut* (hard cheese) for the winter.

"It's very cold in the winter time, and we always hope for lots of snow because it's our only source of water. We call it 'Afghan gold,' because without snow our rivers dry up, our crops die and we starve."

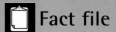

Do you know?

As Shi'ite Muslims, the Hazara are very religious and follow very strict rules. They will eat a meal with Christians or Jews because they're people with a Holy Book. They don't like eating with Buddhists or Communists because they don't have such a book.

Fact file

Countries: Afghanistan; Pakistan; Iran

Numbers: 2,324,000 live in Afghanistan

Others live as refugees in Pakistan and northern Iran.

 To help you pray for the Hazara

You can thank God for:

- each Hazara Christian.
- Christian radio programs in Dari, a language that most Hazara people know.

You can ask God:

- to show the Hazaras that they are important to him.
- to help those who have been crippled, blinded, orphaned or who have lost everything.
- to send Christians to share Jesus' love with Hazara refugees living in Pakistan.
- that Hazara people will read the New Testament in Dari and decide to follow Jesus.
- to help Hazara Christians, wherever they are, to tell others about Jesus.

Uzbekistan

Turkmenistan — Kyrgyzstan

Tajikistan

HAZARA
Afghanistan

Pakistan

Afghanistan

India

A refugee

Once I asked Abdul why he left Afghanistan.

"The more powerful Pushtuns and Tajiks look down on us," Abdul said. "Some Hazaras have gone to live in the cities. It seems natural enough that they would want a better way of life for themselves and their children. Instead, the Hazaras in the cities found they had to work very hard for very little money. Then, in 1979, thousands of Hazaras demonstrated against the government and a lot of them were taken as prisoners. It is as if they disappeared from the face of the earth – they've never been heard from since.

"A year later, the Soviet army arrived. They burned our houses and fields. Muslim soldiers, the *mujahidin*, were also fighting for power. There wasn't much left for us to live for. My father sent me across the mountains here to Quetta where many other Hazaras live. He wanted me to keep on studying."

Abdul looked around him, frightened, and then came closer. "I studied English," he said, "because I knew that would help me get a good job. It did, and I started to work in a hospital. Some people I worked with invited me to join an English club, where I learned about Jesus, the Son of God. Sometimes it just amazes me that he loves even the homeless and the poor. And that means Jesus loves the Hazara." Abdul whispered, "I'm a follower of Jesus. If the *mujahidin* knew that, they would kill me. Please pray for me."

A few months later, Abdul was forced to return to Hazarajat. The *mujahidin* were hunting for him and several other new Christians.

In 1996, a Muslim group called the Taliban took over the country, defeating some of the *mujahidin* groups. At first people thought they would bring peace, but thousands of Hazaras have suffered under their rule. One reason is that the Hazara are Shi'ite Muslims and not Sunni Muslims, like most other people in Afghanistan.

Please pray that God will help Abdul and the other Hazara Christians be faithful to Jesus – no matter what.

Herero

Children of the Omumborumbonga Tree

Questioning the tree

The Herero people, who live in Namibia, South West Africa, have a legend that, at the beginning of time, a man and woman came out of the Omumborumbonga tree. This is a large, twisted, ancient-looking tree that grows in the dry bush country where the Herero graze their cattle.

The man was called Mukuru, the first ancestor, and his wife was Kamungarunga. Even today, when some Herero pass the Omumborumbonga tree, they will bow, put a bunch of grass into the branches and ask it questions.

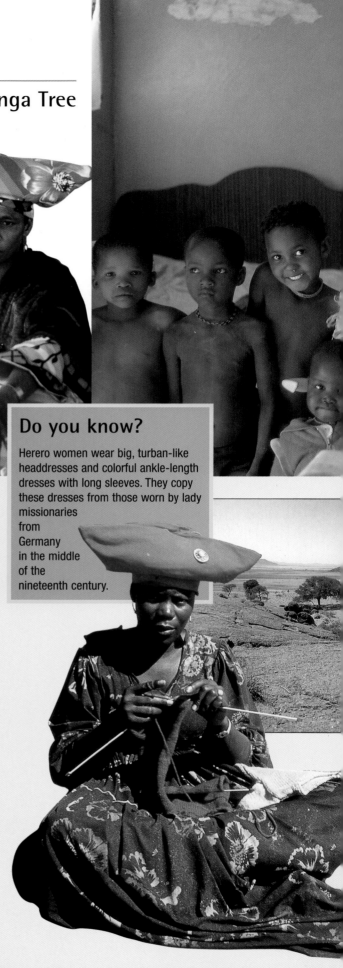

Africa

Angola

HERERO

Botswana

● Windhoek

Namibia

South Africa

Do you know?

Herero women wear big, turban-like headdresses and colorful ankle-length dresses with long sleeves. They copy these dresses from those worn by lady missionaries from Germany in the middle of the nineteenth century.

The Herero believed that a god named Karunga was present everywhere and that people had souls that went to heaven after death. They wanted to say and do only good things so they could go to Karunga as clean and fresh as the rain. Karunga, they believed, sent a flood to punish people for quarreling. Do these ideas sound familiar? It isn't surprising that the Herero people quickly understood when missionaries told them about God the creator who is everywhere, and about heaven, Adam and Eve and the great flood of Noah. But they were amazed to learn that we don't have to be clean and pure before we can talk to Jesus. They could hardly believe that if we do or think or say something wrong, we can ask him to forgive us. He's the only one who can make us clean.

To help you pray for the Herero

You can thank God for:

- each Herero Christian.
- the Herero Bible.

You can ask God:

- to help evangelists explain to children who are poor, unhappy or afraid that God loves them.
- to send teachers to help people know Jesus and follow only him.
- to help each Herero Christian who is studying at Bible school.
- that Herero Christians will forgive those who have hurt them, particularly during the war for independence from South Africa, just as Jesus forgave them.
- to help Herero Christians care for refugees and those who have no work.

Fact file

Main country: Namibia, with a smaller group in Botswana

Numbers: About 181,000 (Namibia); 18,000 (Botswana)

Main religions: Christianity; traditional African religion

Traditional occupation: Cattle breeding

Holy fire

Some of the Herero people still follow their old beliefs. They have many taboos that sometimes make people afraid – for example, they aren't supposed to look at twins or at their chief in case something really bad happens to them. They worship their dead relatives at a sacred fire and believe that if that fire ever went out, the tribe would die out, too.

Alphonso and Poppi, a young Herero couple, had come to know Jesus as their savior and friend. On their wedding day, they refused to worship at the sacred fire. The village elders were very angry with them because they were afraid that some terrible disaster would come to the village. "We can't worship at the fire," Alphonso and Poppi said, "because we belong to Jesus. The Bible tells us that as Christians we must worship God and follow only him."

Maybe they'll be brave and tell lots more people about Jesus like Ananias did. Ananias was a poor Herero shepherd who went to South Africa in 1945 to preach about Jesus. Full of joy and love for Jesus, he was the first Herero missionary.

War and peace

Between 1904 and 1907 there was a terrible war in Namibia as the people fought for independence from Germany. More than 70,000 of the Herero people were killed or died in the desert and only 20,000 were left alive. It has taken them many years to recover from that war, but now there are as many Herero as there were then. Most live in Hereroland, East Namibia, while some live near the capital, Windhoek. South Africa governed Namibia from 1920 until 1990, but Namibia fought for freedom from the apartheid laws (that kept black and white people apart). In 1990, Namibia became an independent country.

The first missionaries translated the New Testament into the Herero language, and the whole Bible was completed in 1988. Please pray that as Herero men, women, boys and girls read the Herero Bible, they will come to know that they really are sons and daughters of the living God.

Hui

Chinese Descendants of Warriors and Merchants from Arabia

Dumplings and noodles

"Come and eat momo (dumplings) with us," my friends invited me, *"or you could have lamien (noodles). We're going to a Hui (whey) restaurant. The food's great, but whatever you do don't ask for pork, because they're Muslims."*

As we walked along the busy street in a city in north central China I saw people who looked Chinese and who dressed like most of the other people I'd seen here. But the men had white caps on their heads, and the women were wearing short veils of fine black or dark green cloth.

Fact file

Population: About 9,500,000

Country: China

Language: Chinese (Mandarin)

Religion: Islam

Number of Christians: 20–30

"These are Hui people," my friends told me. "They live in this part of the city near the main mosque. We'll bring you back here on Friday so you can see the hundreds of men come to the mosque to pray and listen to the sermon."

Merchants and warriors

Who are the Hui? Where did they come from and why are they Muslims?

More than a thousand years ago, hundreds of Arab and Persian merchants made the long journey along the Silk Road, right across Asia to China. Arab warriors also came to China to help Chinese emperors fight against their enemies. Still more Arabs traveled to China by sea. Many of them never returned to their homelands.

These men were Muslims, and they were proud of their Arab background. Wherever they settled in China they built mosques, married local Chinese women and brought their children up as Muslims. They became known as the Hui.

Hui Muslims live in different places all across China. In the country they often work as farmers. In towns and cities they

Friday prayers

To help you pray for the Hui

You can thank God for:

- the Hui Christians.
- those who prepare Christian radio broadcasts.

You can ask God:

- to help Hui children and young people to understand that they will never know his love simply through keeping their traditions, customs and laws.
- that many Hui people will tune in to Christian radio stations and discover for themselves that they can only have hope and eternal life by trusting in Jesus.
- that when the Hui receive Christian leaflets or booklets, they will read them and learn about Jesus' love for them.
- that Han Chinese Christians will make friends with Hui people and share God's love and care with them.
- that many people around the world will pray that Hui people will come to know him as their savior and friend.

Hui women wear short black or green veils

live around their mosques. A lot of them work in their own Hui shops and restaurants, but most of them have jobs like anyone else.

In many parts of China the Hui seem no different from the Han, the people we usually think of as being Chinese. These Hui speak Mandarin, have Chinese names and look and dress like them. But they are different. They are Muslims.

There are more than nine and a half million Hui in China. Many of them live in north central China, where the Chinese government has set up a special region for them called the Ningxia (*ning-shia*) Hui Autonomous Region. About a third of the people who live in this region are Hui. There they can follow their own religion and culture.

Learning Arabic

Liang is a young Hui boy. His father goes to the mosque every Friday and has even been on pilgrimage (H*ajj*) to Mecca. "Sometimes I go to watch the men pray," Liang said, "but I don't think I want to go to the mosque with them yet, because there aren't many other boys and young men who go. I'm quite happy to follow our other Islamic customs, though.

"My father wants me to learn to read Arabic so I can read the Koran. We speak Mandarin Chinese at home, but we use a few Arabic words as well. I've

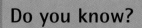

seen Arabic words written on the walls of the mosque. The writing looks beautiful, but I think it's going to be hard to learn. I'm still learning to write Chinese ...

that's hard enough!"

There are very few Hui Christians – perhaps no more than 20. The Hui's traditions are very important to them, and probably only a quarter of them have ever heard about Jesus. How will they hear about the Savior who loves them and wants them to follow him? Who will tell them?

Restaurant worker

Do you know?

The Hui are the largest of the ten Muslim people groups in China. About three-quarters of them have never even heard about Jesus.

On the Edge of the Arctic Circle

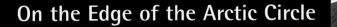

Land of fire and ice

Iceland is a large island, about 500 miles north of Scotland. It's called the land of fire and ice because it has a lot of active volcanoes as well as huge glaciers and ice fields that cover large areas. Much of the ground is black with volcanic ash and rocks. Iceland also has the largest lava bed on earth. In 1963, some fishermen out in their boats were amazed when the sea seemed to be boiling. A few weeks later, a volcano under the sea erupted, shooting steam, fire and ash high into the air. In a very short time, the volcano became the new island of Surtsey.

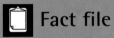

Workers in a fish processing factory

Icelandic girl in traditional costume

Fact file

Area: 39,768 sq. mi.

Population: 280,969

Capital: Reykjavik

Religion: Christianity (Lutheran)

Chief exports: Fish and fish products; aluminum

Because Iceland is nearly as far north as the Arctic Circle, it's almost never dark during the summer. But it's dark almost all the time in the winter, when people stay inside their snug, warm houses to read, tell stories and play games like chess. Most of the houses in Reykjavik (*raik-ya-vik*), the capital of Iceland, get their heat from hundreds of hot springs that occur there naturally.

1,000 years of Christianity

"Please tell me a story," Erik asked as he sat down beside his father. "Tell me how Iceland became a Christian country." His father smiled. He loved to tell this story.

"We've been a Christian country now for a thousand years," Erik's father began. "It all started a long time ago when the first settlers came to Iceland. They were great adventurers and made long and dangerous journeys across the sea. Some came

To help you pray for Iceland

You can thank God for:

- each Icelander who is discovering that Christianity is far more than just a part of their tradition.

- the new translation of the Bible.

- university students who are deciding to follow Jesus.

You can ask God:

- that a lot of children will choose to follow Jesus at Christian camps.

- that those who study in the Bible school will share the good news about Jesus wherever they go.

- that there will be more pastors and evangelists who will teach the Bible clearly.

- to help those who follow Jesus to tell others about him.

Geysers (right), and sulphurous gases escaping from the ground (below) are evidence of Iceland's volcanic activity

Iceland chose to be a Christian country more than a thousand years ago

Christian country or go on following the old gods. So they called a special meeting in the year AD 1000. They elected a man everyone respected very much and gave him the huge responsibility of choosing for them. He chose to follow Jesus and, for the past thousand years, Iceland has been a Christian country. In nearly every home, families have always met together every night to pray and read the Bible ... just like we do."

"Hardly any of my friends at school go to church except when there's a wedding, a baptism or a funeral," Erik said, "but a lot of them still say the Lord's Prayer at home every day."

"That's right," his father replied. "Nearly everyone in Iceland would call themselves Christians because it is part of our culture and tradition."

"That's why my friends think the Christian camp I go to in the summer sounds fun, but they don't want to go. They never want to come to church with me when I invite them, either. They don't understand when I tell them that Jesus is my friend, who promises to be with me all the time," Erik said. "Are we still a Christian country, then?"

"Well," said his father, "some of us are praying that God will make the whole country excited about following Jesus. We've seen God beginning to answer those prayers. We have a new edition of the Bible that everyone can understand, some of the churches have been running a three-month Bible school, and Christians are telling others the good news about Jesus. Some people from here have even gone to tell people in other countries about Jesus."

from Norway, while others were Norsemen who had married Christian women. They brought the good news of Jesus with them, and soon almost half the people in Iceland had decided to follow Jesus. There were still a lot of people who followed the old Norse gods like Thor and Odin.

"Our ancestors knew they had to choose whether we should become a

Land of a Million Gods

A festival

"Come on, wake up!" Sanjay said, shaking his brother. "It's almost dawn. The sadhus are already on their way down to the river. It's time for us to go!" Sanjay and his brother had spent the last two nights huddled together beside a small dung fire waiting for this very moment. All around them were the tents of millions of people who had also come for the Maha Kumbh Mela.

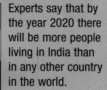

Hindu artist holding her image of a god

Colored dyes for sale at a bazaar

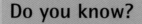

Fact file

Area: 1,237,060 sq. mi. (about a third the size of the United States)

Population: 1,013,661,777 (almost four times the number of people living in the United States)

Capital: New Delhi

Languages: Hindi; English and 16 other official languages including Urdu, Tamil and Telegu. Altogether, there are 1,652 languages!

Religions: Hinduism (about 78%); Islam (about 12%); Christianity (about 3%); Sikhism (1.92%)

Chief exports: Gems; jewelry; cotton; textiles; clothes; tea

Sanjay and his brother had started their adventure a week ago, when they left their village to walk all the way to Allahabad, "city of God." They were going to the great *mela*, or festival, at the holy place where the Ganges and Yamuna Rivers meet. Sometimes a farmer had given the two boys a ride on his bullock cart. And once or twice they'd traveled a few miles on crowded buses. But mostly they had walked – along the hot and dusty paths and roads.

As they finally neared the river, Sanjay and his brother were caught up in the huge crowd of pilgrims. Everyone was pushing, slipping and sliding, dodging sacred cows and wandering goats, on their way down to the river. At last they reached the mighty river and stepped into the water. Sanjay faced the rising sun and poured water over himself, hoping that the water's flow would wash his sins away.

Do you know?

Experts say that by the year 2020 there will be more people living in India than in any other country in the world.

The Maha Kumbh Mela is one of India's great religious festivals. Although it is held every four years, it only comes to this sacred place every twelfth year. Hindus, whether high or low caste, rich or poor, come from all over India, hoping to wash away their sins in the Ganges. Most of them have never heard that Jesus is the only one who can truly wash their sins away and make their hearts clean.

A million gods

Indians are very religious. Most are Hindus, but others are Muslims, Christians, Sikhs, Buddhists, Jains or animists. Wherever you go in India,

Most missionaries in India today are Indians, telling their own people about Jesus

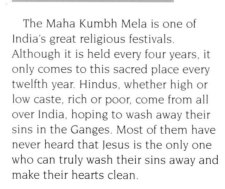

To help you pray for India

You can thank God for:

- every Indian Christian.

- the thousands of missionaries and preachers, from other countries as well as from India, who have told people there about Jesus.

- Indian missionaries.

- the Christians working among the millions of people who are poor and homeless, blind and sick, drug addicts and lepers.

You can ask God:

- that both adults and children would read and understand the millions of Scripture portions, New Testaments and booklets that are given out each year.

- that many Indians will listen to the Christian radio programs beamed into India and follow Jesus.

- that one day Jesus will truly be king, the one and only God, over all India.

Women preparing offerings

The cow is a sacred animal in the Hindu religion and is often seen in the streets

you will find temples and shrines. There are more than a million Hindu gods. Some of these gods are very important and are worshipped all over India. Every day the Hindu priest has to wake up the gods in his temple, bathe them with milk and honey, dress them, offer them food and pray to them.

When people worship at a temple they bring offerings of food or flowers for the brightly painted gods. They ring the temple bell to make sure the god or goddess is awake. Even after they have made their offerings and prayed, they're still never sure the god will be kind to them.

Sharing the good news

Christian missionaries have worked in India for hundreds of years. One of the best known is William Carey, who went to India more than 200 years ago. He lived there for almost 40 years, translating the Bible into several Indian languages and teaching many people to follow Jesus.

There aren't many missionaries from other countries who can get visas to work in India now, but that doesn't mean that there aren't missionaries there. Although militant Hindus have threatened and attacked some of them, thousands of Indian missionaries and Christians are bravely talking to people about Jesus. They work in towns and cities, in hospitals, schools and churches. Some are helping the millions of people who have no homes and live on the streets. Others go into the thousands of villages. They give out Christian books, show films about Jesus and teach children to read.

But there are still millions of people in India who have never heard about Jesus. India is a country with a million gods and a billion people. But there is only one God ... who loves every single one of those billion people.

Indonesia

An Island Nation

700 languages!

The country of Indonesia has at least 13,500 islands. That means that if you tried to visit a different one every day, it would take you 37 years to visit them all! The islands are spread out over an area of the Indian and Pacific Oceans as large as the United States. Java, where 60% of Indonesians live, Sumatra and Sulawesi are three of the biggest islands. There are about 213 million people living in Indonesia. They belong to so many different people groups that about 700 different languages are spoken. (You can read about the Balinese, Dayak, Minangkabau and Sundanese in this book.) At school everyone has to learn Indonesian, the national language.

For almost 350 years, the Dutch ruled most of Indonesia. But the country declared its independence in 1945. War broke out in 1965, when Communists tried to take over the country.

Choosing a religion

Petrus, who was eight years old then, still remembers how frightened he was. "There were the Communists fighting on one side," he said, "and Muslims on the other. The Muslims didn't want the Communists to take control, so they killed anyone they thought might be a Communist. We just wanted peace. Then everything changed when the government defeated the Communists. They brought back an old law that said everyone had to choose a religion.

A lot of people were animists, who had no real religion. Some chose to become Muslims, Hindus or Buddhists. My father had seen how kind and forgiving Christians were to others during the war, so he decided we should become Christians. About two million people chose Christianity as their religion, but a lot of us didn't really understand what being a Christian meant. We were glad that missionaries and evangelists taught us how to follow Jesus."

There has been terrible fighting in Indonesia, but Christians there are reaching out with God's love

Do you know?

Indonesia has the fourth largest number of people of any country in the world — after China, India and the United States.

To help you pray for Indonesia

You can thank God for:

- all the Indonesians who know and love Jesus.
- Bible colleges where Indonesians can study to become evangelists, pastors and missionaries.

You can ask God:

- to send evangelists and missionaries to every inhabited island in Indonesia to tell people about Jesus.
- for pastors and church leaders to teach the truth of the Bible.
- that all Christians will want to learn more about Jesus and how they can follow him.
- that he will help Christians forgive those who hurt them, instead of trying to hurt them back.
- that the government will lead the many different peoples wisely and fairly.

You can speak Indonesian

Good morning is "Selamat pagi"
   (si-**lah**-mat **pah**-ghee)
Goodbye is "Selamat tinggal"
   (si-**lah**-mat **tin**-gahl)
Please is "Tolong" (**toh**-long)
Thank you is "Terima kasih"
   (**te**-ree-mah **kah**-see)
Yes is "Ya" (yah)
No is "Tidak" (tee-**dak**)

[Map showing: China, Taiwan, PACIFIC OCEAN, Philippines, Indonesia, Sumatra, Jakarta, Java, Timor, INDIAN OCEAN]

Trouble in the islands

"What happened then?" we ask him. "Is there peace now?"

"Indonesia isn't a peaceful nation," Petrus tells us, "and we have lots of problems. A man named Suharto was president for 32 years, but people were tired of him being so unfair. He resigned in 1998. We could be a rich country, but some people are wealthy while millions of others don't have enough food to eat.

"The government would like us to think of ourselves as one people instead of many people groups. They want us to be one nation, with one language and with a belief in God. But some parts of the country, like Aceh in Sumatra and Ambon in Maluku, want independence. There has been terrible fighting in these places and in East Timor, which voted to become independent, and a lot of people have

been killed. Some Muslims want Indonesia to become a Muslim nation with Muslim laws. They're afraid that a lot more people will become Christians, so they've burned down churches and stoned and killed Christians. It's sad that, in some places, Christians have done the same things to Muslims."

The good news

"Are churches still telling people the good news about Jesus?" we ask. "With so much persecution, maybe people won't even want to hear about him."

"Let me tell you a story," Petrus says. "A boy called Enjang was six years old when he started to study the Koran. He got really scared when he read about hell. His uncle showed him where he could read about Isa, Mary's son. Enjang loved reading about Isa and realized that Isa is the Muslim

name for Jesus. Little by little, Enjang began to love Jesus. He started to tell other Muslim children about him, but that made their parents very angry. Enjang's own brother was so angry that he made him leave his home. But Enjang knew that Jesus loved him so much that he told people about Jesus wherever he went.

"Because of people like Enjang, the church in Indonesia is growing. We're praying that soon every part of our country will hear about God's love. Christians are sharing the good news about Jesus in lots of different ways. They're helping people who have been hurt in the violence or who have lost their homes and jobs. They're praying that people will forgive each other for all the bad things that have been done and that our country will live in peace. Please pray for us, too."

Between the Tigris and Euphrates Rivers

A Bible land

Did you ever wonder where in the world the Bible begins? Genesis 2 talks about a place called Mesopotamia, between the Tigris and Euphrates rivers. Hundreds of years later, the Jewish people were taken into exile in Babylon (you can read about this in 2 Kings). Both Mesopotamia and Babylon were part of the country that is now called Iraq. It was in Babylon that Daniel served Nebuchadnezzar and Balshazzar and went into the lions' den. And, hundreds of years after that, people from Mesopotamia were in Jerusalem on the day of Pentecost and heard the disciples speak about Jesus in their own language (in Acts 2, in the New Testament).

Fact file

Area: 169,238 sq. mi.

Capital: Baghdad

Population: 23,114,884

Official languages: Arabic; Kurdish in the Kurdish region

Religion: Islam

Chief export: Oil

Woman selling produce at a market in Baghdad

These people took the good news about Jesus back to their own country. Although Iraq is now a Muslim country, there are people there who know and love Jesus.

Iraq is a large, oil-rich Arab republic in the Middle East. Almost three-quarters of the people living there today are Arabs. Kurds live in the northern mountain region, and a people known as the Marsh Arabs live in the south.

A troubled land

"I just can't believe this," Paul said as he showed his father a magazine. "The United Nations says that between five and six thousand children are dying every month in Iraq. How can this be happening?"

"It's a sad story,"

Paul's father said. "Iraq has had problems for a long time. In July 1958, the king and prime minister were killed during a violent revolution. After several coups, a man called Saddam Hussein came to power in July 1979.

"In 1980, Iraq invaded Iran. They had been fighting over control of a waterway to the Persian Gulf for a long time. Millions of Iraqi and Iranian people were killed. The war lasted for eight years, but no one really won."

"But if that war ended in 1988, why are so many children still dying?" Paul asked.

"Well," his father continued, "in 1990, Iraq invaded Kuwait. Among other things, Iraq accused Kuwait of stealing oil from oil fields along the border between the two countries. Many countries, including the United States and Britain, took part in the short but terrible Gulf

War at the beginning of 1991. And again, Iraq wasn't really defeated.

"Not long after that, the Kurds in the north of Iraq, who want a country of their own, revolted again. Many Kurds were killed and their homes destroyed. It was awful to watch long lines of Kurdish refugees on television as they trudged hopelessly across snow-covered mountains, away from the ruins of their villages. And far away in the south of the country, where the Tigris and Euphrates rivers meet, the Marsh Arabs were being driven out of the swamps which had been their home for hundreds of years. A lot of them died, and

Do you know?

Mesopotamia, "the land between the rivers," was the birthplace of civilization. Agriculture, animal farming and writing were all first developed here.

اجل البناء . وراءك ياصدام

To help you pray for Iraq

You can thank God for:

- every person who has discovered that, no matter what happens, Jesus loves them and helps them.
- the thousands of Bibles and New Testaments that have been sent into Iraq.
- Christian radio broadcasts in Arabic and Kurdish, and the *Jesus* film.

You can ask God:

- that enough food and medicine will reach the people who need it.
- to send people to take care of all the children who are hungry, sick or dying.
- that Iraqi Christians training to become church leaders will return to help the churches in Iraq.
- for a government that will lead Iraq towards peace and rebuild the country.

Children sing praises to Saddam Hussein at an orphanage

Ancient world in 1350 BC

Iraqi soldier during the Gulf War

The good news of Jesus

Paul sat quietly for a few minutes. "Are there any Christians in Iraq?" he asked.

"Yes, some have gone to other countries as refugees," his father said. "When the Gulf War started, the evangelical church in Baghdad decided to meet every day to pray and read the Bible together. Muslims joined them sometimes, and some of them became Christians. Surprisingly, the *Jesus* film has been shown several times on national television. Christians used to be persecuted in Iraq. But now, perhaps because they've suffered so much, people want to hear about Jesus and his love."

"Can they buy Bibles there?" Paul asked.

"Thousands of Bibles and New Testaments have been brought in from

only a few have been able to continue their way of life."

"That's terrible," Paul said. "Is anything being done?"

"Other nations didn't want Saddam Hussein and the Iraqi government to ever be able to form such a strong army again. So they stopped trading with Iraq. Iraq is allowed to sell a certain amount of oil in exchange for food, but most people are very poor. There isn't enough food or medicine. That's why so many children are dying. A lot of people think we should start trading with Iraq again because it's ordinary people, especially children, who are suffering most. I read that some Iraqis have become very rich, and that Saddam Hussein has at least 50 palaces. It seems so unfair."

Jordan," his father told him. "The government has also given permission for Arabic Bibles and Christian children's books to be published in Baghdad and for thousands of New Testaments to be given to Christian children in state schools. The churches need trained pastors and leaders, but training is expensive."

"Isn't there anything we can do?" Paul asked.

"The Bible tells us that God loves the poor, the homeless and the downtrodden. The situation is too big for us, but not for God. We can pray that, in the midst of their suffering, people in Iraq will experience Jesus' love and care."

The Holy Land of Jews, Christians and Muslims

The Promised Land

"Why do people say that Israel is the homeland of the Jewish people?"
Tanya asked her father. Tanya's family are Messianic (Christian) Jews who
emigrated to Israel from Russia.

"It's a long story that started thousands of years ago," her father replied.
"This is the 'Promised Land' God gave to his people, the Hebrews, and it
was here that famous kings like Saul, David and Solomon lived. Jesus was
born and lived and died here, so it's special to Christians. And Muslims
believe that Mohammed traveled from Jerusalem to heaven on his winged
horse to speak with God. So
Jews, Christians and Muslims
all call it the Holy Land."

The Dome of
the Rock,
Jerusalem

 Fact file

Area: 8,000 sq. mi. (plus
3,000 sq. mi. of the West
Bank, Gaza and the Golan
Heights which Israel has
controlled since 1967)

Population: 5,121,683 (plus
West Bank 155,000; Gaza
6,000; Golan Heights 17,000)

Capital: Jerusalem

Official languages: Hebrew;
Arabic

Religions: Judaism; Islam;
Christianity

Chief exports: Machinery;
chemicals; textiles; cut
diamonds;
fruit and
vegetables

Conquered

"A long time ago, this land was called
Palestine. Every time another country
invaded Palestine, Jews left the country
– sometimes just a few, but often quite
a lot left at a time. They settled in
almost every country on earth but,
wherever they went, they were usually
persecuted. And they longed and
prayed for the day when they could
return to their own land – but not
many ever returned.

"After the Arabs conquered Palestine
in AD 641, Arab Muslims settled here.
Twelve centuries passed by.

Lebanon
Syria
MEDITERRANEAN SEA
Tel Aviv
Jerusalem
Israel
Jordan
Egypt

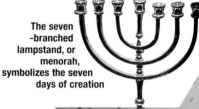

The seven
-branched
lampstand, or
menorah,
symbolizes the seven
days of creation

Arab and Jewish Christians
are setting an example of how to live
together as part of God's family

Orthodox Jews praying at
the Western Wall in
Jerusalem

Then, at the
end of the
nineteenth
century, some
Jews arrived
from Europe
and started
farming.
More and
more
Jews returned to Palestine, but
it wasn't really their own country.
In 1922, Britain was asked to govern
the country. It split the country in
two. The eastern part was put under
Arab rule, and Jews were allowed to
settle in the west."

 ## To help you pray for Israel

You can thank God for:

- the *Jesus* video in both Hebrew and Arabic that explains how Jesus really is the promised Messiah.
- Christian books, magazines and Sabbath (Sunday) school materials.

You can ask God:

- for many in Israel, both Arabs and Jews, to come to know Jesus as the true Messiah, the Son of God.
- to help Messianic (Christian) Jews and Arab Christians learn to trust each other.
- that Israeli and Arab Christian parents will teach their children to love Jesus.
- that tourists in Israel will not only visit historic places but will also pray for the country.
- for peace and understanding between Arabs and Jews in Israel.

Palestinians at a sheep market in Beersheba

A new State

"Was that the beginning of the State of Israel?" Tanya asked.

"Not exactly," her father said. "It wasn't until 1948 that the United Nations voted to divide the western part of the country into a Jewish State and an Arab State. And on May 14th, 1948, the new Jewish State of Israel was formed. Ever since, thousands of Jews have come to Israel from countries all around the world."

"I have friends at school from Europe, America, Asia and Africa. If we didn't all have to learn Hebrew, we'd never understand each other!" Tanya said.

"Yes, it's wonderful to see Jews from all these different places returning to Israel," her father said. "But because so many people are coming to live here, there isn't enough work for everyone."

"Is that why you work in a laboratory now, even though you were a doctor in Russia?" Tanya asked.

"That's right," her father said, "And I'm grateful to have a job."

"What about the Arabs?" asked Tanya.

"During the more than 50 years since the Jews were given their own country there have been wars and a lot of fighting between Jews and Arabs," her father said sadly. "Thousands of Arabs have had to leave their homes. They're still looking for a country of their own. It's sad that we can't all learn to live together, but some of our leaders are trying to work towards peace."

Christians

"Some of the kids at school say I can't be a Jew because I'm a Christian," Tanya said. "Why do they say that?"

"The Old Testament tells us about God's promise of a Savior," her father said. "A lot of Jewish people are longing for this Savior, or Messiah, to come and bring peace to his people. But they don't understand that *Yeshua* (Jesus) is the Messiah that God promised. That's why some of them

Do you know?

The Jews living in Israel have come from 102 different countries. One person in every six has come from Russia, so stores often have signs in Hebrew, English, Arabic and Russian.

feel we can't be Jews if we follow *Yeshua.*"

"Aren't there some Arabs living in Israel who are Christians, too?" Tanya asked. "There are only Jewish Christians in our church."

"There are whole villages of Arab Christians, but we don't often meet them," her father replied. "A friend of mine recently went with some other members of his church to visit an Arab church. It was a big step, because usually there isn't much friendship between Jews and Arabs. He said they were kind, and made them feel at home. As he told me about their visit, I thought about what the Bible says in Galatians 3:28: 'we are all one in Christ Jesus.' If we follow Jesus, we're all members of one family – God's family."

Land of the Rising Sun

Japan is a chain of four main islands and about 4,000 smaller islands in the North Pacific Ocean. Mountains and hills cover many of the islands, and most of Japan's nearly 130 million people live crowded on the narrow plains along the coasts.

The rising sun on Japan's flag symbolizes the sun goddess. The Japanese call their country "Nippon," which means "the land of the sun." The Japanese tradition is that their emperor descended from the sun goddess and was himself a god. He was made emperor in a special ceremony as part of a secret meeting with the sun goddess. Emperors used to be very powerful, but the emperor today has little power and his role is mainly ceremonial.

The cherry blossom has special significance in Japan

Fact file

Area: 145,870 sq. mi.

Population: 126,714,220

Capital: Tokyo

Language: Japanese

Religions: Shinto; Buddhism (but freedom of religion is guaranteed)

Chief exports: Machinery; vehicles; ships; electronic equipment; textiles

Shinto

The main religion of Japan is called Shinto, "the way of the gods." Its followers worship the emperor, the sun, Mount Fuji, the fox god, the snake god, spirits of water and fire and many other things. Children visit Shinto shrines to learn more about their culture and beliefs.

Do you know?

The islands of Japan are really the tops of a huge range of mountains under the Pacific Ocean. Some of them are volcanoes! Every year, about 1,500 earthquakes are recorded in Japan. Most of them are minor, but once in a while a very strong one causes a lot of damage.

If the influence of Shinto becomes really strong, people could be stopped from preaching about Jesus. This has happened before. Shintoists can't understand why Christians refuse to worship at Shinto shrines, since they don't see a problem with worshipping more than one god. Many Japanese people feel that if they became Christians and worshipped only Jesus, they would be turning against their family and culture.

There are even more Japanese Buddhists than Shintoists. Although many people don't really believe in Buddhism, they're afraid to give it up.

The flag of Japan shows the rising sun, symbol of the sun goddess

Children wearing kimonos, traditional Japanese dress

Lighting a candle at a shrine

✋ To help you pray for Japan

You can thank God for:

- the freedom of religion the Japanese have, and that some have chosen to follow Jesus.
- every Christian who has shared God's love with the people of Japan.

You can ask God:

- to show Japanese pastors and evangelists and missionaries from other countries the best ways to help the people of Japan understand that God loves them and wants them to follow him.
- to help each Christian be brave enough to worship only Jesus and never bow down to idols.
- that many people will learn that he is the one and only Creator-God who loves them and sent Jesus to save them.
- for Christians to have such joyful hearts that wherever they are – at home, or school or work – others will want to discover that joy for themselves.
- that many people will go into Christian bookstores to buy Bibles and books to help them learn how to follow him.

Japan makes more cars and electronic toys and products than any other country

Too many lessons!

In the Japanese culture it's very important to be successful, and children have to work hard in school if they want to do well.

Toshio was angry. "I don't want to take classes after school," he complained. "I want time to ride my bike or just play computer games! Why do I have to work all night?"

"Shhh, Toshio! Your father will hear you. Only studying will get you into college and a good job."

"I don't care, and I don't see why he does either – a good job hasn't made him happy. He's always at work. I want to have fun with my friends."

"If you don't pass all your exams, what will our neighbors think of us?" Toshio's mother sighed. Toshio ran out of the house. He felt like crying. His mother was always worrying about what other people might think.

Not all Japanese think like Toshio. Although they have a long day at school, and compulsory school clubs afterwards, many still take extra classes at night to make sure they pass their exams! Some sleep very few hours.

Japan makes more cars and electronic appliances than any other country in the world. The Japanese use thousands of robots to do the work in their factories, clean sewers, wash windows and pick oranges.

The family shrine

Japanese people often live to be very old. Toshio's mother takes care of his great-grandmother, who is very religious. She worships at the family shrine every day, and she scolds Toshio's mother for not doing so.

Jolas

Who Pray to the Spirits in Poems

Praying to the spirits

Ampa's week-old baby brother squirmed as a Jola elder shaved his head. The old man was chewing betel nut and spat some of his red saliva on the baby's head. "This will protect the baby's heart," he said. Then the old man blew and prayed into the baby's tiny ears. They also sacrificed a chicken to please the spirits so that they would look after the baby.

Ampa stood and watched this ceremony for his little brother and remembered when he was 10 years old and very sick. His father had asked the priest to pray to the spirits for him. The priest prayed a poem he made up. He told the spirit that Ampa was sick and that his father had brought palm wine and a chicken as a gift. In his poem he asked one spirit to tell another spirit, and so on, until eventually a spirit told the creator god. Ampa didn't really understand how all of this talking to the spirits worked. He had heard about some missionaries who said they could talk directly to the true Creator God. Ampa thought that would be amazing … if it was really true.

The Jolas

Most Jolas are farmers who grow rice, vegetables and groundnuts (peanuts). They live in the West African countries of Senegal, Gambia and Guinea-Bissau. Ampa's family lives in Gambia, which is one of the smallest countries in Africa. Gambia is a narrow strip of land (rarely more than 30 miles wide) that runs along either side of the Gambia River for about 300 miles. Apart from its Atlantic coast, Gambia is completely surrounded by Senegal.

You can speak Jola

Hello is "saafi" (sah-fee)

Peace is "kasuumaay", which you use to ask how someone is, or tell them you are okay (kah-soo-my)

Goodbye is "ukatoolaal" (oo-kah-tolal)

Do you know?

Jola kings always wear long red gowns and tall red felt hats to worship their gods. No one else who worships the Jola gods is allowed to wear red or to sit on a stool after a king has sat on it. So, wherever he goes, a Jola king carries a small stool with him. He also carries a brush made of palm leaves, which is the symbol of his authority. Whatever he touches with it belongs to him.

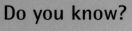

She was so beautiful, and I knew that when she was old enough she would help me look after the house. Then I had another baby, a little boy. I was very happy because I knew your father and his family would be pleased. But the baby died, and everyone was very sad.

"Soon I was expecting another baby. Your father's family took me to the *marabout*, the local holy man, who told them I'd been cursed by evil spirits.

He said I had to change my name and keep out of the spirits' way. When the baby was born, the *marabout* tied charms around his hands, waist and neck to protect him from the evil spirits. But he died, too."

Mariama's family had sent her away from her home in Senegal because they believed she had been cursed. "In Sibanor," she said, "a small village in Gambia, I met a Jola Christian who invited me to church. There I heard about Jesus, who loves and cares for everyone who follows him, and who is much more powerful than any evil spirit.

"I came back to Senegal, and before long there was another baby on the way.

My family took me to the *marabout* again, who gave me a special charm so the baby wouldn't die. I went back to Sibanor because I knew the nurses at the Christian hospital there would look after me and my baby. You were that precious baby, Samuel. One day I took you to the church and the elders prayed for you and gave you the name Samuel. I took off all the charms you were wearing, and from then on I trusted Jesus to look after you."

"What happened then?" Samuel asked.

"I asked Jesus to be my friend," his mother said. "My family was very angry and afraid, but God helped me to follow him. Now he has

Preparing the ground for planting

given me another beautiful baby daughter. I'm glad that I can serve God in the church as a deaconess. There are only a few Jolas who are Christians, Samuel, and I pray that our people and the rest of our family will come to know Jesus, too."

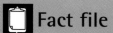

Fact file

Main countries and numbers:
Senegal (430,000)
Gambia (120,000)
Guinea-Bissau (15,000)

Religions: Animism; Islam

Occupation: Mainly farmers

To help you pray for the Jolas

You can thank God for:

- the Jolas who are following Jesus.

- the beautiful songs and poems Jola Christians make up to worship him.

- the Sunday schools and youth clubs where children learn about Jesus.

You can ask God:

- for Christians to be faithful to Jesus even when others get angry because they're following him.

- to help the Jola Christians share his love and power with others.

- to bring many more Jolas to trust in Jesus and be free from the power of evil spirits.

- that Jola Christians would become evangelists, pastors and leaders in their churches.

Sunset in the "bush"

Kal-Tamashaq

Blue-veiled Guardians of the Sahara

Famine of no hope

The Kal-Tamashaq, or "the people of Tamashaq", live in the Sahara Desert. Let's talk to Amud, who's hoeing between the millet plants over there in the hot sun. "Our lives are very different now," Amud told us. He pulled his long blue veil across his mouth as he spoke. "Slaves used to work in our gardens while we traveled across the desert with our camels, herds and families. Then came the worst famine we'd ever seen. There wasn't any rain for six years, and lots of people and animals starved to death. We called it 'the famine of no hope.' Now we're poor and we don't have slaves to grow our millet and vegetables. At least I still have my own tent."

Algeria   Libya
KAL-TAMASHAQ
Niger   Chad
Mali
Burkino Faso   Nigeria
Africa

A nomad's tent

We look over at Amud's ragged, oval tent made of leather. "That tent has been my home for a long time. When I was young, we used to carry our tents and belongings from place to place on the backs of our camels. We were so proud that we were called 'the Lords of the desert.' In our own language we call ourselves *Imashagan*, which means 'noble and free.' But now, sometimes, we feel like God has abandoned us."

Proud nomads

The Kal-Tamashaq are descendants of the Berbers of North Africa. Hundreds of years ago, the Arabs drove them out of their homeland and south into the Sahara Desert and the Sahel. Even though they were treated this way, the Tamashaq were strong and powerful. They weren't afraid of anyone. It wasn't long before they forced the black Africans, who lived in the lands where they settled, to become their slaves.

The Kal-Tamashaq became very rich. They spent their days raiding, trading and herding. They moved through the desert with their herds of camels, cattle, sheep and goats. Traders gave the Kal-Tamashaq money or other valuables to guide and

 ## To help you pray for the Kal-Tamashaq

You can thank God for:

- the few Tamashaq who follow Jesus.
- the parts of the Bible that have been translated into Tamashaq.

You can ask God:

- to help the many Tamashaq people who are very poor.
- that Christian workers would show his love and care to the Tamashaq.
- for more evangelists, pastors and missionaries who can show the Tamashaq that they're important to him and who can teach Christians how to follow Jesus.
- to give Tamashaq Christians the courage to tell others about how he has helped them.
- to send enough rain each year so they'll have enough food for themselves and their animals.

Do you know?

The blue turban and veil (*litham*) that the Tamashaq man wears is about six yards long. He covers his mouth with his veil when he meets anyone he respects, and when he eats he uses his left hand to lift the veil from his mouth.

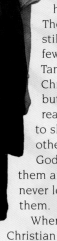

protect them as they traveled across the Sahara between west and north Africa. Everyone was afraid of these blue-veiled guardians of the desert, but they weren't afraid of anyone.

When France took control of large areas of West Africa in the nineteenth century, they banned raiding, which had always been a part of the Tamashaq way of life. They also enforced the boundaries between countries, so the Tamashaq couldn't move freely from place to place. The proud Tamashaq weren't so powerful anymore.

No longer powerful
The last 50 years have been very hard for the Kal-Tamashaq. When Mali became independent from France in 1960, the black

Africans in the south of the country took over. The Tamashaq fought the government in a civil war. They were defeated, and many of them were killed. The harsh climate defeated them, too. There's never much rain in the Sahel, but since "the famine of no hope" (which lasted from 1968–74), there have been lots of droughts and famine, and thousands of people have died. Many Tamashaq had to abandon their nomadic life and go to refugee camps, where they sometimes felt they were treated unfairly.

The Tamashaq are Muslims, but because they moved around so much they didn't build many mosques, and most of them don't keep Ramadan. But when they moved to a new

place, a Muslim holy man traveled with them to pray for them. Until recently, most of the Tamashaq had never heard about Jesus.

Not abandoned
Biga listened carefully to the tape about Jesus. He had never heard such a wonderful story. Did God really love people so much that he sent Jesus, his only Son, to die for them? Was he powerful enough to actually change people's lives? Would he really help them every day? When Biga decided to follow Jesus, some people laughed at him for following the white man's religion. But it didn't take them long to realize that Biga was a different person because God had

changed him. There are still only a few Tamashaq Christians, but they really want to show others that God loves them and will never leave them.

When Christian organizations started to send food and aid to the Tamashaq, the Christians made sure that the neediest people got their share. "How can we follow Jesus, too?" some of them wanted to know. "Life is very hard, but now we know that God hasn't abandoned us!"

Nomads, Space and Jesus

Kazakhstan is a large Central Asian country stretching from the Caspian Sea in the west to China in the east. High grassy plains called steppes roll across the northern part of the country, but there are dry, sandy deserts in the south. In the east, towards Kazakhstan's border with China, are the soaring Altai and Tien Shan Mountains.

For many centuries, the Kazakh people were nomads. They never lived in one place for very long but traveled across the steppes with their herds of cattle, sheep, horses and camels looking for pasture. About a hundred years ago, Russia conquered Kazakhstan. Thousands of Russians then came to live in Kazakhstan, forcing the Kazakh nomads off their land. Many nomads were made to live in villages and towns, but others fled to China with their animals.

Fact file

Area: 1,049,150 sq. mi.

Population: 18,588,000

Capital: Astana (until 1995, Almaty was the capital)

Language: Kazakh is the official language, but people speak Russian whenever they are doing business.

Religions: Islam; Russian Orthodox

Chief exports: Oil; wheat; wool

Kazakh nomads

The Russian settlers planted wheat on the land that had been used for grazing animals, and they started to mine iron and lead. In 1957 *Sputnik I*, the world's first space rocket, was launched from Baykonur in Kazakhstan.

Kazakhstan is once again independent from Russia. It could be a wealthy country because there is so much oil, coal and gold, and it has the world's largest chrome mine, but many Kazakhs are very poor. A few people have all the money, and there are lots of people who can't find jobs. Many children don't bother going to school, and there is more and more crime.

Some Kazakhs are hearing about Jesus on their radios

The Kazakhs are Muslims, but many of them are afraid of evil spirits. Christians are telling Kazakhs about God's love and about how they don't have to be afraid if they ask Jesus to protect them. Christian radio broadcasts and the *Jesus* film are also sharing the truth about Jesus with Kazakhs.

A Bactrian camel

"No one cares about me!"

Aibek shivered. He wanted to cry. No one in the bazaar was interested in a little boy begging for food. He should have been at school but he was much too hungry, cold and miserable. At home there was never enough food for him and his five brothers and sisters. His

 ## To help you pray for Kazakhstan

You can thank God for:

- Kazakhs who are becoming Christians and who want to share Jesus' love with their friends and families.

- Christians who have gone to Kazakhstan to tell the people about Jesus.

- the New Testament and some other parts of the Bible that have been translated into Kazakh.

You can ask God:

- to build Christian churches and fellowships throughout Kazakhstan where people can worship God and learn more about being Jesus' followers.

- to help Kazakh Christians to be brave and tell their friends, families and co-workers about Jesus.

- to send more Christian workers to Kazakhstan so that as many Kazakhs as possible will hear about God's love for them.

- to use the Christian radio broadcasts and the *Jesus* film to tell more people about Jesus.

Muslim prayers

As Aibek listened, he realized that someone *did* care about him. God loved him so much that he sent his Son Jesus to die on the cross so that Aibek could be forgiven for all the bad things he had done and go to be with God in heaven one day. In heaven there would be no hunger, cold or beatings. Aibek learned that Jesus would always be with him and be ready to hear his prayers. Aibek decided that following Jesus should be the most important thing in his life.

One very cold day, when there was no electricity, he told his mother and brothers and sisters that he was going to pray. As he said "Amen," the electricity came on again. Aibek is excited because he knows Jesus loves him and he wants his family and friends to know Jesus, too.

mother had a job, but sometimes she was paid in cabbages, or even socks, instead of money. His father was often drunk and would beat Aibek. Aibek felt as if no one cared what happened to him.

One day Aibek's big sister came home and said, "I've decided to become a Christian. Come along to the meetings with me to hear about Jesus." Aibek didn't know what a Christian was, but he went with her and had fun singing. It was warm in the meeting room, so he stayed to listen to the Bible stories.

God heals a little girl

Nurgal went up to her big sister Akmaral and whispered in her ear. A little later, Akmaral stood up in the meeting and said, "Nurgul would like us to ask Jesus to make the painful sores on her hands and feet go away."

Every day for two weeks Akmaral prayed for her. At first Akmaral was not sure that God would heal Nurgul but, as she prayed, her faith grew.

One day Nurgul told her, "It doesn't hurt any more! The sores are gone!"

Kurds

Sharing the Good News

Persecuted and ill-treated

There are probably about 30 million Kurds. They have their own culture, traditions and languages. But they don't have a country of their own. Most of them live in the rugged, mountainous area in the heart of the Middle East. Although this region is often called Kurdistan, "the land of the Kurds," it doesn't belong to them but to the countries of Turkey, Iran, Iraq and Syria.

The governments of these countries have often treated the Kurds cruelly and persecuted them. They want them to forget they are Kurds and to think of themselves as ordinary citizens of the countries where they live. Because of this, the Kurds have often been involved in long and violent struggles. In Iraq they have been bombed and attacked with poison gas.

Kurdish guard

Kurdish trader

A refugee in northern Iraq
Khaled clapped his hands and jumped for joy. He had finally passed his English exam so he could move up to the next class.

When Khaled was younger, a bomb hit his home in Kirkuk. He

The aftermath of war

In 1991, thousands of Kurdish refugees died while fleeing from Iraq to Turkey and Iran. There are about 15 million Kurds living in Turkey. Nearly all of them live in the eastern area of the country that is part of Kurdistan. Some are refugees from Iraq, but for most of them this is their homeland. They have often been ill treated. Until 1991, the Turkish government wouldn't even allow them to have books in their own language.

Hearing the good news
The Kurds are Muslims. For a long time Christians have wanted to take the message of Jesus' love to them, but it's been difficult to visit the areas where they live. In the past few years, Christians have been allowed to give food, medicine and other

aid to the Kurds in northern Iraq. The Kurds there often want to hear stories about Jesus.

Thousands of Kurds have left their homelands and settled in other countries. Although they often work for very low pay in these other places, they feel life is safer for them and better for their families. Some Kurds in Turkey have become Christians while studying the Bible, and others elsewhere are hearing the good news about Jesus and following him.

📋 Fact file

Total worldwide: About 30 million

Main countries (approximate numbers of Kurds):
Turkey (15 million)
Iran (7 million)
Iraq (4 million)
Syria (1.5 million)
Europe (850,000)
CIS (400,000)

Greet your friends in Kurdish: Good day is "Roj bas" (rawzh baash) (roj = day; bas = good)

has terrible scars on his face where he was burned. His parents fled to Kurdish Iraq with Khaled and his ten brothers and sisters. Thanks to the help of some aid workers, Khaled was able to start school. His father is too ill to work, so every day after school Khaled and his brothers have to work selling cigarettes, candy or sunflower seeds.

Because he was so tired from working and had so little time to study, it wasn't surprising that he failed his English exam. But he really wanted to pass it. A Christian family invited him to come to their home to study English. Every day for two weeks Khaled walked nearly five miles, in the summer heat, to their house. It was worth it, because he passed his exam. Now he and two of his brothers have English lessons with this family every week. These Christians pray that Khaled and his family will come to know Jesus.

A refugee in Europe

One day some soldiers came to the Kurdish village in Turkey where Serhat lived. They destroyed all the houses in the village, including theirs.

Serhat's father decided they should go to Germany. They traveled by bus, then by boat, and finally on foot. They were so glad to finally cross the border into Germany. The Germans took them to a refugee camp where they had to wait for permission to stay in Germany.

Serhat was always delighted when visitors came to the camp to play with the children, especially those who spoke Turkish, which he understood. They

told stories about Jesus, who loves children and wants to be their friend. Serhat had never heard about Jesus before. His new friends gave him a cassette of Christian songs written for children. He listened to these songs again and again and watched the *Jesus* video. Is it really true, he wondered, that Jesus offers a new life to all who trust in him?

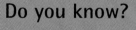

Do you know?

It is thought that the Kurds are descendants of the Medes, who are mentioned in the Bible (for example in Daniel, chapters 5 and 6).

To help you pray for the Kurds

You can thank God for:

- the translation of the New Testament into Sorani Kurdish, and for the translations into each of the main Kurdish dialects that will be completed soon.

- the *Jesus* video, radio broadcasts and Christian song and message cassettes.

You can ask God:

- that wherever Kurdish refugees are living, Christians will help them, and that through their help many Kurds will come to know Jesus as their friend.

- that many Kurds will hear the good news that Jesus offers new life to all who trust in him.

- that governments of all the countries where Kurds are living, and particularly those in the Middle East, will treat them fairly.

- to help children who are hurt and confused by the way in which they and their families have been treated.

- to show Christian workers the best ways to show Jesus' love and care to the Kurds.

A Kurdish village in Iraq

Kyrgyz

Who Live in a Land of Snow-capped Mountains

A Kyrgyz hero

Aigul thought about last night's thanksgiving feast for her uncle. She had especially loved the exciting stories the storyteller had told about Manas, the ancient Kyrgyz hero.

Had Manas really lived, Aigul wondered? Had he really learned to ride a horse as soon as he could walk? And become a mighty warrior by the time he was nine years old and rescued his father from the enemies who had captured him? Was he really the leader of all the nomadic tribes in Central Asia? Whether the stories were true or not, Aigul knew that all the Kyrgyz took great pride in their great warrior-hero.

Aigul wasn't too pleased when her father killed a sheep for the feast. He explained that they had to shed blood to show how grateful they were that her uncle, who had been seriously ill, was well again.

A Kyrgyz shepherd

Her uncle carved up the sheep's head and gave different parts to the guests. "Eat this eye, so your sight will improve!" he said as he gave an eye to an old man. He gave the youngest guest an ear, saying, "This is to remind you to listen to your elders!"

Shepherds and sheep

Manas performed his amazing deeds long ago, when the Kyrgyz were nomads. They used to ride on horseback in the valleys of the snow-clad Tien Shan (or "Heavenly") Mountains with their herds of sheep, goats, yaks and camels. They lived in *yurts*, round tents made from thick, heavy felt. The Kyrgyz haven't been nomads for a hundred years, but the symbol of the top of a *yurt* in the middle of the Kyrgyz flag reminds the people of their history.

Animals are still important to Aigul's people. As long as a family owns a cow and a few sheep and goats, no one thinks of them as poor. Several families join together to employ a shepherd to look after their animals. The shepherd leads the animals from pasture to pasture, and the sheep actually know the shepherd's voice and follow him.

The Good Shepherd

Aigul remembered another amazing story she had heard the week before. Teachers from another country had visited their school and told them that God had sent his only Son, Jesus, into the world to be born as a baby. "When he grew up," the visitors said, "he told the people that he was the Good Shepherd. He wanted them to follow him so he could look after them. He even said he would give his life for the people who followed him. And he did. Cruel men hated him so much that they killed him. But, because he was the Son of God, he rose from the dead to live forever. He's still the Good Shepherd and

Fact file

Country: Kyrgyzstan (population 4,728,000). A little over half the population is Kyrgyz. Other Kyrgyz live in Kazakhstan, Uzbekistan and Xinjiang (China).

Language: Kyrgyz, but many speak Russian as well.

Religion: Islam

Occupations: About 80% of Kyrgyz work in some sort of farming.

wants us to follow him, too."

"Manas died a long time ago," Aigul thought, "but even though Jesus died, the teachers say he rose from the dead and is still alive today! I wonder if I could follow him?"

Changes

Bishkek, where Aigul lives, is the capital of Kyrgyzstan (*Ker-ger-stan*), a small Muslim republic in Central Asia. It's a modern city with broad, tree-lined streets and colorful parks. During most of the twentieth century, Kyrgyzstan was under Russian or Soviet rule.

Russian settlers took over a lot of the best land and forced many of the nomadic Kyrgyz to settle on big collective farms. Although the Russians made it possible for everyone to go to school for free, they changed the way the Kyrgyz language was written from Arabic letters to the Cyrillic script used in Russia. The Communist rulers also banned the teaching of religion and closed mosques and churches. Kyrgyz Muslims and Russian Christians sometimes met in secret, but often children grew up knowing only what their grandparents taught them about Allah or Jesus. Very few Kyrgyz had ever even heard of Jesus.

In 1991, Krygyzstan once more became on independent country. Christians from other countries arrived to offer their help and

Traditional headdress

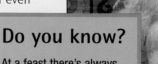

Do you know?

At a feast there's always plenty to eat. The Kyrgyz national dish, called *besh-barmak*, is made from mutton mixed with noodles. Its name means "five fingers," because the Kyrgyz used to eat it with their hands!

to tell the Kyrgyz about God's love for them. Some have started to follow Jesus, the Good Shepherd, who takes care of them.

Hunting with a hawk

Selling *shyrdak* (felt mats)

To help you pray for the Kyrgyz

You can thank God for:

- every Kyrgyz man, woman, boy and girl who has started to follow Jesus.
- the New Testament and children's Bible in the Kyrgyz language.
- the Christian bookstore in Bishkek.

You can ask God:

- to help all the local Christians, whether they are Kyrgyz, Russian, German or from some other country, to work together and love one another.
- for Christians to tell Kyrgyz boys and girls about Jesus through songs and stories.
- that as the Kyrgyz church grows, pastors and church workers will teach Christians how to obey God and how to tell others about Jesus.
- to give the leaders of Kyrgyzstan wisdom as they govern this country which has few natural resources and where many people are poor and don't have jobs.

The Switzerland of Africa

Lesotho is a small country completely surrounded by the Republic of South Africa. If you visited Lesotho you would see lots of mountains, fast-flowing streams and rushing rivers. Although it's thousands of miles away, Lesotho reminds some people so much of Switzerland that they call it "the Switzerland of Africa." Because it's usually cool and damp in Lesotho, the people wrap up in warm, colorful blankets. They wear cone-shaped hats made of woven grass on their heads.

Most of the two million people living in Lesotho are Basotho, and they speak a language called Sesotho. Because there aren't enough jobs in Lesotho, many men go to South Africa to work in the gold mines.

Children walking to school

Lesotho
• Maseru

South Africa

Shepherd boys

In many countries boys go to school while the girls stay at home to help their families, but not in Lesotho. A lot of Basotho boys, especially those from poor families in the country, begin to look after flocks of sheep and goats and herds of cattle when they're only seven years old. Wool from the sheep and mohair, which is made from goats' hair, are two of Lesotho's main exports. That means that the animals are very valuable.

Imagine what it would be like to be a shepherd boy in Lesotho. You would spend many weeks away from home, all by yourself, looking after the sheep and goats in the mountains. In the

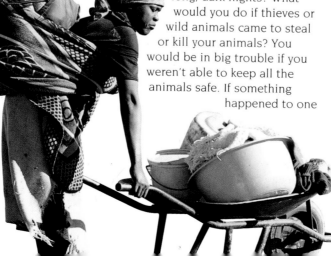

Would you walk many miles to learn about the Bible? Lots of Lesotho church leaders do!

summer it rains, and in the winter it's very cold. The frost and snow might feel even colder because you wouldn't have a warm house or fire or even dry clothes to wear. What would you think about during the long, dark nights? What would you do if thieves or wild animals came to steal or kill your animals? You would be in big trouble if you weren't able to keep all the animals safe. If something happened to one

of your sheep, your family might not have enough food to eat. You can read in the Bible about the adventures of another shepherd boy – the story of David and Goliath is in the Old Testament, in 1 Samuel 17. David knew that God would keep him safe in every situation.

Some of the shepherd boys who know how to read and write are learning how to teach their friends who are also

 To help you pray for Lesotho

You can thank God for:

- the many people in the capital city, Maseru, who are coming to know Jesus as their friend.
- all the boys and girls who are learning about Jesus through Scripture Union.
- new Christians who go into mountain villages to share the good news of Jesus' love with others.

You can ask God:

- to protect MAF pilots as they fly into remote villages with supplies and medical care and share Jesus' love with people there.
- to keep the shepherd boys safe and bring many of them to know Jesus, a friend who is with them all the time.
- to help the Christian leaders with their Bible lessons so that they will know how to teach others about Jesus.
- to look after the men who have to go to South Africa to work in the mines to earn money for their families, and to keep their families at home safe.

Traditional homestead

MAF airplane

Fact file

Area: 11,740 sq. mi.

Population: 2,152,553

Capital: Maseru

Main languages: Sesotho; English

Religion: Christianity (mainly Roman Catholic)

Chief exports: Wool; mohair; diamonds; livestock

shepherds. The boys who know how to read will be able to get better jobs in Lesotho when they grow up.

In the towns, most of the boys and girls go to school. An organization called Scripture Union is teaching many of the children about Jesus.

Teachers who ride on horseback

Most Basothos belong to the Roman Catholic or the Lesotho Evangelical Church, but many of them don't really understand that Jesus died to forgive their sins. Missionaries are training church leaders to explain to the people what the Bible says. The missionaries send these leaders homework to do, and once a month they travel many miles (on horseback, by bus or on foot!) to attend a special class.

There are lots of villages scattered throughout the mountains. Christian workers, often riding on horseback, visit these villages to tell the people about Jesus. They have also shown the *Jesus* film to thousands of people in Lesotho. Many people watch this film about Jesus' life and teaching, the miracles he did and his death on the cross, and they ask Jesus to be their friend.

A flying ambulance

The Missionary Aviation Fellowship (MAF) has built 40 runways throughout Lesotho. Their planes carry supplies to areas that are difficult to get to, and sometimes they fly patients to the hospital. "It was lots of fun but kind of scary flying in the plane," recalls Mokeane, a little Basotho boy. "I broke my arm and an MAF pilot flew me to the hospital in Maseru. I loved looking out of the plane to see all the little rivers and trees! It only took us 25 minutes to get there. If we had gone on horseback and bus, it would have taken nine or ten hours!"

Lobi

Who File their Teeth to Points

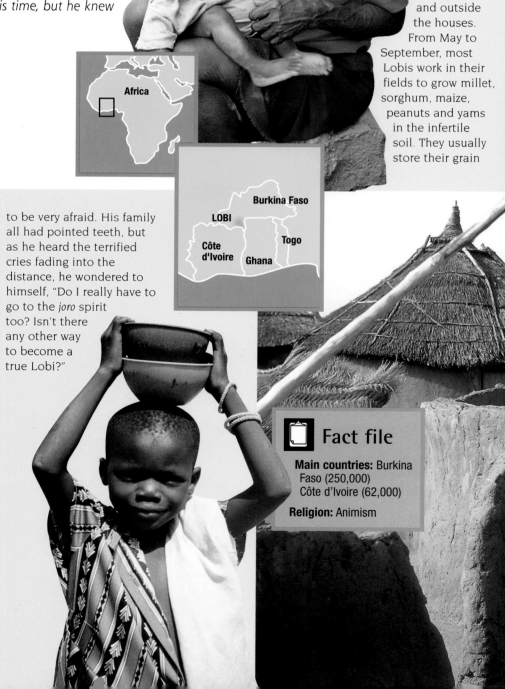

Children who vanish

Sie watched the long line of people hurrying down the road. There were children, some not much bigger than himself; women carrying cooking pots and sacks of food on their heads; men cracking whips so that everyone moved quickly. He shivered as he heard the cries of the children. These cries are heard only once every seven years, at the time of the joro. Sie was afraid. He was too young this time, but he knew his turn was coming.

Africa

Burkina Faso

LOBI

Côte d'Ivoire

Ghana

Togo

Slaves no more

The homes of the Lobis are big and built of mud, and the inner rooms are very dark because there are no windows. There are life-sized idols made of clay both inside and outside the houses. From May to September, most Lobis work in their fields to grow millet, sorghum, maize, peanuts and yams in the infertile soil. They usually store their grain

The *joro* is the initiation ceremony of the Lobi people who live in Burkina Faso in West Africa. Tribal leaders take children who are seven years old and older from their parents and go into the bush for two or three months. After many frightening tests of bravery, each child is brought before a large idol of the *joro*, the evil spirit who controls the initiation. The children's teeth are then filed to points as a sign that they are true Lobis. Some children never return, and their families aren't allowed to ask what happened to them. It is enough to know that the *joro* spirit took them.

Although anyone who has been through the *joro* is forbidden to talk about it to those who haven't been initiated, Sie knew enough

to be very afraid. His family all had pointed teeth, but as he heard the terrified cries fading into the distance, he wondered to himself, "Do I really have to go to the *joro* spirit too? Isn't there any other way to become a true Lobi?"

Fact file

Main countries: Burkina Faso (250,000)
Côte d'Ivoire (62,000)

Religion: Animism

on the flat roofs of their houses in round bins which have cone-shaped covers made of thatch.

There are very few Lobis who are Christians, but more and more are coming to know Jesus. There are 80 churches and meeting places in Burkina Faso where Christians worship on Sundays. One of these churches is in Nako, near the main center where the initiation ceremonies take place. About 100 Christian Lobi men and women have been trained to share the good news about Jesus with their people and teach them to follow him. They're also telling other animistic and Muslim peoples in Burkina Faso about Jesus.

The New Testament was translated into Lobi and published in 1985. Although most children and young people are learning to read, only one Lobi adult out of every 10 can read.

Perhaps Sie will not have to go to the *joro* to become a true Lobi. Each time the initiation ceremonies are

Do you know?

Many years ago, Lobi women had their faces scarred to make them look so ugly that slave traders wouldn't want them. They pierced holes in both lips and inserted round pieces of wood into them. A few women still wear lip rings.

held, Christians pray that the spirits will lose their power over the people. There are signs that God is answering these prayers. Please join them in praying that the slaves of the *joro*, who takes life, will become the children of God, who gives life!

 ## To help you pray for the Lobi

You can thank God for:

- the Lobi New Testament.
- Christian Lobis studying at Bible school.
- Christians leading camps and programs for young people.

You can ask God:

- that Lobis learning to read will read the New Testament for themselves.
- to help those translating the Old Testament into Lobi to find the right words so the meaning is clear.
- that young people will understand that they don't have to be afraid of the *joro* if they trust in Jesus.
- that the church in Nako will become so strong that the initiation ceremonies will come to an end.

Where Christians Gave up their Lives for Jesus

A bird's-eye view

If you look at a map of Africa, you'll see a long, narrow island in the Indian Ocean about 250 miles off the coast of southeast Africa. This is Madagascar. It's the fourth largest island in the world, more than twice the size of the state of Colorado.

Peter is on an airplane about to take off from Mahajanga, on the west coast. Let's fly over the island with him to see what it's like. "There are fields of rice and sweet potatoes, and quite a few cattle, on this part of the island," he tells us. Soon we're flying over the large central plateau where most of the people live.

Manambold Gorge

Fact file

Area: 226,650 sq. mi.

Population: 15,941,727

Capital: Antananarivo

Official languages: Malagasy; French

Religions: Christianity; traditional religions

Chief exports: Coffee; cloves; vanilla; sugar

Christians in Madagascar are teaching people about Jesus in hospitals, prisons and schools

"The hills and steep valleys of the plateau used to be covered in forests," Peter says, "but the people have cut down a lot of the trees for firewood and clear a new patch of land every year to grow their crops. Since these forests have been cut down, the heavy rains wash away a lot of the red soil each year. This is called erosion, and it makes it more difficult to grow crops in the soil." Now we see a big city on a mountain. "Look," Peter says, "there's Antananarivo, the capital city. Look for the old churches and palaces."

Suddenly, it looks like the land is disappearing from under us as we leave the central plateau and fly across the forests of the eastern plain to the coast. A lot of the forest has been cleared for farming here, too. "Most of the people in Madagascar are very poor," Peter says. "There isn't much rain in some places in the west, so the crops don't grow well. Cyclones pass through Madagascar nearly every year, destroying the forest and crops and causing flooding. There aren't many good roads, so it's difficult to get help to the people who need it most."

Risking their lives for Jesus

Almost 200 years ago, two brave Welshmen took the good news about Jesus to Madagascar. They brought their wives and babies with them, but

Africa

Diego Suaréz

Mahajanga

Antananarivo

Madagascar

INDIAN OCEAN

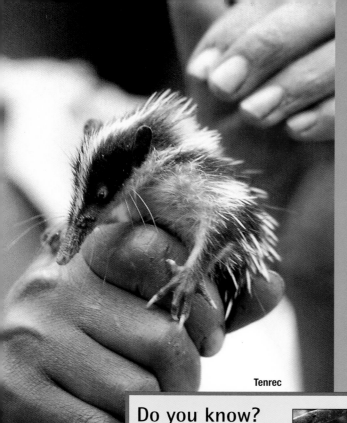

Tenrec

 ## To help you pray for Madagascar

You can thank God for:

- every missionary and church leader.
- the groups that teach young people about Jesus.
- the Malagasy Bible Society.

You can ask God:

- to help Christians today to be faithful to Jesus.
- for many young people to know Jesus and to tell others about him, too.
- for Christians to go to places where the people have never heard about Jesus.
- that Christian radio programs will reach many people with the good news about Jesus.

Do you know?

There are many different plants and animals found only in Madagascar. These include lemurs (relatives of monkeys), tenrecs and the Malagasy mongoose. Some of them are in danger of dying out because they live in the forests that are being destroyed.

Lemur

a few months later only one, David Jones, was still alive. It would have been very easy for him to go back to Wales and forget all about the people of Madagascar! But he knew God wanted them to hear about Jesus, so he stayed. He set up a little school, and the king's son was one of his first students. There were no books because their language, Malagasy, had never been written down. When other missionaries joined David Jones, they put the language into writing and taught the children and their parents to read and write. They taught them about Jesus, too, and translated the Bible into Malagasy. A lot of people asked Jesus to be their savior and friend.

Then a new ruler, Queen Ranavalona, decided that the people of Madagascar should worship their dead kings and queens. She said that anyone who worshipped or prayed to

Jesus would be put to death.

Many of the Christians met secretly – in houses, caves or on mountaintops – to pray and read the Bible. The queen had thousands of them tortured and killed because they wouldn't stop following Jesus. She reigned for 33 years, but when she died there were far more Christians than when her cruel reign began. God is so much more powerful than any human ruler.

Remembering God's help

Although more than half the people in Madagascar are Christians, many of them want to worship other gods as well as being Christians – but it doesn't work.

Some of the Christians do love and follow Jesus, just as the Malagasy

martyrs did long ago. Lots of young people, too, are learning about Jesus and following him. Some of them work with the Malagasy Bible Society, which trains them to tell others about Jesus. They bring the Bible to people in hospitals, prisons and schools. They know it's important for people to have the Bible and read and understand what it says. Some of these volunteers teach reading with special Bibles for people just learning to read.

But there are still people groups in Madagascar who have never heard of Jesus because their villages are so remote and there aren't any roads into the mountain areas where they live. Please pray that someday they, too, will hear about him and put their trust in him.

Beautiful Islands in the South Indian Ocean

Holiday paradise

Peter's father pulled a world atlas down from the bookshelf and opened it to show him the map of India. "Look, Peter," he said, pointing to a chain of tiny islands in the Indian Ocean. "These are the Maldives. I thought we could go there this summer. We'll have to fly to India and then about 300 miles southwest to get there." He traced the chain of islands with his finger. "We won't be able to see all the islands, though – see how they stretch right down here to the equator? That's about 500 miles." He handed Peter a travel magazine. "See for yourself how beautiful they are."

Fact file

Land area: 115 sq. mi.

Population: 286,223

Capital: Malé

Language: Divehi

Religion: Islam

Economy: Fishing; tourism

"Wow!" exclaimed Peter. "Coral islands! Coconut trees! And sandy beaches! The islands look like they're floating in the sea." Peter started to read the magazine. "I can hardly wait to go! We'll have to bring our snorkels, and we'll do lots of swimming ... oh, and wind surfing! And scuba diving!"

Every year, thousands of people visit the Maldives to bask in the sun and swim in the clear blue sea. They stay in hotels built for tourists, but often the only Maldivians they meet are those who work in the hotels.

Over 1,000 islands

"Hey Dad," Peter said a few nights later, "I've been reading more about the Maldives. Did you know that there are at least 1,200 little islands, but only 202 of them are inhabited? Most of the islands are so flat that if the sea level rose only a little, they would be flooded. That's why their government is really concerned about global warming.

Do you know?

Although the Maldives are very beautiful, some Maldivians believe that Allah, the Muslim god, sent all the *jinns* of the world to live in their islands.

Decorated ceramic

"Malé, the capital island, is less than a square mile in area. It must be very crowded with 60,000 people living there! The international airport is on the nearby island of Hulule."

"Very good," his father replied, "I've found out a few things too. The people call themselves Di*ve*hi, which means 'islanders.' Their language is called Di*ve*hi, too ... and they write from right to left! Most children go to school, and in Malé there are schools where the children study in English. If they want to go to college or university they have to go to another country.

"Boat building is an important business, and more than a third of the people are fishermen. Some people say the Maldives is among the 20 poorest countries in the world. They must be very glad to have the money they earn from tourists."

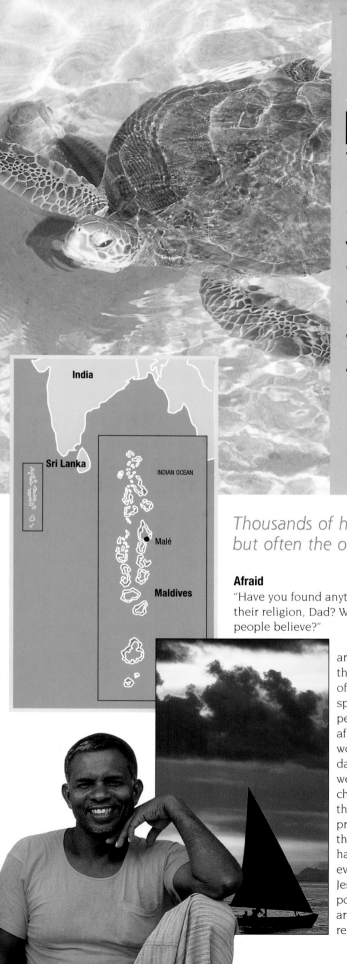

 ## To help you pray for the Maldives

You can thank God for:

- the parts of the Bible that have already been translated into *Divehi*.

- the Christian radio broadcasts that are being beamed into the islands.

You can ask God:

- to take away any fear that Christians working there may have and to give them joy as they share his love by caring for others.

- for Maldivians to discover that through trusting in Jesus they can be set free from fear and the power of evil spirits.

- to lead Maldivians studying in other countries to meet Christians who will share God's love with them.

- that the leaders of the country will allow each person to worship in the way he or she chooses.

Thousands of holiday-makers visit the Maldives every year but often the only Maldivians they meet are hotel workers

Afraid

"Have you found anything out about their religion, Dad? What do the people believe?"

"The Maldivians are Muslims, but they're also afraid of *jinns*, or evil spirits. Many people are so afraid that they won't go out after dark. They often wear blue glass charms around their necks to protect them from the *jinns*. We don't have to be afraid of evil spirits because Jesus is more powerful than they are. Do you remember what we read in church on Sunday about Jesus casting out demons in Luke 4:31–36? Jesus will always protect us."

Peter shivered. "I know, but all this talk about evil spirits is scary. Aren't there any Christians there?"

His father shook his head. "Only a few," he said. "The government doesn't allow missionaries, but Christians from other countries do go there to work. They can read the Bible and pray in private, but they can't speak about Jesus to Maldivian people. Some foreign Christians have been expelled from the country and some Maldivian Christians put in prison. It's not easy to be a Christian when that happens!"

"But Jesus can change the world, can't he?" asked Peter. "Let's start praying that the people of the Maldives will hear the good news that Jesus saves them and protects them from evil spirits."

World Map

Countries which are featured in this book are shown in red.
People groups are shown in orange.

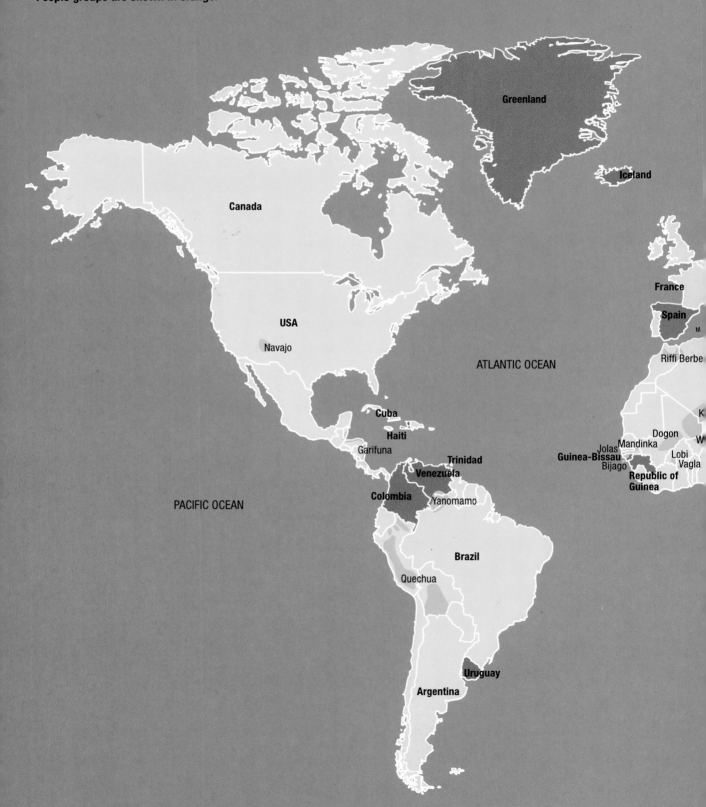

Greenland

Iceland

Canada

France

Spain

M

Riffi Berbe

USA

ATLANTIC OCEAN

Navajo

K

Cuba

Dogon

W

Haiti

Mandinka

Garifuna

Jolas

Lobi

Guinea-Bissau

Vagla

Trinidad

Bijago

Venezuela

Republic of
Guinea

PACIFIC OCEAN

Colombia

Yanomamo

Brazil

Quechua

Uruguay

Argentina

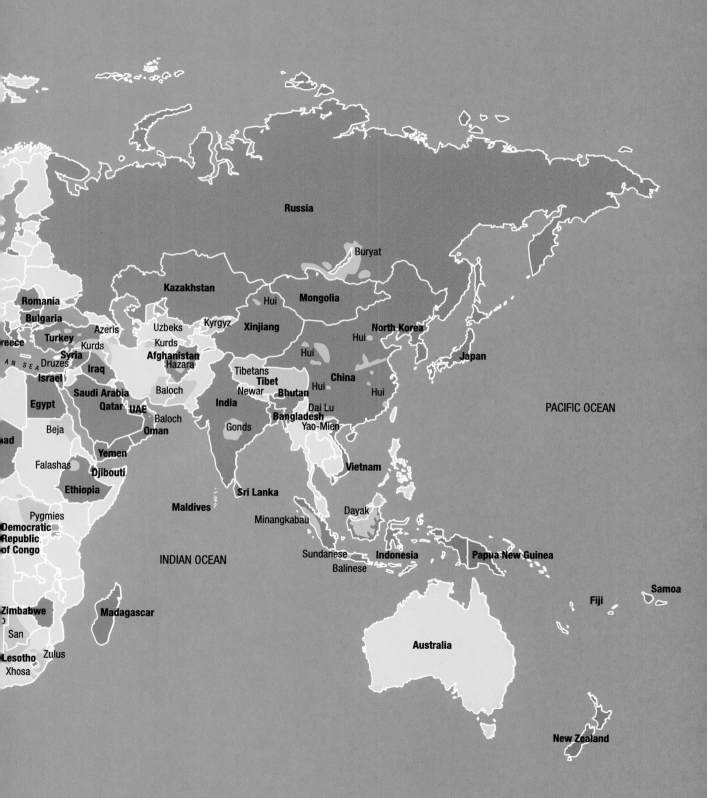

Russia

Buryat

Kazakhstan

Hui

Mongolia

Romania

Bulgaria

Azeris

Uzbeks

Kyrgyz

Xinjiang

North Korea

reece

Turkey

Kurds

Kurds

Hui

Syria

Druzes

Afghanistan

Hazara

Hui

Japan

Israel

Iraq

Tibetans

China

Egypt

Saudi Arabia

Baloch

Newar

Tibet

Hui

PACIFIC OCEAN

Qatar

UAE

India

Bhutan

Hui

Beja

Baloch

Bangladesh

Dai Lu

ad

Oman

Gonds

Yao-Mien

Falashas

Yemen

Djibouti

Vietnam

Ethiopia

Sri Lanka

Pygmies

Maldives

Dayak

Democratic

Republic

of Congo

Minangkabau

INDIAN OCEAN

Sundanese

Indonesia

Papua New Guinea

Balinese

Zimbabwe

Fiji

Samoa

San

Madagascar

Lesotho

Zulus

Australia

Xhosa

New Zealand

AN SEA

Mandinka

Who Hope Charms Will Keep Them Safe

Charms for a baby

Nene cuddled her baby son. Outside her mud and thatch house, the village people were singing and dancing. The marabout (Muslim teacher) had come, and Nene had paid him to tie ten jujus (charms) around her baby's arms, neck and waist. She hoped these would keep him safe from sickness and evil spirits. Nene was very worried. The charms hadn't worked for her other three babies, who had all died. Nene had wanted to take the children to the Christian nurse at the nearby clinic, but her husband wouldn't let her. "If you do," he told her, "they'll make you take off the jujus and burn them. That's against our Mandinka ways, and the children wouldn't be protected from the evil spirits.

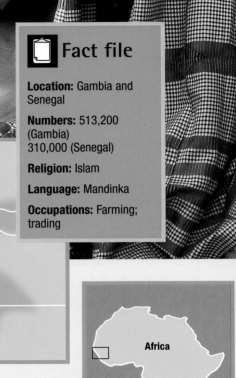

Fact file

Location: Gambia and Senegal

Numbers: 513,200 (Gambia) 310,000 (Senegal)

Religion: Islam

Language: Mandinka

Occupations: Farming; trading

Senegal

Gambia

Banjul

MANDINKA

Senegal

MANDINKA

Africa

The *marabout* makes *jujus* by writing verses from the Koran on bits of paper. Then he sews them into little leather pouches and hangs them on a string. The Mandinka believe that the power of these *jujus* comes from Allah, the Muslim God.

Followers of Islam

Almost half the people living in the small West African country of Gambia are Mandinkas. Many centuries ago, they left their homeland in Mali and traveled west in search of better farmland. Eventually they settled in Gambia and the surrounding countries.

The Mandinkas were animists. Traders passing through the region converted some of them to Islam, but a lot of the Mandinkas continued to follow their traditional religion. Now most Mandinkas say they are Muslims, like nearly all the other people in Gambia. But many of them are still afraid of the spirits.

"I'm so afraid!"

Oumar sat near the fire and listened to the grown-ups tell scary stories about beautiful women who were really witches and sold children for meat. He had lots of strange dreams and was scared to go anywhere in the dark.

"I'm always afraid," he told his mother one day. "I can't even sleep. I wish there was a god who was more powerful than the bad

To help you pray for the Mandinka

You can thank God for:

- the Mandinka New Testament.
- the clinics, youth centers and other places where people can feel God's love and learn about him.
- the Mandinkas who are helping to translate the Old Testament.

You can ask God:

- that Mandinkas who are learning to read will understand what the Bible says.
- to help Mandinka Christians to always follow Jesus, help others and tell them about God's love and care.
- to show the Mandinkas that he is far greater and more powerful than all the gods and spirits that they fear.
- to send more missionaries to Gambia to help the Mandinkas and to tell them about Jesus.

Mandinka Scriptures

Do you know?

Only two out of every ten Mandinka people can read. So programs teaching them to read are very important.

witches and spirits and who would take care of me."

"We're Muslims, Oumar," she said. "We believe in the great God Allah. He'll help you." So Oumar learned as much as he could from the Muslim teachers. He prayed five times every day and fasted during the month of Ramadan, but he was still afraid.

Oumar wanted to do well in school so he could get a good job and help his mother. At the Catholic high school he learned about the Lord Jesus Christ, the Son of God. Oumar was confused. "I wonder which is true?" he asked himself. "Islam or Christianity?"

Oumar started to study the Bible through a correspondence course. He wanted to prove that Jesus was not really the Son of God so he could know that

Islam was true. But he was surprised to learn that Jesus really was the one who could take away his fears. Oumar wanted to follow this God more than anything else, but he was afraid his mother would be very angry. Oumar knew that he had finally found the truth. He had to make a choice to follow Jesus or be afraid forever.

Oumar told his teacher that he wanted to follow Jesus. Now he knows that Jesus is always with him and helps him when he's afraid. His mother was angry with him at first, but when she saw the change in Oumar's life, and that he wasn't afraid anymore, she wanted to follow Jesus too.

Showing God's love

There aren't many Mandinka Christians yet, but missionaries are showing them God's love and helping them in a lot of different ways. They provide medical care, reading classes (there are even special classes in prisons), and youth centers where young people can learn new skills.

There's a Mandinka New Testament, and a team translating the Old Testament. The missionaries pray that a lot more Mandinkas will put their trust in Jesus, who will take away their fears.

Minangkabau

The People of the Water Buffalo

The weak triumphs over the strong

The Minangkabau (mee-nahng-kah-bow) people, who live in West Sumatra in Indonesia, enjoy telling a legend about the water buffalo. (Minang means "winning," and kabau means "water buffalo.") About 600 years ago, the king of the nearby island of Java tried to conquer West Sumatra. The people of West Sumatra knew they weren't strong enough to win a war, but they had another idea.

Pick your best water buffalo to fight our best buffalo," they told the king. "If your buffalo wins, we'll serve you; but if ours wins, you must never attack us again." The Javanese king agreed and found the biggest, fiercest water buffalo in Java. He was sure they would win!

Do you know?

All Minangkabau children learn two languages. They speak Minangkabau at home, but at school they speak Indonesian, the national language.

On the day of the contest, this enormous buffalo stomped out onto the field. The Javanese army laughed and laughed when they saw the buffalo the people of West Sumatra sent out onto the field. It was just a tiny calf. How ridiculous to think such a little creature could beat their giant!

What the Javanese didn't know was that their enemy had a sneaky plan. For three days, the West Sumatrans had kept the baby buffalo away from its mother and her milk. As you can imagine, he was very hungry indeed. They had also tied sharp knives to his head. When the calf saw the big water buffalo, he thought it was his mother and rushed towards it. He pushed his head under the Javanese buffalo's belly, searching for milk. As he did so, the knives on his head cut into the big animal again and again. Bellowing with pain, the big buffalo ran away and finally fell down dead!

"*Minang kabau!*" the West Sumatrans shouted. "Our buffalo is the winner!" Since then, the people of West Sumatra have called themselves the Minangkabau because they're proud that they were so smart. They even make points shaped like the horns of a water buffalo on the roofs of their houses.

The Bible is full of true stories like this, where the weak triumphs over the strong. One of the best known is the story of David and Goliath (you can read about this in 1 Samuel 17 in the Old Testament).

The family name

The surnames of most people in the world come from their father's

China

Malaysia

MINANGKABAU

Sumatra

Indonesia

INDIAN OCEAN

Planting rice in a paddy field

Water buffalo

To help you pray for the Minangkabau

You can thank God for:

- the Minangkabau who know Jesus.
- Christian radio programs.
- the New Testament in Minangkabau.

You can ask God:

- for more Christians to share the good news about Jesus with the Minangkabau.
- to show these people that they can be Christians and still be Minangkabau.
- that Minangkabau all over the world will meet Christians and hear about Jesus.
- that the government and local people will be fair to the Minangkabau Christians and not hurt them.

Fact file

Country: West Sumatra, Indonesia

Numbers: 8,000,000

Occupations: Rice farming; business; restaurant owners

---

family – yours is probably the same. But the Minangkabau use the mother's name. They're unusual in other ways, too. The men are leaders within the bigger family (called a clan) and in the village, but it's the women who own the rice fields and houses. Because they don't own land, the men often leave their villages to find work in the towns, only returning to help at harvest time. Some of them never go back, which is why there are Minangkabau in every part of Indonesia. A lot of them open restaurants, where they serve their very hot spicy food called Nasi Padang.

A wonderful discovery

There are about eight million Minangkabau. About four million of them live in the mountain region of West Sumatra, and the rest are scattered throughout Indonesia. Almost all of them are Muslims, but many of them still also believe that spirits living in the forests and mountains cause sickness and trouble. Those who become Christians know that they'll probably lose their jobs, their families will disown them, and they may even be thrown into prison. The government even closed down a hospital, that was helping a lot of people, just because it was run by Christians. And nearly all the copies of the New Testament in Minangkabau were taken and burned soon after they were printed.

There are only about 200 Minangkabau Christians. How will the rest of the Minangkabau hear the good news about Jesus? God will answer your prayers to make that happen. Some hear about Jesus as they listen to radio broadcasts. Some, like Pak Iman, hear about him when they work in other parts of Indonesia or the world.

On a business trip in America, Pak Iman found a Bible in his hotel room. He had never seen one, but he started to read it and then took it home with him. For six years, Pak Iman read the Bible and watched the Christians where he worked. He finally decided to follow Jesus, but he was afraid to tell his wife and children. He was surprised and happy to discover that his wife had been reading the Bible, too, and that she and their children all wanted to become Christians. God is answering prayers for the Minangkabau.

117

Missionary Kids

Belonging to Two Worlds

Two countries

"What's America like?" Paul asked his friend David. *"I was only four the last time we were there. Were you scared to go there?"*

David remembered how confused he felt when they arrived at JFK Airport in New York. Everything was so big, exciting and a bit frightening. Riding on the moving sidewalks and going up and down escalators had been fun, but there were so many people rushing around that he made sure he kept close to his father.

"Yes, I was a bit scared," David admitted, *"even though I knew I'd be seeing my grandparents and all the rest of our family. I wondered how I'd get along with them, but they made me feel right at home. We had lots of treats, like hamburgers at MacDonald's and going to Disney World … that was awesome!"*

Two schools

"What about school?" Paul asked. "Our school here is so small, and all the teachers are our friends. We're just like a big family and we do everything together. Maybe I won't find any friends in America."

"I know how you feel," David said. "At first my new school seemed too big.

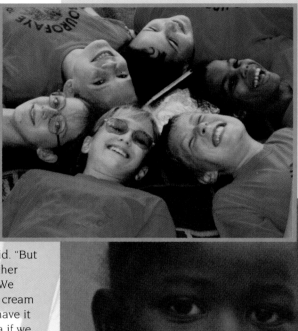

Paul and David are both nine years old, and they go to a small, international boarding school for MKs (missionaries' kids) in West Africa. David and his family recently returned from a year of "home leave" in America, and Paul and his family are about to go home.

Paul grinned. "I can't wait for things like that, and television. There'll be lots of big stores and things to buy, but I probably won't know what to choose! What's the food like? Is it very different?"

David laughed. "Well, I missed peanut stew!" he said. "But there were lots of other good things to eat. We hardly ever have ice cream here, but we could have it every day in America if we wanted! In hundreds of different flavors! I didn't like shopping in the big malls at first. They were too big and there were so many things to choose from that I couldn't decide what I wanted. But it was great being able to buy the newest computer games and bring them back here – especially now that we have electricity all the time."

There were almost as many kids in my class as we have in the whole school here. I wondered whether I'd make friends, and if the other kids would think I was weird because I didn't know much about life in America. I wondered whether I would know as much as the kids in my class did. But I didn't need to worry, because sometimes I even got the best grades in my class. And it was great having enough kids for a soccer team!

"My class really liked hearing about Africa – the different animals, village life and my African friends. They liked hearing about our school here, too. I told them about the fun we have, and about our games and sports and some of the tricks we play on each other. They wanted to hear about our visits to the cotton fields and markets. I told them about some of the difficult things as well, like the heat and insects, how much I miss my parents at the beginning of each term, and how sick I felt when I had malaria. I told them how lonely I am sometimes when I go home to the village during school holidays because even though I still play with my African friends, it's not the same since I've gone away to school. My life is so different from theirs because they never leave the village except to go to their fields or to the market.

"They couldn't believe that we studied the Bible every day and had our own church service on Sundays – and that we actually enjoyed it! Most kids I met didn't even go to Sunday school."

Two cultures

MKs have lots of unusual experiences. Their parents often teach them at home until they're old enough to go away to school. Sometimes they travel a lot and live in fascinating places. They meet all sorts of people and have friends from all around the world. But they can also feel very lonely. "It's really hard to say goodbye to friends who go on home leave or move to other places," said an MK called Mary, "but we stay in touch through letters and e-mail. MKs understand each other, because none of us really belong to the country where we grow up. And we don't always feel at home in the country our parents call 'home.' Sometimes we feel like we don't really belong anywhere, although we seem to belong everywhere. But we can understand other people, no matter where they come from."

If you know a missionary family, you could be a friend to the children. You could write to them about the things you do so that when they come home everything won't seem quite so strange. They'll write to you, too, and tell you about their school and the things they do.

 To help you pray for missionary kids

You can thank God for:

- the friends MKs have from different countries.
- their missionary parents, who show Jesus' love and care to others.
- schools where MKs can study and learn the same things as children in their home countries.

You can ask God:

- to help MKs find friends and not to feel lonely.
- to keep them safe and well.
- to help them adjust when they return to their home countries.
- that they can use their experiences to understand and help others.

Very Hot or Very Cold

From mountains to desert

The country of Mongolia is sandwiched between Russia and China. In the north you will find windswept mountains, plains, forests and lakes, but the Gobi Desert in the south is a vast wilderness of sand and gravel. The winters are long and cold, but the summers are very hot.
There are only a few towns in Mongolia. More people are moving into these towns, but most people still live in the country. Those who still follow the traditional way of life move to the pastures in the mountains during the summer with their flocks of sheep, goats, camels, yaks and horses. In the cold winter months they move down to the grassy plains. Their homes are felt-covered gers, or tents, which they take with them. The gers protect them from both heat and cold.

Fact file

Area: 604,250 sq. mi.

Population: 2,662,020

Capital: Ulaanbaatar

Language: Khalkh Mongolian

Religion: Buddhism

Chief exports: Minerals; meat; wool

Buddhism and Communism

For many centuries Mongolia was a Buddhist country and most families sent their eldest sons to be Buddhist monks. Few people were ever allowed to preach about Jesus there, and those who did rarely met anyone who wanted to learn anything about him.

In 1924 Mongolia became a Communist republic and, for the next 65 years, Mongolia was closed to the outside world. The Communist government destroyed many of the Buddhist monasteries and banned religion. In 1990 a miracle happened: the Communist government lost power and the people were given the freedom to choose which religion they would follow. Some returned to Buddhism, but others became Christians.

Growing up in Mongolia

Jill was excited to meet a Mongolian student and had lots of questions about this mysterious country. Udbal grew up in Ulaanbaatar, Mongolia's capital. "It's the only large city in the country," she told Jill. "Some people live in apartments, but many still prefer to live in *gers*. In the city, you'll often see tall buildings and *gers* next to one another. The city *gers* have electricity, but they don't have running water. My parents both worked, so my brothers, sisters and I helped carry water, chop wood, shop, cook and clean."

Jill wanted to know if it was true that they drank fermented horses' milk. Ubdal laughed. "Mares' milk, yes. It becomes fizzy after a few days and is very refreshing. We make cheese from the milk of sheep and

 To help you pray for Mongolia

You can thank God for:

● those Mongolians who have come to know Jesus.

● the New Testament in Mongolian.

You can ask God:

● for Mongolian Christians to share God's love.

● to help students in Bible school.

● that Mongolians will read and understand the New Testament.

● to help those translating the Old Testament.

● to bring help for the poor and the sick, especially the street children.

Nomad woman

Young monks

Russia

Mongolia
● Ulaanbaatar

Japan

China

In the city, you'll often see tall buildings and gers next to one another

A group of tent-like homes called *gers*

goats. Lots of people keep animals, even in the towns where it's against the law."

"Did you learn about Buddhism as a child?" Jill asked her.

"It was never mentioned at school, and the Communists only allowed one Buddhist monastery to stay open. My father is an atheist and doesn't believe in God. When I was little I wondered about the world: Who made

it? Where do people come from? How can there be no God, as the Communists say? Most children wonder about these things, but when we asked questions, we were told to be quiet."

Jill wanted to know how Udbal became a Christian. "When I was at school," she answered, "a man from overseas asked me to help translate the New Testament. I thought it was a children's book because of the exciting stories. Gradually I realized it was a special book about God and his son Jesus. I believed what the Bible said, and I began to trust in Jesus."

New Christians

The church in Mongolia has grown in the years since 1990. By 1999, there were more than 30 churches. Most of them are in Ulaanbaatar, but there are churches in the other towns as well. Lots of young people have become interested in Christianity through seeing the *Jesus* film, and many have decided to follow him. Now there is a Bible school, where young Christians can study and train to be leaders in the churches.

The New Testament has been translated into Mongolian and printed in the Russian alphabet. It's also being printed in the Mongolian alphabet. Some of the Old Testament has already been translated and the whole Bible should be published soon.

Navajo

Craftsmen of the American West

Skilled workmen

The Navajo (nah-vuh-hoh) are the largest group of American Indians in the United States. They live in the western states of Arizona, New Mexico and Utah. Although most of them now live in modern houses, almost every family still has at least one "hogan." The hogan is a traditional one-room home made of wood and mud or stone. A Navajo storyteller explains the hogan like this: "Long, long ago, our Holy People told us that the door of the hogan must always face east towards the rising sun. Inside, there's a special place for everyone and everything. The area for the mother and her little children is on the north side, the father and older boys use the south side for their things and any special guests are honored with a place on the west. We hang our belongings from nails in the walls or tuck them into crevices in the walls or up in the domed ceiling."

Navajo hogan

USA

NAVAJO

USA

Utah

Colorado

NAVAJO

Arizona

New Mexico

The Navajo are very artistic. They color wool with dyes made from desert plants and then use it to weave beautiful rugs on handmade looms. They also make beautiful silver and turquoise jewelry. The Navajo medicine men use an amazing mixture of pollen, corn meal, crushed flowers, charcoal and ground minerals to make sand paintings for their ceremonies. Today, the Navajo make framed sand paintings to sell to art collectors and tourists.

Turquoise and silver earrings

Ceremonies, songs and celebrations

As part of their religion, Navajo memorize and recite songs and chants. Some ceremonies last for nine days, and they can't make any mistakes. The Navajo who perform these ceremonies are often called Singers, and the ceremony itself is often called a "Sing" or "Chant."

When a baby laughs out loud for the first time there's a special celebration for the whole family, and the person who made the child laugh pays for the party! It's no wonder visitors are careful to ask if the babies have

Navajo boy at a pow-wow

laughed out loud yet before playing with them, because grandparents, uncles, aunts and cousins are all included in the celebration. During the party, the guests all walk past the mother and baby, and the baby gives each one a piece of rock salt. Salt was always a prized item for the Navajo, and by giving it

 To help you pray for the Navajo

You can thank God for:

- the Navajo Bible.
- every Navajo pastor and church leader.

You can ask God:

- to help older people as they learn to read, and to give their teachers patience.
- that the Navajo who can't read will listen to the Bible on tape.
- that Navajo Christians will share Jesus' love with their families and friends.
- to help them spread the message about Jesus in America and other countries.
- that all Christian leaders in the Navajo Nation will be wise and faithful.

Navajo woman weaving at a loom

Monument Valley

away the mother is teaching her child to be generous and share with others. This is important to the Navajo, because to be stingy is to be a bad Navajo.

The Navajo are afraid of evil spirits and witches, and they're always trying to be careful not to make the spirits angry by doing wrong things. They have special ceremonies to heal themselves from the power of evil, "Sings" to protect them from harm, and other rituals to ask the spirits to bless them. When Christians told the Navajo that there is a God who is good and loves them, they found it hard to understand.

Today, Navajo are coming to know Jesus as their friend who sets them free from the fear of evil spirits. Pastors and teachers are helping them to understand God's love. They're also learning to sing the praises of the one true God, who doesn't mind if they make mistakes when singing.

The Bible in Navajo

Because the Navajo language is one of the most difficult languages in the world to learn, very few people outside the tribe know how to speak it. The Americans knew this, and during the Second World War Navajo soldiers played an important role by sending radio messages in their own language. Only those who were meant to receive them could understand them.

Although it's a very difficult language, the Navajo are the only North American tribe with the whole Bible in their own language. It took 40 years to translate and was published in 1986. One of the translators was a blind Navajo man, Geronimo Martin. He knew English and had learned to read Braille. As he read an English Braille Bible with his fingers, he translated it aloud into Navajo, and other people recorded his words. It's amazing to think that a blind man was able to help his own people see the truth of Jesus by giving them the Bible.

Many older Navajo speak only their own language and have never been to school. Some are now being taught to read, but learning to read when you are older is very difficult. The Navajo like to listen to stories, so Geronimo's wife and some other Navajo Christians are reading the Navajo Bible aloud and making cassettes for them.

New Zealand

Aotearoa: Land of the Long White Cloud

Kiwis

New Zealand has two main islands that are simply called the North Island and the South Island. It's a beautiful country with long, sandy beaches, rolling hills, steep mountains, volcanoes, giant trees and hot, bubbling pools and springs. Some plants, animals and birds that live in New Zealand aren't found anywhere else in the world. One of them is the kiwi, a large bird that isn't able to fly but looks like a hen. "Kiwi" is also a nickname for New Zealanders. The people love sports and are known all over the world for their skill in rugby, cricket and water sports.

Maori wood carving

Maoris

The Maori name for New Zealand is Aotearoa, which means the "land of the long white cloud." It's usually not too hot or too cold in New Zealand, and there's plenty of rain, so it's an ideal place for sheep farming. There are three and a half million people living there, along with more than 45 million sheep: that's over twelve sheep to every person!

Most of the people living in New Zealand are descendants of British and European settlers, but about 10% are Maoris. Twelve or more centuries ago, the Maoris traveled vast distances from the Pacific islands of Polynesia. They came in 60-foot-long canoes, each carved from a single log. They built beautiful meeting places in New Zealand, where the tribes still meet. On special occasions they cook food in leaves buried in the ground between hot stones. Sweet potatoes, cabbage, beef, lamb and pork taste delicious cooked this way.

When the settlers arrived from Britain and Europe in the

Do you know?

In the North Island there are four active volcanoes and it's a common sight to see geysers and clouds of steam rising from hot bubbling springs that well up from volcanic rocks in the area.

You can greet one another in Maori
Hello is "Tena koe" (**Ten**-a kway)
Goodbye is "Haere ra" (hy-**air**-ay rah)

📋 Fact file

Area: 103,500 sq. mi.

Population: 3,861,905

Capital: Wellington

Language: English

Religion: Freedom of religion, but mainly Christian

Chief exports: Meat; dairy products; wool; fruit

There are more than twelve sheep for every person living in New Zealand!

 ## To help you pray for New Zealand

You can thank God for:

- the many Christians in New Zealand who know Jesus and want to tell others that Jesus loves them and died on the cross to take away their sins.

- each Christian who volunteers to teach Bible-in-school classes and to run camps, after-school clubs and other activities so that children will learn to follow Jesus.

You can ask God:

- to help Christians talk about Jesus in a loving, caring way to people of other faiths.

- that as Maoris bring back some of their old customs and traditions, Maori Christians will be faithful in following Jesus.

- for Christians to give money to Bible schools so that Maori and Kiwi evangelists, pastors and missionaries can be trained to teach about Jesus.

- to bring many people in New Zealand to follow Jesus.

- for all Christians in New Zealand to love and care for each other, because they all belong to God's family.

City skyline, Auckland

Long boat, Matauri Bay

The Maori people came to live in New Zealand more than 1,000 years ago

Many countries, many faiths

Although many people in New Zealand say they are Christians, only one person out of nine reads the Bible regularly. Few of them believe that Jesus is the only way to God. People of different faiths have come to live in New Zealand from many other countries. Some are refugees; others have come seeking work. Among them are Buddhists and Muslims from South East Asia, Hindus from Fiji and Confucians from Hong Kong. They have brought their own religions with them and have set up their own places of worship.

Maori cooking pits

nineteenth century, they fought fiercely with the Maori people over land. A lot of Maori people lost the land where their people had lived for hundreds of years. In school, Maori children were often punished for speaking their own language instead of English, until their leaders demanded their rights. "We've been here more than 1,000 years, so why shouldn't we speak our own language?" they asked. Now Maori artists, painters, craftsmen and film producers are reviving old customs and traditions, and children often learn their history in action songs. Some Maoris have become strong Christians, and some are studying in Bible schools.

Newars

Who Have a Living Goddess

Fact file

Country: Nepal

Location: Kathmandu Valley, but there are also Newars scattered throughout Nepal.

Numbers: About 400,000

Language: Newari

Religions: Buddhism; Hinduism

Occupations: Businessmen; tradesmen; craftsmen; farmers

The Kathmandu Valley

"Look! The Himalayas! They're even higher than I thought they'd be. Do you think we'll see Mount Everest?" We gazed out of the plane's window at the distant snow-covered mountains that straddle the northern border of Nepal. We had already flown over the Terai, the flat, fertile plain along Nepal's southern border with India. Below us now, encircled by mountains, we could see the towns and villages, rivers, green fields and temples of the Kathmandu Valley. In a few minutes we would be landing at Kathmandu, Nepal's capital city.

The people in the fertile Kathmandu Valley grow rice, corn, wheat and many different fruits and vegetables. The cities of Kathmandu, Patan, Bhaktapur and Kirtipur are full of ancient Hindu temples and huge Buddhist stupas (shrines). There are also lots of houses and palaces with beautifully carved wooden doors and shutters.

The door shuts … and opens again

Nepal is proud of being the only Hindu kingdom in the world. But the people have actually mixed their Hindu beliefs with Buddhism and animism. In 1816, after a war with the British over the borders of the Terai, Nepal shut itself off from the rest of the world. For many years, Christians on India's border with Nepal told the Nepalis they met about Jesus. And they prayed for the day when they could go into Nepal.

At last, after a short revolution in 1951, Christians were among the first to go in to help the new king and his country. At first, Nepalis who became Christians were often put in prison. But democracy was introduced in 1991, and since then Christians have had greater freedom to worship God. Now there are more than 250,000 Christians in Nepal! But there are still many villages all over Nepal where the people have not yet heard about God's love.

Many different peoples

Almost 100 different people groups live in Nepal. A lot of them live in remote villages in deep river valleys or on the sides of mountains. There are very few roads in these areas – only rough, narrow trails. If these people need food, medicine or anything else, men or donkeys have to carry it in to them.

The Newars are one of Nepal's people groups. About half of them live in the Kathmandu Valley, and the rest live throughout the country.

Many different gods

Maya, a Newari girl living in the city of Bhaktapur, finished sweeping the floor. Then she picked up the empty brass water pot and joined some other girls going to the water tank. Talking and laughing, they passed temples where people were worshipping and making offerings to the gods. In the city square,

The Himalayas

To help you pray for the Newars

You can thank God for:

- every person in Nepal who loves and follows Jesus.
- the Christian books available in several of the languages spoken in Nepal.

You can ask God:

- that many Newari children will hear about Jesus and understand that he is the only God.
- that Newars will discover that Jesus is far more powerful than all the gods they worship.
- that Christians visiting the Kathmandu Valley will talk to Newari people about Jesus.
- that many young Newars, especially those who will lead their country someday, will come to know and follow Jesus.
- that many more Christians will go to Nepal to tell the Newars and the other people groups about Jesus.

Ganesh, the Hindu elephant god

Do you know?

The Newars worship hundreds of gods, and they set aside over 150 special days each year to worship them.

potters were forming new pots on their wheels. At the water tank, Maya washed herself and then filled the pot.

As she went back into her house, Maya looked up at the figure of Ganesh, the Hindu elephant god. The Newars believe that Ganesh brings wealth and wisdom to their homes. Maya knew that Newars were supposed to be Buddhists and worship Buddha. But they worshipped other gods too, so she wasn't sure if they were Hindus as well.

"Why do we have so many gods everywhere?" Maya asked her mother. They were mixing red vermilion powder, rice and flower petals to make offerings for the Buddha and the other gods in their house and at the temple. "We have gods for every part of our lives," her mother told her. "There's a god for everything you need."

The Living Goddess

As she helped her mother, Maya asked her to tell the story of the Living Goddess.

"The Newari girl who is chosen to be Kumari, the

Living Goddess, always comes from a family belonging to the gold and silver-smith's caste," Maya's mother told her. "She's only five years old when she's chosen, and she has to be perfect in every way. She has to pass lots of difficult and frightening tests to show that she really is the Living Goddess. Once she has been chosen, she always wears beautiful clothes and jewels and lives in Kathmandu, in Kumari Bahal, the House of the Living Goddess. People worship her, and even the king comes to her for advice. She doesn't stay a goddess forever, though. When she reaches her teens she becomes an ordinary person again. That must be quite hard for her. Be glad you're an ordinary Newari girl, Maya!"

Clay pots drying at Bhaktapur

Kumari is only a goddess for a few years. But Jesus has always been God, and always will be God. And he promises that he'll always be with those who follow him.

Following a God-king

A first god-king

Once upon a time, says a Korean legend, Hwanung, the son of the Great Creator, decided to come down from heaven and become king of everything he could see. As he looked around at the beautiful country he heard a bear praying. "Make me into a human being," it said. "I'm tired of being a bear."

Hwanung felt sorry for the bear and told it to eat 20 pieces of garlic and some mugwort (a plant with a bitter taste) and stay in a cave for 100 days. The bear obeyed, and turned into a woman!

The woman longed for a son and gave birth to Tangun. According to the legend, Tangun was the first king of Korea, thousands of years ago. He reigned for more than 1,000 years and his people worshipped him.

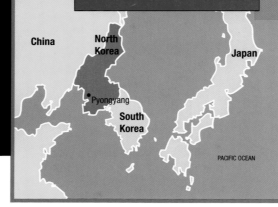

China
North Korea
Japan
Pyongyang
South Korea
PACIFIC OCEAN

Fact file

Area: 46,540 sq. mi. (slightly smaller than England)

Population: 24,039,193

Capital: Pyongyang

Language: Korean

Religions: Buddhism; Confucianism (but it is a Communist state)

Chief exports: Coal; iron; copper; oil; grain

A second god-king

Not long ago, there was another man who thought he was a god-king. In 1945, when Korea was divided into two separate countries – North Korea and South Korea – at the end of World War II, Kim Il Sung, the "Great Leader," came to power in North Korea.

At that time there were so many Christians in North Korea that Pyongyang, the capital city, was sometimes called the "Jerusalem of Korea."

But Kim Il Sung expected everyone to worship him. He made everyone wear a badge with his picture. Every building in Pyongyang had his picture above the doorway. All over the city, there were posters of Kim Il Sung. And high on a hill outside the city, he built a 330-foot-tall statue of himself with his arms outstretched, smiling down on the city.

No other god

The "Great Leader" was a Communist and wanted to get rid of every trace of religion in North Korea. He had all the church buildings destroyed, and nearly three million Koreans were killed, including thousands of Christians.

At school, the teachers showed the children a little black book and asked,

North Korean soldiers

 ## To help you pray for North Korea

Remember that many people there have never heard of Jesus because the country has been closed to the outside world for more than 50 years.

You can thank God for:

- the many secret believers in North Korea.

You can ask God:

- that the Christians will know he is near them despite the threat of punishment or even death if they are betrayed.
- that Christian businessmen who visit North Korea, and those who take food into the country, will speak of Jesus' love.
- that Christians will help the children abandoned on the streets.
- to prepare the hearts of North Koreans for the day when the good news about Jesus can once more be shared openly.
- to work a miracle in the hearts of Kim Il Yong and his government so that they will know that he alone is God.
- for Christians around the world to pray faithfully until people can once more share the gospel in North Korea.

A poster in honor of Kim Il Sung

Buddhist monastery

Do you know?

Just north of the demilitarized zone which separates North and South Korea is a beautiful mountain region which can be visited by boat. Christians often go on the journey to pray for North Korea.

"Are there any books like this hidden in your house? Search for them, even in your parents' bedroom, then tell us." Some children did find that book and told their teachers. They never saw their parents again. The little black book was the Korean Bible.

Some brave people continued to follow Jesus and met in secret to worship him. They knew they couldn't worship another god. Two million people fled to South Korea, but Kim Il Sung attacked the South, too. Everyone was afraid. Korea was no longer like its name "Chosun," the "Land of Morning Calm."

The children were taught to worship Kim Il Sung. They sang, "He is our Great Leader and we keep his image in our hearts." You can read in the Bible (in Daniel chapter 3) about some other people who were expected to worship an image. They refused, and God protected them.

Death of the god-king

In 1994 Kim Il Sung died. The people wept because the one who had made himself their god was dead. His son, Kim Jong Il, the "Dear Leader," took his place.

But floods, hail and drought destroyed the crops. People starved. Aid agencies were allowed to bring food into the country, but the government arranged how it was distributed. It is thought that at least two million people died from starvation during the next five years or risked their lives escaping into China.

The one true God

Christians have tried all sorts of ways to tell the people of North Korea about God's love. They've beamed in radio broadcasts, although most radios in North Korea can receive only government broadcasts. They've even sent Christian literature to North Korea by balloon, and in plastic envelopes that they've thrown into the ocean.

In South Korea, many Christians are praying that the North Koreans will see that they've been worshipping a false god. God is answering their prayers. There are now three official churches and more than 500 registered "church-service houses" where people can meet for prayer, as well as many more underground churches.

Where Oil has Replaced Frankincense

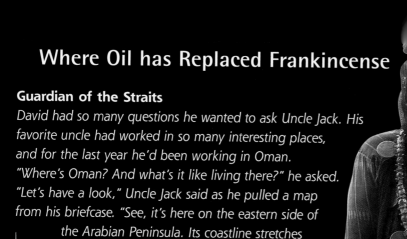

Guardian of the Straits

David had so many questions he wanted to ask Uncle Jack. His favorite uncle had worked in so many interesting places, and for the last year he'd been working in Oman.
"Where's Oman? And what's it like living there?" he asked.
"Let's have a look," Uncle Jack said as he pulled a map from his briefcase. "See, it's here on the eastern side of the Arabian Peninsula. Its coastline stretches along the Arabian Sea and the Gulf of Oman and it has land borders with Saudi Arabia, Yemen and the United Arab Emirates.

Frankincense tree in the desert

"Can you see the Musandam Peninsula that sticks out into the Straits of Hormuz? It belongs to Oman, too. But the United Arab Emirates here," he pointed, "separates it from the rest of the country. The peninsula's really a line of razor-sharp peaks … some of them are a mile high! It's a very important place, because from there Oman protects the 20,000 ships, many of them oil tankers, which pass through the Straits of Hormuz each year from the Persian Gulf."

Past and present

"What's the rest of Oman like?" David asked. "And what about the people who live there?"

"It's almost twice as big as the state of New York, but only about two and a quarter million people live in Oman – compared with almost 20 million in New York. The one and a half million local Omani people are all Arabic-speaking Muslims. But about a third of the people living in Oman are guest workers from other countries. A lot of them are from India, Pakistan or

Bangladesh and work in low-paid jobs. Others, like myself, are experts in our professions who go there to train Omanis. I work with people in the oil industry.

"When I flew over Oman," Uncle Jack continued, "all I could see were bare, rocky mountains, oil wells in the sandy desert, and a few green oases. As we came in to land at Muscat I could see gardens and fields all along the coast, where most of the people live. I even caught a glimpse of the twin forts built into cliffs on either side of the bay. There are actually over 1,000 forts in the country.

"Oman is a rich country now because of oil, but a long time ago it was frankincense that made people in Oman wealthy."

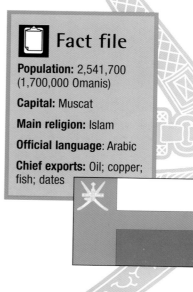

Fact file

Population: 2,541,700 (1,700,000 Omanis)

Capital: Muscat

Main religion: Islam

Official language: Arabic

Chief exports: Oil; copper; fish; dates

To help you pray for Oman

You can thank God for:

● the few Omani Christians.

● the Bibles in Arabic that have been given to some Omanis.

You can ask God:

● for Christians working in Oman to have opportunities to talk with their Omani friends about Jesus.

● to send Arab Christians to Oman who can clearly explain the good news about Jesus to the Omani people.

● that many Omanis will listen to Christian radio and television shows.

● to encourage Arab Christians to write books that will help children understand who Jesus is.

● for Christians in the west to show God's love and care to Omani students studying in their countries.

Life is much more comfortable for Omanis now, but they still don't know the peace and love of Jesus

A new day

"If oil has made Oman rich," said David, "what was it like before?"

"By the 1950s, Oman had become the poorest country in Arabia," Uncle Jack said. "Even when oil was discovered in the 1960s the ruler, Sultan Sa'id, didn't use the money to modernize his country right away. He even told people they weren't allowed to ride bicycles or wear sunglasses. So many Omanis went to other countries to find work, and those left behind weren't very happy. In 1970, Sultan Qaboos took control from his father. He told the people: 'Oman in the past was in darkness ... but a new day will rise.'"

"What does that mean?" asked David.

"Well," said Uncle Jack, "there were only three schools in Oman in 1970,

and one hospital. Today, there are many modern hospitals, hundreds of schools and a university. The government has built good roads, new harbors and airports. There are new industries and many people now own expensive cars, mobile phones and televisions. The government wants Omanis to be trained so that they will become the experts in the industries in their own country. I suppose the new day means that Omanis have a better life and hope for the future."

Christian guest workers

"If Omanis are Muslims, does that mean there aren't any Christians there?" David asked.

Do you know?

There's an amazing network of underground and surface irrigation canals in Oman. They're called *falaj*, and some are over nine miles long and nearly 400 feet deep. They were built over 1,000 years ago! Some have been restored and are in use today.

Hill fortress overlooking Muscat

"There are a few," Uncle Jack replied. "Missionaries built the first hospital, clinics and schools in Oman, and so the people really respect them. Most Christians in Oman are guest workers who want to tell Omanis about Jesus. They can meet together to worship God. But only about 40 Omanis have ever become Christians, and those who do follow Jesus know that their families, friends and the authorities will be angry and try to stop them. You can pray that an even greater 'new day' will come for the people of Oman, when they'll see the light of Jesus' love, forgiveness and new life."

A Wild Place!

"Tok Pisin"

Papua New Guinea (PNG for short) occupies half of the world's second largest island (there's a country called Irian Jaya on the other half). If you wanted to visit someone in another part of PNG, you would have to climb steep mountains, cross fast-flowing rivers and trek through tropical jungle! You wouldn't need a car, since there aren't many roads outside the towns. There are lots of small airstrips around the country, but even if you did have a plane it would still be hard to travel because many of the airstrips need to be repaired.

Do you know?

Since more than 870 languages are spoken in PNG, each language is spoken, on average, by about 6,000 people. That would be a bit like each town having its own language!

Speak "Tok Pisin"
(If you say the words out loud, you will see how much they sound like English.)
Good morning is "Moninnau" (**moh-nin-nau**)
Goodbye is "Lukim-yu" (**look-im-yoo**)
Please is "Plis" (pliss)
Thank you is "Tenku" (**tank**-yoo)

There are over 800 different groups of people in PNG – and each group speaks its own language! Even people living in valleys quite close to one another often don't speak the same language. It's a good thing everyone also speaks "Tok Pisin," a kind of pidgin, or simplified, English. Everyone can also read the Bible which has been translated into "Tok Pisin."

Sometimes in PNG everyone in a village becomes a Christian all at once! Although this seems wonderful, very often people don't really try to change to be more like Jesus. Instead, they carry on with their traditional witchcraft and fighting. But many who are truly following Jesus are working together to teach people what God says, so they will learn to live at peace with one another.

Fear of spirits

One day John, a missionary in PNG, had a haircut and some of his hair fell on the ground. "Don't leave your hair there," his friend Aiyako warned him. "A witch doctor could use it to put a curse on you."

Another day Aiyako and John were eating with people from a different tribe. "Don't leave any food on your plate," whispered Aiyako. "Someone might use it to attack us through the spirits."

A church in Papua New Guinea

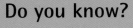

Fact file

Area: 178,703 sq. mi.

Population: 4,806,640

Capital: Port Moresby

Official languages: English; Tok Pisin

Main religions: Christianity; animism

Chief exports: Gold; coffee; timber; copper

Women studying the Bible

To help you pray for PNG

You can thank God for:

- the New Testament that has now been translated into "Tok Pisin" as well as into several other languages spoken in PNG.

- teachers who are helping people learn to read in their own languages so that they can read the New Testament.

- Christians from PNG who have gone to other countries to share God's love with other men and women, boys and girls.

You can ask God:

- to help Christian leaders in churches and in the government be a good example to those they serve.

- to help pastors to faithfully teach the Bible to their people so that they will learn to follow and obey Jesus and not be afraid of spirits.

- to give people understanding when they watch the *Jesus* film in their own language so they will know that the Bible is not a fairy tale but is about real people and God's son, Jesus.

- to encourage people to keep the airstrips in good repair so that books and other goods can arrive safely in the remote parts of the country.

Papua New Guinea

Indonesia

Port Moresby

Australia

Girls carrying roots in *eles*

People in PNG carry everything in bags – from babies to Bibles!

Although John wanted to laugh, he knew Aiyako was really scared and he felt sorry for him. John explained that the Bible tells us that when we trust in God we don't need to be afraid of anything. God is bigger and stronger than anything that could hurt us. Thousands of people in PNG are full of the same sorts of fears.

Carrying babies in bags

Most people in PNG carry their belongings in net bags. One of the people groups, the Nabak, call this bag an *ele*. They hang these bags from the walls and use them as drawers or shelves. A Nabak boy carries everything in an *ele* slung over his shoulder, and his sister's *ele* hangs down her back from a strap around her head. Mothers even carry their babies in *eles* on their backs.

Nabak women sometimes make the bags from tree bark, but often they use strands from the yucca plant. First they pull the yucca plant through a slit in a big piece of bamboo to scrape off the outside part, which is green. Then they spread the strands that are left out in the sun to dry. When the strands are dry enough, the women make them into a coarse thread. They rub cold ashes from the fire on their thighs and roll the strands back and forth across their thighs until they form a thread. It takes a long time to make thread this way, so it's not surprising that it takes several weeks to make just one bag. When they have enough thread, the women start "crocheting" the bag with needles made from the bones of the wings of bats and flying foxes.

God's *ele*

People all around the world have prayed for PNG, and God has been changing the country. Pastors are teaching the people what God says in the Bible so they can learn to love and serve God in everything they do. Hundreds of Nabak people now have a special *ele* for carrying their Nabak New Testament. Christians from PNG are going all over the world to tell others about Jesus. God is using these people as his *ele* to carry the good news of Jesus around the world.

133

Pygmies

Children of the Forests of Central Africa

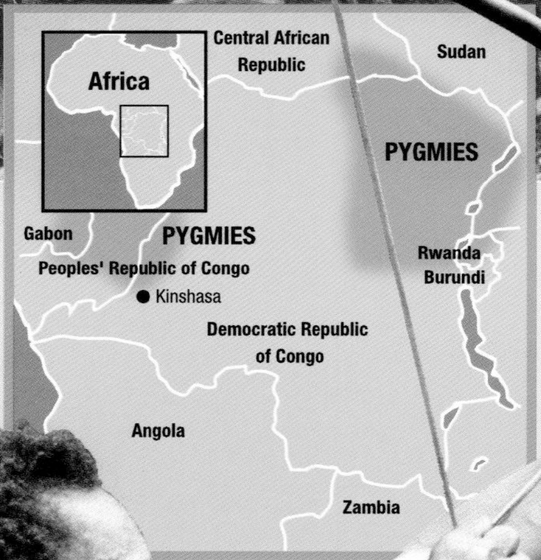

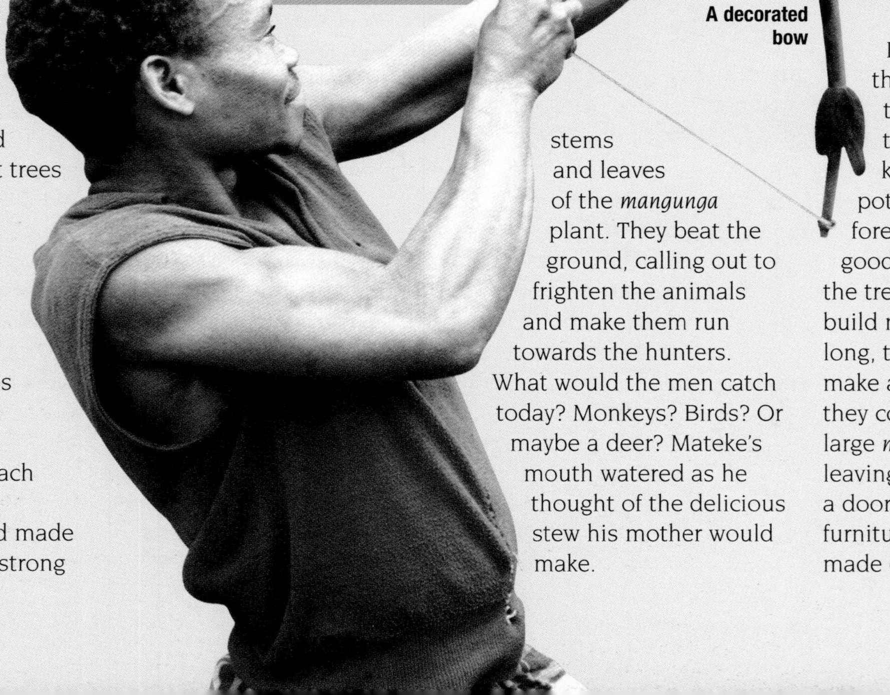

Hunting in the forest

"You'll be ready to come hunting with us soon," Mateke's father told him. Mateke tried to hide his excitement. He couldn't wait to go hunting with the men rather than taking care of his little brother and gathering fruit, nuts, leaves and grubs. He was so proud that every arrow he'd shot at the tree stump that morning had hit the target. He and his friend Matedu spent a lot of time shooting at big spiders, rats and frogs, and it had paid off.

Do you know?

The name "pygmy" comes from a Greek word that means 'elbow high." A true adult Pygmy is only about four and a half feet tall. They call themselves "children of the forest."

A decorated bow

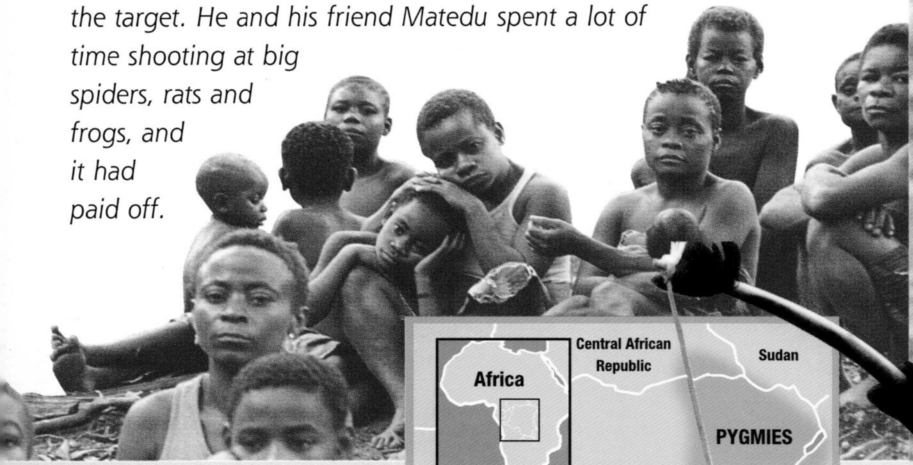

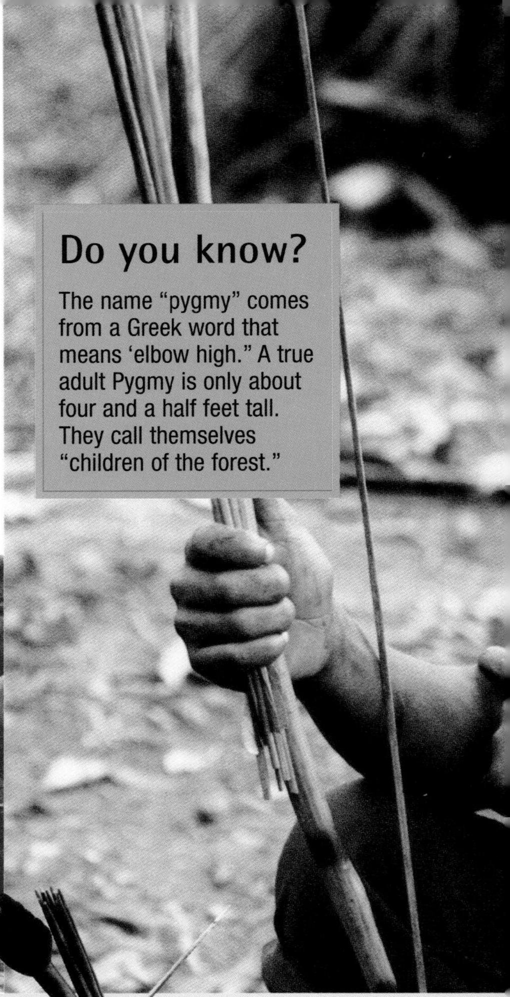

Mateke watched as the men got ready to go hunting. They dipped their sharpened arrows into poison from the bark of the *anga* tree. Then they dried the arrows over the fire.

When they were all ready to go, two women went into the forest. The men followed silently. The giant trees were so tall that they shut out the sunlight, and huge vines hung from their branches. On the ground, enormous twisted roots and young trees were tangled around each other.

The women had made beaters from the strong stems and leaves of the *mangunga* plant. They beat the ground, calling out to frighten the animals and make them run towards the hunters. What would the men catch today? Monkeys? Birds? Or maybe a deer? Mateke's mouth watered as he thought of the delicious stew his mother would make.

New huts

Mateke looked around at his village. There were nine small huts. He had heard the men say that they would have to move again soon, because there weren't many animals left in that part of the forest.

Every time they move, the Pygmies collect their few belongings – their bows and arrows, knives and cooking pots – and travel into the forest. When they find a good place, the men clear the trees and the women build new huts by bending long, thin tree branches to make a small dome. Then they cover the dome with large *mangunga* leaves, leaving a small opening for a door. They don't need any furniture –just a mattress made of *mangunga* leaves.

You can thank God for:

● the Pygmies who are learning to follow Jesus.

● the Pygmies who are studying to be pastors and evangelists among their own people.

You can ask God:

● for more Christians to be willing to live and travel in the forests with the Pygmies.

● to help evangelists explain to the Pygmies who Jesus is and how much he loves them.

● to help evangelists learn the Pygmy languages so that the Pygmies will understand what they say.

● that many Pygmies will listen to Christian messages on cassette tapes and understand what it means to follow Jesus.

● that lots of Pygmy boys and girls will hear about Jesus and follow him and help others to know him, too.

Fact file

Numbers: Between 150,000 and 200,000

Location: The tropical rain forests of Burundi; Cameroon; Central African Republic; Democratic Republic of Congo; Gabon; Peoples' Republic of Congo and Rwanda.

Occupation: Semi-nomadic hunter-gathers

Languages: Bantu or Sudanic dialects; the languages of the people they mix with.

God's book

"Do you think the preacher will find us again when we move?" Mateke asked Matedu. "I hope so," Matedu said. "I love listening to his stories about the God who made us. Do you remember how we all hid in the forest the first time he came? I can't believe we were afraid of him!"

"I remember that," Matedu said, "and he knew that we needed salt, so he

A Pygmy house

brought us some. He asked my father if he ever prayed to God."

"Yes," Mateke remembered. "And your father said that he did. He told the preacher that the forest is our God and our father and mother. It gives us all we need – houses, food and clothing – and when a big storm comes, it protects us."

"And then the preacher showed my father 'God's book' that says there's only one God," Mateke said. "I still remember how amazed I was when the preacher told us that God made our forest, the trees, the animals, and even us. He told us about how we've all broken God's laws. But God wants us to follow him, so he sent his Son called Jesus. I'm so glad that Jesus died for all of us, and that he forgives us if we ask him to. My father says his heart tells him it's true."

Mateke and Matedu are Pygmies. There are about ten different Pygmy groups living in the forests of central Africa. They're nomadic hunters and gather food from the forest. They also trade meat and honey with neighboring peoples for things they need like salt, clothing, tools and vegetables. Mateke's tribe lives in the great Ituri forest of northeast Congo. Although Pygmies live in the forests far away from anyone else, they're hearing the good news about Jesus and learning to follow him. Some Pygmies are going to school now, and a few are studying in Bible schools to become pastors and evangelists. It's not easy for them to leave their homes to go to school and live in buildings when they've lived in the forests all their lives. But they want to learn how to tell their people about God's love.

The Thumb of the Arabian Gulf

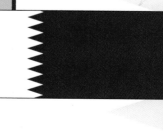

Serving guests

Six-year-old Ahmed felt important. He was old enough now to help his father entertain his guests in the majlis, *a room set apart for male visitors. Dressed in his* thaub *(ankle-length shirt) and embroidered cap, he carefully served coffee to his father's guests, speaking only when spoken to.*

Ahmed was very interested in their conversation. His father had a special guest today – a foreigner from America who had just started working in his father's company.

Do you know?

Qatar has the third largest natural gas reserve in the world. Only Russia and Iran have bigger reserves.

"Thank you very much," said Jim, the man from America, when Ahmed handed him his coffee. Jim asked Ahmed how old he was and what he liked to do. Ahmed liked Jim. Because he was only a child, none of the other men ever spoke to him.

A wealthy country

Ahmed's country, Qatar, sticks out like a thumb into the Arabian Gulf. It's a small desert country, with a population of about 600,000. Ahmed was used to seeing foreigners, since only a quarter of the people living in his country are true Qataris – the rest are guest workers from other countries. But he had never talked to one before.

"Yes, we feel at home here. It's nice to have our own newspaper, radio and TV channel," Jim was saying. Ahmed knew that his father sometimes thought these foreigners felt too much at home in Qatar, especially when they wore jeans, tee shirts and shorts in public.

Soon the men were talking about oil again. "Did you know that most of the

people living in Doha, the capital, moved here after 1940, when oil was discovered?" his father asked Jim.

"Yes," added one of the other men, "life's very different here since they found all those reserves of natural gas offshore. Our country is so wealthy now that it provides free schooling and medical care, and even free housing for the poor."

"What did people do for work before oil was discovered?" Jim asked.

"Most Qataris tried to make a living from fishing, camel herding and pearl diving. Our main trade items used to be pearls and guano, a kind of manure

The few Qatari Christians all live outside Qatar

Fact file

Area: 4,247 sq. mi.

Population: 599,065

Capital: Doha

Language: Arabic

Religion: Islam

Chief exports: Oil; gas; fertilizers

To help you pray for Qatar

You can thank God for:

- the few Qataris in other countries who follow Jesus.
- Christians from other countries working in Qatar.

You can ask God:

- that Qataris in other countries will meet Christians who will show them Jesus' love.
- to help Qatari Christians when their families reject them and they can't live in their own country.
- that Christians will pray for Qataris to hear about Jesus.
- to use each Arabic Bible and New Testament taken into Qatar to bring someone to know him.
- that soon there will be Qatari people living in Qatar who will follow Jesus.

Modern buildings reveal Qatar's wealth

At the *souk* (market)

produced by sea birds that makes very good fertilizer," one of the men explained.

"Is there any farming in Qatar?" Jim wanted to know.

"Yes, but it's difficult," Ahmed's father told him. "There isn't much land, it's too hot and water is scarce. But now that sea water is being distilled to remove the salt, the farmers have more water. The government provides the farmers with free seeds and fertilizers to help them grow more and better crops. There are even some experimental farms that use greenhouses to keep plants cool, not warm!"

"How does the government work?" asked Jim.

"Well," said one of the men, "the ruling Sheikh chooses most of the leaders from his own family. He doesn't have to explain his actions to anyone, but he does have to keep Islamic law and listen to the Muslim religious leaders."

"Has life changed a lot for young people since the country became rich?"

Jim asked. There was a long silence. Ahmed's older brothers wanted their freedom and liked speeding around the desert in their cars and drinking illegally. His father had even beaten one of his brothers because he hadn't said the Muslim prayers. But Ahmed also knew his brothers were afraid of the future, of not passing their exams, and of punishment by Allah or their parents because of bad habits and not keeping Islamic laws. How could his father tell a stranger all this?

As a Christian, Jim really wanted to tell his host that riches don't bring peace, happiness or hope for the future. He remembered the story of the first known Qatari believer.

One day in 1985, some young evangelists in England met a man from Qatar and talked to him about Jesus. Afterwards, since they didn't know anything about Qatar, they looked it up

in the book *Operation World*. "Wow!" one of them said. "It says there are no known Qatari believers! Let's pray for that man – he could be the first."

He was, but the evangelists didn't realize how much suffering their new friend would go through when he gave up Islam and decided to follow Jesus. His wife divorced him, his children were taken away and he wasn't allowed to return to Qatar. Since then, a few other Qataris living outside the country have come to know Jesus. They've suffered for their faith, but they all agree it's worth sacrificing everything for the hope and freedom they have in Jesus.

Jim prayed that one day he would know his host well enough to tell him that only through trusting in Jesus would he know real freedom, peace and hope.

Quechua

Children of the Incas

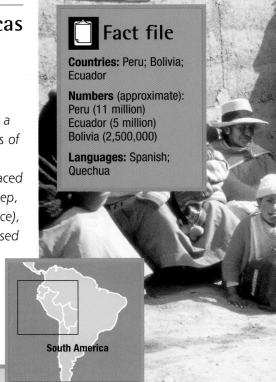

Fact file

Countries: Peru; Bolivia; Ecuador

Numbers (approximate):
Peru (11 million)
Ecuador (5 million)
Bolivia (2,500,000)

Languages: Spanish; Quechua

Living on a mountain

"Hey, Pedro, how much further do we have to climb to get to your house?" John panted. "I'm out of breath!"

"Not much further," Pedro grinned. "Only about an hour!" Pedro is a Quechua boy whose family lives in a village in the Andes Mountains of Peru. Wrapped in warm ponchos, the two boys continued climbing along the steep path. As they walked, Pedro pointed out small terraced fields of maize, wheat and potatoes as well as sheep, alpacas (which are bred for their fine soft fleece), llamas and a condor. "You might be surprised when you see my house," Pedro told his new friend. "It only has one room, with a dirt floor. We don't have electricity or running water, either. But you'll be very welcome, and my mother's a great cook!"

South America

Ecuador

Peru

QUECHUA

Bolivia

SOUTH PACIFIC OCEAN

Chile

At last they reached Pedro's village. "Here it is," Pedro said, as he stopped at a small thatched hut built of stone. "Come on in." Soon they were eating maize and potatoes that Pedro's mother had cooked over a fire in the corner of the hut. "A lot of Quechua are poor," Pedro said, "but we have some sheep, a few llamas and a little land.

Because a lot of our people don't have any land, they go down to the cities. Even if they do find jobs, they don't earn much and usually have to live in the slums."

The Incas

There are about ten million Quechua people in Peru. They are descended from the Incas, who built huge terraces, great palaces and temples and an amazing network of roads and cities. The Incas were also famous for their beautiful gold jewelry and pottery. They believed that their king, or Inca, was the sun and that they themselves were the children of the sun and the moon. By the sixteenth century, the Inca Empire spread from Ecuador to Chile – over 2,000 miles. In 1532, when the Spaniards reached Peru looking for new lands and gold, they found two Inca leaders and their followers quarrelling over who should be the next king. Because the Incas were fighting among themselves, a small group of Spanish soldiers was able to defeat them quickly and take everything from them – their country and

"We have the Bible in our own language"

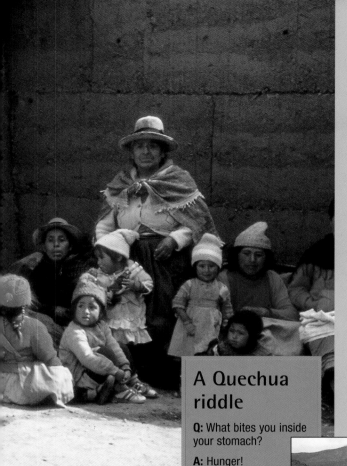

To help you pray for the Quechua

You can thank God for:

- Quechua men, women and children who are learning to know Jesus, the Good Shepherd.

- answering prayers to break the power of the Shining Path. Pray that they will never again be able to hurt people.

- Quechua Christians who, when they were wrongly accused and put in prison, shared Jesus' love with other prisoners.

- Romulo Saune's widow and her work sharing Jesus' love with the women she teaches.

You can ask God:

- that each Quechua Christian will always follow Jesus, no matter what happens.

- to provide training programs to show Quechua Christians how to teach young people about Jesus.

- that every person in the Quechua villages turning to Jesus will read the Bible and follow him faithfully.

A Quechua riddle

Q: What bites you inside your stomach?

A: Hunger!

Llama, kept as a pack animal and for its wool

You can speak Quechua

How are you? is "Imaynalla?" (ee-may-**nal**-yo)

I'm fine, is "Allinmi" (al-**yeen**-mee)

Yes is "Ari" (a-**ree**)

No is "Mana" (**ma**-na)

their rich gold and silver mines. The Spanish brought their Catholic faith to Peru. Today, nearly 500 years later, most of the Quechua people belong to the Roman Catholic Church. But when they need help, they usually turn to priests who still follow their old Inca religion.

Prayer for a troubled country

There have been a lot of problems in Peru since it became independent in 1821. In the 1980s and early 1990s, a Communist guerrilla group called the Shining Path terrorized and killed more than 20,000 people in the mountains. Christians started a movement in 1989 to pray for peace in Peru, and God has been answering the prayers of people around the world.

A good shepherd

When he was a little boy, Romulo Saune looked after his family's sheep. When he came to know and follow Jesus, his favorite verses in the Bible were about Jesus, the Good Shepherd, who gave his life for his sheep (us). (You can read this story in your Bible in the Gospel of John, chapter 10.) Romulo became a well-known Christian leader and spent his life helping his Quechua people. He loved to tell them about Jesus, the Good Shepherd. He knew how important it was for his people to have the Bible in their own language, and so he translated it into one of the Quechua dialects.

The Shining Path guerrillas hated Romulo. Even though he knew it was

dangerous, Romulo often visited Christians in remote mountain villages because he loved them and wanted them to learn more about Jesus. One day in September 1992, as he was returning home, Shining Path guerrillas killed Romulo and four others who were with him. He was another good shepherd who had given his life for his sheep, the Quechua.

Is that the end of the story? No, because God has been answering the prayers of Christians in Peru and around the world. Romulo Saune's widow teaches women so they can read the Bible for themselves. And high up in the Andes Mountains, whole Quechua villages like Pedro's are coming to know Jesus, their Good Shepherd, and are learning to follow him.

Inca ruins at Machu Picchu

Refugees

Looking for Help and Safety

Homeless ... Sierra Leone

"Run, run as fast as you can!" screamed 12-year-old Finda. "We have to get away from here!" She ran with her baby brother in her arms as her frightened little brothers and sister ran after her. They came home from playing to find that Sierra Leonean rebels had murdered their mother, and their father had disappeared. For seven days Finda led the little ones through the forest to a refugee camp in the neighboring country of Guinea.

But Guinea is a poor country and can't really help refugees like Finda. There's no water in the camp, so Finda has to walk three miles to get water three times every day. She also has to look for firewood in the forest. Sometimes she's able to earn a little money to buy food for the family. Her brothers and sister go to school in the camp, but she's too busy looking after them to go herself.

Refugees from Sierra Leone at a camp in Guinea

Refugee child in Sri Lanka

Homeless ... Afghanistan

"Don't make a sound!" Abdul warned his children as he woke them up. "Put on your warmest clothes and come quickly." Silently, the children followed their parents out into the night and started the long, long walk through the rugged mountains from Afghanistan to Pakistan. The Soviet Union invaded Afghanistan in 1978, and millions of Afghans and their families fled in fear to Iran and Pakistan.

Abdul and his family and many others made their homes in tents in refugee camps. Even though that war is over, a lot of refugees are afraid to go home because there's still fighting in Afghanistan.

Homeless ... Sri Lanka

Sri Lanka is a beautiful place. But a terrible civil war is being waged there. "I was only five years old when the Tamil Tiger guerrillas demanded a separate state for Tamils in the north of Sri Lanka," Mohan said sadly. "That happened in 1986. We lived in Jaffna, and there was a lot of fighting there. My family fled by boat to India, but we decided to return home as soon as it seemed more peaceful. When we arrived back, the fighting was worse than ever. We fled again, away

 ## To help you pray for refugees

You can thank God for:

- organizations like the United Nations High Commission for Refugees (UNHCR) who do so much to help refugees.

- churches helping refugees to settle in new countries where things seem strange at first.

You can ask God:

- that many Christians will show God's love to the millions of sad and hurting refugees.

- for caring people to look after refugee babies and children.

- for people to comfort refugee children who feel lonely and frightened because they are lost or their parents have died.

- that governments will help make refugees feel welcome.

- to bring peace to troubled countries so that many refugees can return to their own homes.

Refugees from Kosovo in Albania

from the fighting. I lost my parents and I've wandered around the country ever since, trying to keep out of the way of the fighting. More than anything, I just want my family and to feel safe."

40 million refugees

As you sit in your own comfortable home, can you imagine what it would be like to be a refugee, having to flee from your home and country, hoping to find a place where you could feel safe?

There are about 40 million refugees in the world, and at least half of them are children. That's a big number – more than twice the population of Australia! Refugees are frightened to stay in their own country because of racial hatred, religious

persecution or war. They leave everything behind and try to find a new life somewhere else.

Some have had to leave their homes and villages and find a place to live in another part of their own country. People all over the world have lost their homes because of floods in Bangladesh, volcanoes in Turkey, drought in the Sahel of Africa and hatred and violence in Colombia. These refugees look for another place where they will be safe and have food, care and hope for the future.

Jesus, a refugee

There have always been refugees. History is full of them. In the book of Exodus in the Bible we can read the story of the Israelites' escape from slavery in Egypt. Joseph and Mary,

Feeding program in Colombia

with baby Jesus, were refugees when they fled to Egypt from cruel King Herod.

The Bible says that we should care for the poor, the suffering and the refugees. In Matthew 25:34–40, Jesus tells us that those who feed the hungry, give water to the thirsty, provide clothes for those who have none,

look after the sick and visit those in prison do all these things for him. You can pray for refugees all around the world. You might also think of some practical ways to follow Jesus' command to help refugees.

Republic of Guinea

Where Missionaries were Banned

Rich, but poor

Guinea, in West Africa, is one of the poorest countries in the world. Crops like rice, coffee, bananas and oranges grow easily there. Iron, gold and diamonds are found there. Guinea is also the world's second largest producer of a mineral called bauxite, which is used in making aluminum. Guinea used to be one of France's richest colonies. But when it became independent in 1958, the president wanted Guinea to become a Communist country. Guinea is still trying to recover from the consequences of Communism and the president's harsh and foolish decisions.

Fact file

Area: 95,000 sq. mi. (a little smaller than the state of Nevada)

Population: 7,430,346

Capital: Conakry

Official language: French, but there are 8 national languages and another 20 spoken in the country.

Religions: Islam; animism

Chief exports: Bauxite; fruit; coffee; diamonds

More than three-quarters of the people living in Guinea are Muslims. Although missionaries worked there when it was a French colony, very few people became Christians. In 1967, the president forced almost all the missionaries to leave. The missionaries prayed for the millions of people in Guinea who had never heard about the God who loves them. God answered their prayers. In 1984, when the president died, missionaries were allowed to return to Guinea. Even before that, though, God was at work. The people had become so poor that a lot of them went to work in other African countries so they could buy food and clothes for their families. Sometimes these people heard about Jesus.

Alhaji and his wife want to share Jesus' love with others, but Christians in Guinea often suffer for their faith

Looking for God

Alhaji was a Muslim. He wanted to know more about God, so he prayed, fasted and studied the Koran. He was a tailor, and when he went to live in Gambia he quickly found work sewing

Preparing the celebration feast for the opening of the church

for some missionaries. They gave him a book to read, but he couldn't understand it because it was in English (Guinea is French-speaking, Gambia is English-speaking).

Alhaji learned to read English just so he could know what the book said! The book told him about Jesus, the Son of God. The missionaries also gave him a Bible, which he started to read as well as the Koran. He prayed that God would show him the right way. One day he read John 3:16: "God loved the world so much that he gave his only Son, so that whoever believes in him will have everlasting life." When he read that, he realized that the Bible is the true word of God, and he decided to follow Jesus.

 To help you pray for Guinea

You can thank God for:

- Christians like Alhaji.
- Christian youth centers and training projects.

You can ask God:

- that Christians in Guinea will always show others how Jesus loves and cares for them.
- for more missionaries to share the good news about Jesus.
- that lots of children will follow Jesus, even when others make fun of them.
- that many forest people will realize that worshipping spirits and the devil brings fear, but following Jesus brings peace and joy.
- to show Muslims that Jesus is God.

Africa

Guinea-Bissau
Mali
Republic of Guinea
Conakry ●
Sierra Leone
Côte d'Ivoire
Liberia

God works miracles

When Alhaji told his wife, she was angry. She left him and went back to Guinea. He was very sad, but he didn't stop studying the Bible or following Jesus or praying for his wife. Then God worked a miracle. Alhaji's wife decided to follow Jesus, too, and went back to live with him. They decided to return to Guinea to tell their people about the God of the Bible who loves them all.

When they reached their village, Alhaji told them about God's love and everyone welcomed them at first. They built a house, set up a little tailor's shop, and Alhaji started to teach six young men to make clothes. They studied the Bible with him and

wanted to trust in Jesus, but they all turned back to Islam. Alhaji didn't give up. He knew that God would help him explain the truth about Jesus.

After a while, 15 people had decided to follow Jesus. But each one of them had to leave his own home because of that decision. Alhaji looked after all of them and taught them how to make a living as tailors. He also taught them all about the Bible. Some of the people in the village were very angry, especially when the Christians decided to build a church. They persecuted them and tried to stop them, but God is in control of everything and, in March 2000, the church opened.

The Sacred Forest

The people of the forest region of Guinea are animists. Some belong to the Sacred Forest cult and say they have been "born again" through the devil's mouth. When the leader of the cult comes into the village, everyone is supposed to hide indoors. When the son of one village chief became a

Christian, he refused to hide. This made his father, who was afraid of what would happen, very angry. "I belong to Jesus," the son said, "And he has set me free from the devil's power. He'll keep me safe." The chief was amazed when nothing happened to his son. "It must be true that this Jesus really is more powerful than all the spirits we fear!" he exclaimed.

New life in Jesus

Like Alhaji and the son of the village chief, others in Guinea have decided to follow Jesus. They want everyone to know the good news that Jesus is the Son of God who loves them and sets them free from fear.

143

Riffi Berbers

Berbers of the Rif Mountain Range

A sacrifice and a feast

Jamina, a ten-year-old Riffi (Reef-ee) Berber girl from north Morocco, was busy helping her mother prepare for the feast of Eid el-Kabir. This is a special day when Muslims sacrifice a sheep and then eat it to celebrate Abraham's willingness to sacrifice his son Ishmael, and God's provision of a sheep to sacrifice instead. Are you thinking that the son was Isaac, not Ishmael? You're right! (You can read the Bible story in Genesis 22.) Muslims believe that it was Ishmael, from whom all Arab people are descended, that Abraham took to Mount Moriah.

Do you know?

There were many Berber Christians during the first centuries after Jesus died. Some were even martyred for their faith. Sadly, the church grew smaller, and by AD 1100 there were no Berber Christians. But Berbers are coming to know Jesus again!

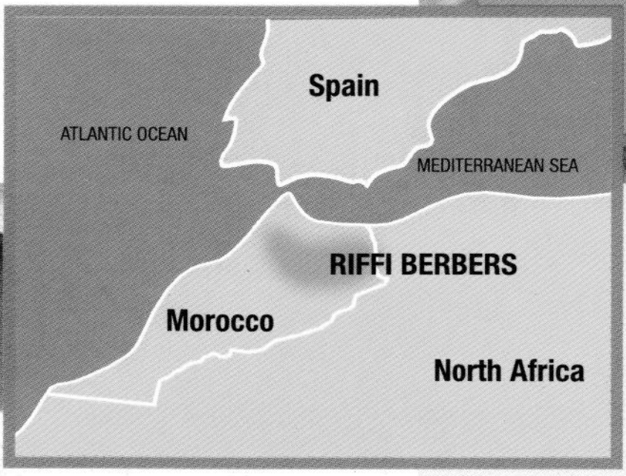

Spain

ATLANTIC OCEAN

MEDITERRANEAN SEA

RIFFI BERBERS

Morocco

North Africa

Jamina's birth

Jamina cleaned the lentils and soaked them. Then she kneaded dough for the flat round loaves, to be cooked over the fire.

As she worked, Jamina's mother told her the story of her birth again. "I wanted a baby so much and was afraid your father would take another wife because I couldn't have a baby. I cried and cried.

To help you pray for the Riffi

You can thank God for:

- Christian radio broadcasts in Arabic and Riffi and the Bible correspondence courses.

- Christian films that have been dubbed in Riffi, and for cassettes in Riffi of stories from the Old Testament.

You can ask God:

- to help the people producing the Christian radio broadcasts and dramatized stories to make them really interesting.

- that those who listen to the broadcasts will find them easy to understand.

- that the teachers for the Bible correspondence courses will know how to answer the questions the students ask about Jesus.

- to help Christian parents encourage their children to learn Bible passages just as Muslim children learn passages from the Koran.

- to fill each Riffi Christian with such love and joy that their friends will want to know Jesus as well.

Fact file

Homeland: The Rif Mountain range of North Morocco. About 1,500,000 Riffi live there.

Occupation: Mainly farming

Other countries where they live: France, Netherlands, Belgium, Spain, Germany and England, where they have gone to look for work.

Then my mother took me to a saint's tomb where I was told to jump three times through the window. Not long after that, I had a beautiful baby!" Jamina's mother is very superstitious, like a lot of Riffi Muslims. Few of them have heard that God promises to help us. You can read about how God does this in the story of Hannah in the Old Testament, in 1 Samuel 1.

No school today!

Mohammed, Jamina's little brother, was glad it was Eid el-Kabir so he didn't have to go to school and study Arabic. Some boys made fun of him for making mistakes when reciting from the Koran. Like most Riffi girls, Jamina had only been to school for three years. Her mother needed her at home to fetch water and wood, look after her baby sister (whom she carried on her back), clean and work in the fields.

Jamina's father had prepared the sheep for the sacrifice. Her brother and sister blew up the sheep's lungs like a balloon and were laughing and shouting. Jamina was looking forward to eating meat. Usually they ate just bread and olive oil, and sometimes lentils or sardines.

Jamina's father worked in Spain, but he had come home for the feast. He loved his family and always made sure they had enough money. He had lots of interesting stories to tell. This time he had seen a film about Jesus. "Muslims believe Jesus was a prophet," he said, "but the film showed us how good he was and it said he was the Son of God. But I'm not sure why he died. I'd like to know more about him."

Arab rulers

The original people in North Africa were called Berbers. There are three main groups of Berber people in Morocco, including the Riffi Berbers, whose home is in the Rif Mountain range.

Almost all Berbers are Muslims. There are more than two million Riffi Berbers, but only about 40 are Christians.

Moroccan market

Free at Last

A ride on the train

Imagine you're taking a train ride through Romania. You see flat land and farms, thick forest, high mountains (with wolves and bears!), deep gorges and the River Danube, the longest and most important river in Romania. You could wear a tee shirt in the summer, but you'd want lots of warm clothes in the winter.

A Romanian grandfather sits next to you on the train, telling stories about how this beautiful country used to be a wonderful place to live. Romania used to be famous for its fine flour and wines.

Romanian Orthodox church

Fact file

Area: 91,700 sq. mi.

Population: 22,326,500

Capital: Bucharest

Language: Romanian

Religion: Orthodox Christian

Chief exports: Petroleum products; heavy machinery

"But it's not like that anymore," he says, "not since Ceausescu."

"Who's Ceausescu?" you ask. And he tells you a sad story …

"For 24 years," he begins, "a Communist dictator called Nicolae Ceausescu ruled Romania. He and his family lived in luxury, but the rest of us were often hungry, cold and very afraid. People in villages were forced to leave their homes, and their land was made into big farms owned by the government. Unwanted children, orphans and the sick and elderly were neglected. Ceausescu sold the fuel and food we needed desperately to other countries to pay his debts.

"But God was still with us," the man continues. "A brave Christian pastor called Laszlo Tokes spoke out when villages were destroyed and Christians were persecuted. He and his wife were arrested and beaten by the secret police, and the windows of their church and home were smashed. Thousands of church members and their friends gathered to protest. The protest quickly spread and turned into a revolution.

Finally, on Christmas night, 1989, Ceausescu was overthrown."

"Did life get better for everyone then?" you ask hopefully.

"I'm afraid not," the old man says sadly. "Even today, many people are still very poor, without proper food or shelter. Thousands of children your age still live on the streets. But God is helping

To help you pray for Romania

You can thank God for:

- the Christians from Romania and other countries who are showing Jesus' love and care to the thousands of destitute orphans and street children and to the homeless, sick and elderly.

- all of the Romanians who are learning to follow Jesus.

You can ask God:

- to give the government leaders wisdom as they rule the country, so that everyone in need will receive help.

- to help Christians in Romania learn to forgive, love and trust one another after the many years of persecution.

- to show people from other countries working with churches in Romania the best ways to help them grow and glorify God.

- to give wisdom to church leaders in Romania as they teach the Bible and reach out to those who have no hope.

- to provide for each Romanian who is studying at Bible school to become a pastor.

Can you imagine not having a Bible – and giving up your most prized possessions to get one?

You can speak Romanian

Hello is "Salut" (sah-**loot**)

Goodbye is "La revedere" (lah reh-veh-**dair**-ay)

Please is "Va rog" (vah-**rog**)

Thank you is "Multumesc" (mool-tsoo-**mesk**)

us to rebuild our lives. After Ceausescu was gone, people all around the world found out about the conditions here during those 24 years. Many churches and other groups brought in truckloads of food, clothes and other supplies. Nurses and care workers came to love and look after the many children in the orphanages.

"I will tell you one more story," he says, "to help you remember that even when everything seems very dark, God brings light to people."

"Ceausescu didn't like Christians. He picked on them, put them in prison and even killed them for believing in God. But the church still grew because people found strength through trusting in God. One day, an

American Christian visiting Romania was sitting in his car waiting for a friend. A woman holding a brown paper bag asked him for something and showed him the bag, but he didn't understand. Finally, his Romanian friend arrived. 'She's asking for a Bible,' he said, with tears in his eyes. 'In the bag are her best clothes. She wants to exchange them for a Bible. That's all she has to give.'"

Construction in Bucharest

The Romanian grandfather turns to you. "How many Bibles do you have in your house?" he asks.

You can't remember and look away, ashamed at what you take for granted.

"Ah," he smiles, "Then you probably can't even imagine this woman's joy when she received that Bible. And, of course, she was able to keep her best clothes too.

"Just after the revolution, there was a cartoon version of the Bible shown on TV called 'Superbook.' A million people in Romania saw this and wrote asking for books and Bibles. Since the revolution, at least a thousand churches have been started. Christian schools, colleges, Bible schools, bookstores and radio stations have also been set up. More and more Romanians are coming to know Jesus every day."

"What can I do to help?" you ask.

"Please pray for us," he said.

A Thousand Years of Christianity

Christ is risen!

"Christ is risen!" The priest called out in the crowded church. "He is risen indeed!" the people replied. Olga was glad to be in church with her grandmother on Easter Sunday. She couldn't help smiling when she saw the joy on her grandmother's wrinkled face. Olga admired her grandmother's strong faith in Jesus, even when life was difficult and she had so little money for food and rent.

As they left the church, with its golden, onion-shaped domes, Olga said, "I can't imagine what it must have been like when churches were closed. Was it really against the law for children to learn Bible stories?"

They sat together on a park bench, and Olga's grandmother told her the story.

Do you know?

Russia is the largest country in the world. It takes seven days to travel by the Trans-Siberian Railway from Vladivostok in the east to Moscow in the west. It's a distance of 5,600 miles, which makes it the longest train journey in the world.

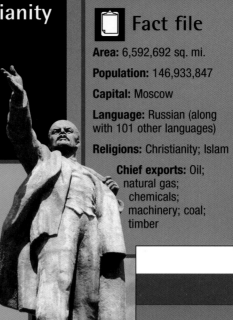

Statue of Lenin, a Communist leader of Russia

Choosing a religion

"Yes, it's hard to believe now, isn't it?" Olga's grandmother said. "I suppose it all started more than a thousand years ago, when a prince called Vladimir lived in this country. He wanted our country to follow a great religion and decided to find out all he could about Judaism, Islam and Christianity. There's a legend that says that, in AD 988, Prince Vladimir saw a light shining over the city of Kiev. He thought this bright light came from Jesus Christ, and he decided to follow him. So Russia became a Christian country. Poor peasants, rich nobles, and even the tsar (king) himself, worshipped God in the same way. The way we worship God in the Orthodox Church has never changed.

"Although some Russians were rich, most were very poor. At the beginning of the twentieth century, workers felt they weren't being treated fairly. Finally, in a revolution in 1917, a group called the Bolsheviks drove the ruler, Tsar Nicholas II, and his family from power. They took control of the government and all the farms and factories. They turned Russia into a Communist country. Life became harder than ever before."

ARCTIC OCEAN

SIBERIA

St. Petersburg

Moscow

Russia

PACIFIC OCEAN

Novosibirsk

Kazahkstan

Vladivostock

China

Mongolia

For 70 years Russians were taught atheism, but now people are hearing about Jesus

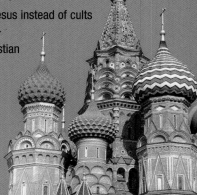
Religion banned

"What happened to the churches?" asked Olga.

"Religion was banned," her grandmother replied. "Very few people had Bibles and most churches were closed down. Our beautiful church was turned into a cowshed. I was very sad – until I remembered that Jesus was born in a stable.

"There were a lot of us who didn't want to stop worshipping God. But the secret police closely watched the few churches that the government allowed to stay open. Many Baptists and other groups formed 'underground' churches that met in secret, often outdoors. The secret police often found them and took away their pastors. Some of them were tortured, put in prison or sent far away to Siberia, in the east of Russia. Although the Communists made life very hard for Christians and punished many of them, they just couldn't get rid of Christianity."

"I'm glad it's different now," Olga said as she looked up at her grandmother and smiled. "We can go to church and have our own Bibles, and I learn about Jesus at school and at Sunday school. What happened to make it all change?"

New freedom

"In 1985, Mikhail Gorbachev was elected as General Secretary of the Communist Party. He knew many things were wrong in our country and started to make changes," Olga's grandmother answered. "He lifted the ban on religion and started to give us back some of the church buildings.

"In 1988, Christian leaders from around the world came to Russia to celebrate a thousand years of Christianity here! Since then, we've been free to worship God again."

"Some of my friends go to Baptist churches," Olga told her grandmother. "They said that sometimes Christians from other countries visited their churches when the government tried to get rid of religion in our country. They said that people all around the world were praying for us. God must have heard their prayers."

"That's right," her grandmother said. "Since 1991, a lot of Christians have come to help the churches. Even though we can buy Bibles now, a lot of people still don't know what it says. They were taught atheism for 70 years, and now followers of all sorts of cults and religions have come into our country and are trying to get people to follow them. We still need prayer, and we need people who can teach us to follow Jesus."

149

A Land Founded on God

Fact file

Area: 1,093 sq. mi. made up of the two large islands of Savai'i and Upolu and seven very small islands

Population: 180,070

Capital: Apia

Official Languages: Samoan; English

Major Religions: Christianity (Congregationalism, Roman Catholicism, Methodism)

Daily prayers

At the end of Ben and Mary's first day on Samoa, they heard church bells ringing. It sounded like they were ringing all over the island. "We have to be very quiet now," their hostess Tili whispered. "It's the time for prayer. Every day, when the church bells ring at dusk, everyone in Samoa stops what they're doing to pray and read the Bible. Let's go back to my house – we can be quiet there." Samoan houses are called fales, and they're all open to the sea breezes. Samoans only lower the canvas sides of their houses in very bad weather.

Savai'i

Samoa   Apia● Upolu

Samoa

Australia

SOUTH PACIFIC OCEAN

New Zealand

An island nation

Samoa, which was called Western Samoa until 1997, is one of the island nations in the South Pacific Ocean. Most Samoans live on the two main islands, Savai'i and Upolu. There are also seven much smaller islands. These mountainous islands were formed thousands of years ago when volcanoes in the South Pacific erupted. Mangoes, coconuts, pineapples and breadfruit (which grow on a tree but taste like potatoes) grow all over the fertile valleys. Coral reefs surround the islands, and there are lots of fish, shellfish and turtles.

A missionary king

"Are all the people in Samoa Christians?" Mary asked Tili later. "Is that why everyone has to stop to pray and read the Bible every day?"

"It's been almost 200 years since people in Samoa first heard about Jesus," she told them. "One of our chiefs became a Christian when he was visiting Tonga, another island nation in the South Pacific. When he came back to Samoa, he wanted everyone to know about Jesus. Lots of Samoans decided to follow Jesus. The King of Tonga even sent people to teach the people here how to follow Jesus. Missionaries came from other countries, too, and soon there were thousands of Christians all over the islands. And there were

Almost all Samoans go to church, but not all of them really understand how to follow Jesus

churches in every town and village. We wanted more and more people to know Jesus, so Samoan missionaries sailed to other Pacific islands to tell them about God's love."

"That's amazing! Are the Samoans still excited about following Jesus?" Ben asked.

"Most Samoans would say they're Christians," Tili replied, "but not all of

To help you pray for Samoa

You can thank God for:

- the Samoans who have told other people in the South Pacific about Jesus.
- the time Samoans have every day to pray and read the Bible.

You can ask God:

- to help the churches in Samoa teach families how they can all follow Jesus.
- that people will listen to the daily Christian radio broadcasts.
- that Samoans will realize that following Jesus is more important than going to church just because everyone else is going.
- to help young people find true happiness in knowing Jesus.
- to help Samoan Christians from the different churches work together.

Climbing a palm tree

them really follow Jesus. Some still want to practice old Samoan customs and ceremonies that honor evil spirits as well. And for some people, being a Christian is just part of our culture. Nearly everyone goes to church on Sundays and to two services during the week as well as to the early morning prayer meeting. We're still sending missionaries to other places, but here in Samoa Christians from all the different kinds of churches need to learn to work together."

Founded on God

"We heard that thousands of Christians from all the different churches in Samoa took part in a March for Jesus," Mary said.

"Yes," said Tili. "It was a very special event. Even members of the government marched. Their motto is, 'The whole government is founded on God.' But I wish all of our people were really 'founded on God.' We were very glad that people from all the different church groups took part in the march. That doesn't always happen."

"What about young people?" Ben asked. "I've heard that a lot of them leave Samoa. You must be sad to see them go."

"Most Samoans don't have a lot of money, but we're happy people and proud to be independent," Tili said. "But a lot of young people are leaving the country because they think they'll find a more exciting life and earn more money in countries like Australia and New Zealand. Some also go to American Samoa, which is just 60 miles to the

In a *fale*

Do you know?

Samoans hold lots of feasts. They wrap the food in leaves and cook it among hot stones, then announce what each delicious dish is before they place it before the guests. Guests wear turtle shell combs, coral necklaces, coconut shell brooches and *lapa lapas*, skirts worn by both men and women. And, despite the heat, men wear shirts, ties and jackets in church but have bare feet and wear *lapa lapas* instead of trousers.

east. The people there are much richer than we are. But although they have their own government, they're not independent like we are because they're ruled by the United States.

"Sometimes," Tili continued, "there doesn't seem to be the love, joy and peace we might expect in a country where nearly everyone says they're a Christian."

151

San

Bushmen of the Kalahari Desert

Rescue in the desert

A hundred years ago, a missionary named Frederick Arnot was traveling through the Kalahari Desert in Botswana to reach the Zambezi River. He and his African helpers were almost fainting from thirst, but they struggled towards a water hole and knelt by its side. They could almost taste the water … but it was completely dry. They lost all hope and some of them collapsed, unconscious, on the sand. Without water they could not go on. They knew they might die.

A group of San Bushmen had seen them from a distance. They ran over and began to dig furiously, scooping up handfuls of sand. Their leader took several lengths of reed and slid them into the hole. Carefully he pushed the reeds, skillfully jointed together, into the ground. After sucking and blowing for some time, he smiled – water!

Lighting a fire by rubbing sticks together

He began to suck steadily on the reed, and as the water rose slowly up the stem he spat it into a tortoise shell. Ten minutes later the shell was full. He gently poured this precious water over Arnot's tongue and down his throat until Arnot was able to swallow. For six hours, the sweating Bushmen worked without stopping to get water for the whole group. Then, without waiting for thanks, the Bushmen left as silently as they had come.

In those days, the people who lived around them wanted the Bushmen's land for themselves and hunted them like wild animals. Having received nothing but cruelty from others, the Bushmen still saved the lives of strangers. As a result of their kindness, and because he saw how God had looked after them, Tinka, Arnot's chief guide, became a Christian. Most Bushmen live in fear of the spirit world. But their painful history and their kind ways would help them to understand the forgiveness and love of Jesus, who sacrificed himself to save others who didn't always treat him as they should.

Do you know?

The San love eating sweet honeycomb, which provides them with energy. When they see a bee's nest in a tree, they climb the tree and smoke out the bees. The bee grubs are considered the tastiest part of the comb and are kept for the elders of the group.

Poisoned arrows

It scarcely ever rains in the Kalahari Desert, and not much besides thorn bushes and coarse grass grows there. Wild animals such as giraffes, lions, impala and wildebeest roam the desert.

Fact file

Total number: About 55,000

Main countries: Botswana (29,000); also Namibia and Angola

Occupations: Very few still live as nomadic hunter-gatherers. Most now work as laborers on farms or in towns.

When the San moved around the desert hunting wild animals and gathering roots and berries, they built shelters of branches, twigs and grass and ate what they killed the same day. They could go without food or water for long periods, which was a great advantage as they often had to follow animals for long distances before killing them. The San hunted the animals with poisoned arrows.

The Bushmen used to roam freely over southern and eastern Africa. They left beautiful rock paintings, which tell us about their beliefs, the animals they hunted and their way of life. As they were able to find fewer and fewer places of safety from white men and other African tribes, most had to give up their nomadic lifestyle and change their ways to fit in with life on farms or in towns. The Botswana government is doing all it can to help them settle and give them land rights, water and education.

There are about 30 different San dialects. Many of their words contain click sounds, made with the tongue against the teeth or roof of the mouth. One click is like the sound we make to urge on a horse, another is like a "tut tut" of disapproval. An organization called Language Recordings has put Bible talks on tape in some Bushmen dialects,

Bushmen cowboys on a cattle drive in Namibia

and missionaries are telling them the good news about Jesus. Not all San have heard about Jesus, but some have decided to follow him.

To help you pray for the San

You can thank God for:

- the work of Language Recordings.

You can ask God:

- to show the San that he can set them free from fear of the spirit world.
- to send missionaries who will understand, love and teach the San.
- that the leaders of the San will follow Jesus.
- to send people to learn the San dialects and translate the Bible.
- to help the San settle on farms and in towns without losing their gentle ways.
- that the San will always be ready to help others.

A San legend

Have you heard that the moon is made of green cheese? Well, according to a San legend, the moon is an ostrich feather, thrown up into the sky by a mantis (insect)!

The Birthplace of Mohammed

Pilgrimage

"It's nearly time for the Hajj," Hassan told his son Abdul. "You're 12 years old now, so this year you'll be coming with me on pilgrimage to Mecca."

Abdul was excited about traveling hundreds of miles from Riyadh, where they lived, to Mecca. Riyadh may be the royal capital and the largest city in Saudi Arabia, but Mecca is the birthplace of Mohammed himself.

Abdul had been studying Islam for years, and he knew that the Hajj was one of the five pillars, or duties, of their religion. Every Muslim should make this pilgrimage at least once, if possible. Abdul's father had already been three times.

"I can hardly wait to go," Abdul told his father. "Tell me what it's like."

📋 Fact file

Area: 830,000 sq. mi.

Capital: Riyadh

Other major cities: Jeddah; Mecca; Medina

Population: 21,606,691

Official language: Arabic

Religion: Islam

Chief export: Oil (Saudi Arabia has the biggest oil deposits in the world.)

Do you know?

Although Saudi Arabia is a desert, if you fly over it you'll see green fields that look like enormous wheels. They're watered by huge sprinklers that rotate from the center of the field. Because of this system, farmers can grow wheat, barley, tomatoes and melons in the middle of the desert!

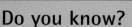

"More than two million Muslim pilgrims from all over the world travel to Mecca every year during the *Hajj*. Everyone wears the same white robe to show that we're all equal in the sight of Allah," Hassan explained. "After our ritual washing and prayer we go to the *Kaaba* and walk around it seven times, keeping it on our left. As we walk around it we have to touch and, if we can, kiss the black stone in the *Kaaba*."

"The *Kaaba's* very old, isn't it?" Abdul asked. "We read in the Koran that Abraham built it at the place where Allah provided water for Hagar and Ishmael in the desert." (You can read in the Bible, in Genesis 21, how God spoke to Hagar and provided water for her and Ishmael.)

"That's right," Hassan said, "and when Allah told Mohammed that all Muslims should turn towards Mecca when they worship him, Mohammed took all the idols out of the *Kaaba* and made it into a holy place. A new black silk cover is put over it every year.

"After we walk around the *Kaaba* seven times, we have to run between two sacred pillars seven times, praying as we go. And the next day we go to the Plain of Arafat, about 10 miles outside Mecca, to

hear the special sermon. There are so many pilgrims, we probably won't be able to hear everything. So we'll take our radios so we can listen to the sermon as it's broadcast. Afterwards we'll collect small pebbles and throw them at three stone pillars to get rid of the evil that's inside us. Then, on our way home, we'll visit the Tomb of Mohammed in Medina."

Students at the Petroleum University

 ## To help you pray for Saudi Arabia

You can thank God for:

- Christian radio and television programs in Arabic that can be received in Saudi Arabia.

- the few Saudis who are following Jesus.

- Christian guest workers in Saudi Arabia.

You can ask God:

- that Saudi and other Arab Christians will help each other follow Jesus.

- that Saudis who go to other countries to work or study will meet Christians who will tell them about Jesus.

- to help guest workers share their faith with other guest workers.

- to use every Bible, Christian book or video taken into Saudi Arabia to bring someone to know Jesus.

Asir Mountains

In Saudi Arabia Christians from other countries often have to meet in secret

Keeping Islam in and Jesus out

Mohammed wanted everyone in Arabia to follow Islam. Shortly after his death in AD 672, the authorities forced every Christian and every Jew to leave Arabia. Today, Islam is the only religion officially allowed inside Saudi Arabia because the government considers itself the keeper of Islam. The religious police make sure that everyone keeps the Islamic laws and that women dress in the right way. They also make sure that all the stores close when the call for prayer booms out five times each day from minarets all over the country.

Maybe someday Abdul will meet Christians who will explain to him that keeping strict laws and following certain customs can never take away our sins. Only Jesus can do that.

Wouldn't Abdul be amazed to learn that he could come to Jesus at any time and know that, wherever he is, God will hear and answer his prayers?

An oil-rich desert

The kingdom of Saudi Arabia is a hot, dry, desert country covering most of the Arabian Peninsula. A strong Arab leader, Ibn Saud, brought together all the nomadic tribes who lived there to create the new Islamic kingdom of Saudi Arabia in 1932. The king's word is law, and the large royal family controls everything.

When oil was discovered, Saudi Arabia became powerful and wealthy. Countries all around the world wanted to buy their oil. Some of the money from oil has been used to build better houses for the people, to set up

schools and universities, to make roads across the desert and to develop industries. The Saudi Arabian government sends huge sums of money to Muslim organizations in other countries to help them publish Muslim literature, train Muslim missionaries and build huge mosques.

Guest workers

Thousands of people from other countries come to Saudi Arabia as guest workers. Some work for the oil companies, and others work as laborers, housemaids and nurses. There are Christians among them, but they often have to meet in secret.

A Land of Contrasts

A big problem

"Come on, Carlos," José said impatiently as they made their way between the busy sidewalk cafés to the entrance of the subway station. They pushed to the front of the crowd listening to a group of young people playing guitars and singing. The boys didn't want to miss the story. "I hope it'll be about one of the people Jesus healed, just like he healed your brother Juan!" Carlos said excitedly.

José and Carlos live in Madrid, the capital of Spain. A lot of people are moving into the city because they're poor and tired of farming. They think it will be easy to get work in the city, but there aren't enough jobs. And, because they have so little money, they're forced to live in very small, crowded apartments.

Fact file

Area: 195,000 sq. mi.

Population: 39,759,775

Capital: Madrid

Language: Castilian Spanish

Traditional religion: Roman Catholic

Chief exports: Wine; fruit; olive oil; vegetables; cars; machinery

When José and his family came to live in Madrid they stopped going to church, because they said they didn't believe in God anymore. They had no work, no faith, and soon José's brothers were stealing and taking drugs. "There's nothing else to do," they complained. One of José's brothers died and another, Juan, became very sick. Their parents didn't know what to do. They felt so alone, and no one seemed to care what happened to them.

One night they stopped at a Christian meeting being held outdoors. A man saw their sad faces and asked if he could help them. When they told him about their sons, he said, "If Juan will come with us, we can help him at the Betel Center where we help people who have been taking drugs." God worked a miracle in Juan's life there at the Center. As he got better, he started to help others who came to the Center. He learned that Jesus is alive and has the power to heal. Jesus forgave him for all the bad things he had done and gave him the strength not to take drugs anymore. Juan had a new life following Jesus!

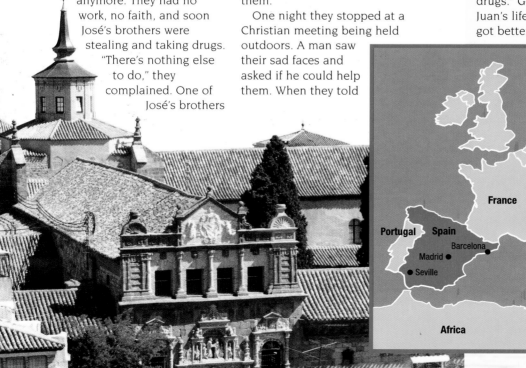

![hand icon] ## To help you pray for Spain

You can thank God for:

- the freedom to preach the good news about Jesus in Spain.

- centers like Betel, which care for drug addicts and share Jesus' love.

You can ask God:

- that people will realize that Jesus is alive and ready to help them.

- for more missionaries, pastors and evangelists to tell people about Jesus and help them to follow him.

- that lots of children will go to the children's clubs and learn about Jesus.

- to help children when others laugh at them or refuse to play with them because they follow Jesus.

- that a lot of people will listen to Christian radio and television programs.

You can speak Spanish

Hello is "Hola" (**oh**-lah)
Goodbye is "Adiós" (ad-ee-**os**)
Yes is "Sí" (see)
No is "No" (no)
Please is "Por favor" (por fa-**vor**)
Thank you is "Gracias" (**gra**-see-as)

Many people in Spain are coming to know Jesus as a friend who is with them always

Crowded Madrid shopping street

Spanish teenagers in Madrid

A feast day

But it's not only drug addicts who need to know about Jesus. Although many people in Spain are still Roman Catholic, there's no longer an official religion. A lot of people have stopped going to church or only go on special occasions, but they still love to celebrate "feast days" of the saints.

In Lidia's village, everyone worked hard cleaning the street and preparing for the feast day of their village saint. When the church bells rang, Lidia and her family went to the church for Mass. Lidia looked at the statue of Christ on the cross and remembered her cousin Marta telling her that she had come to know Jesus as her special friend through a *Club de Amigos* (Friends' Club). Marta had been so excited to tell her that Jesus is alive. Lidia thought that sounded

wonderful, too, and really wanted to know Jesus like her cousin did. "When I visit Marta," she thought, "maybe I can go to the club with her and find out how I can have him as my friend, too."

The church service was soon over. Outside the church, the band started to play. Young men carried gold-covered statues of their saint and Jesus. Everyone joined in the parade and Lidia forgot about her cousin for a while as she and her friends joined in the feasting and dancing.

People in need

The sunny country of Spain lies in the southwest corner of Europe. With its castles, church steeples, colorful fiestas, beautiful beaches and delicious food, it's no wonder many people think of holidays when they

think of Spain! There are people with great needs in Spain but in towns and villages across the country there are some who are discovering that when they ask Jesus to be their friend, he is with them always and helps them all the time.

Island of Beauty and Battle

Golden beaches

Sri Lanka, just south of India, is a beautiful sunny island with many golden beaches lined with palm trees. There are plenty of fish in the sea and all around the coast there are villages where fishermen live. It's a fertile country, too, and all sorts of things grow here – tea, rubber, rice, spices, coconuts and tropical fruits. It's no wonder that almost half the people are farmers. Others work in factories making clothes that are sold around the world. Colombo, the capital, is a busy city and the streets are often jammed with bicycles, small three-wheeled taxis, cars, buses and bullock carts. About 17 million people live in Sri Lanka. Twelve million of them are Sinhalese, who are mostly Buddhists. Another three million are Tamils, whose ancestors came from India. The Tamils are mainly Hindus. There are about a million Muslim Moors, and several other smaller groups of people with different backgrounds and beliefs.

A motorized rickshaw

Violence

Since 1980, there has been lots of violence in Sri Lanka and thousands of people have been killed. Some Tamils believe that the government, made up mainly of Sinhalese, has treated them unfairly. In the north and east of the island, Tamil guerrillas are fighting government forces to make a separate country for themselves. Some have even planted bombs in the city of Colombo.

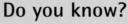

Do you know?

There is buried treasure in Sri Lanka! Sri Lanka has an important gem industry. Some of the gems are mined in the mountains, but some are mined in the paddy (rice) fields. A little shelter with a thatched roof in the middle of a field often covers a mineshaft. Deep in these mines, people find rubies, emeralds, agate, onyx and other stones. They're often polished, ready to be sold, in homes around the fields.

Many children in Sri Lanka have lost their parents in the fighting and live on the streets. Some are involved in the violence, others are abused or abandoned, and some have to work long hours in dangerous jobs to earn a little bit of money.

There is another battle going on, too. Some Buddhists are very angry when Christians tell others about God's love. They have burned down homes and churches to make the Christians afraid so they'll stop sharing the good news about Jesus. But the Christians have stayed and others have started to follow Jesus.

Once Sri Lanka was called a pearl because of its shape, but today it reminds people of a tear. Only Jesus, through the power of the Holy Spirit, can bring peace to this island.

A Buddhist temple in Sri Lanka

 ## To help you pray for Sri Lanka

You can thank God for:

- the Sinhalese and Tamils who are finding a new way of life with Jesus after all the suffering in their land.
- Sri Lankan Christians who are writing books to help Buddhists understand who Jesus really is.
- Christians who aren't afraid to share God's love in villages where people have never heard about Jesus.

You can ask God:

- to help people of all races and beliefs in Sri Lanka learn to live together in peace for the good of their country.
- to speak through Christians to Buddhists, Hindus and Muslims so that, as they hear the truth about Jesus, they will believe and understand it for themselves.
- to so fill the Christians of Sri Lanka with Jesus' love that they will love and help children who are hurt or lonely or abused so that they will know Jesus.
- to show Sri Lankans that the real treasure is not in their precious gem stones, but in Jesus Christ.

Picking tea

Tear-shaped Sri Lanka has seen sadness... but it's also pearl-shaped, a treasure to God

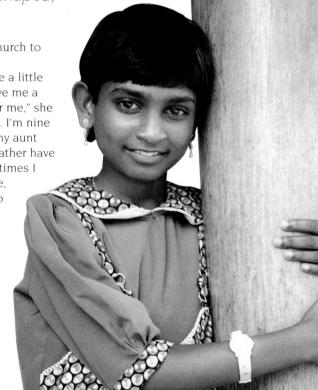

A church in the country

As we drove along the narrow dirt road, Pastor Mahess, who was with us in the van, told us his story. "When I first came to work here," he said, "the Buddhist monks told the people they weren't allowed to listen when I told them about God and his love for them. I tried to help the people, but they burned down my house. I kept telling the people that God wants to help them. One day, a man whose son was very sick came to see me. The doctor couldn't make him better. The monks at the temple couldn't help him either. I prayed for the boy and he got better. Soon the boy's whole family was following Jesus."

The van stopped beside a large, simple stone house. There was a crowd of men and women, boys and girls waiting outside. "This is the church," Mahess said, "and my home."

Everyone went into the church to worship God.

At the end of the service a little girl held my hand and gave me a shy smile. "Please pray for me," she said. "My name is Kumari. I'm nine years old and I live with my aunt because my mother and father have gone away to work. Sometimes I think they've forgotten me, but I'm glad I can come to church where everyone treats me as part of their family."

Sundanese

From Beautiful West Java

Can the gods help?

"Why do I always forget everything I've learned?" Paru wondered. "I can never remember the passages from the Koran I'm supposed to memorize. I feel so stupid. Even my little brother can learn them."

Paru was walking home, up the path between the steeply terraced rice fields. Every time he walked this path, he was amazed when he looked up at the high volcanic mountains that everyone called the "home of the gods." "The gods must have been happy with the offerings we made before we planted our fields this year, because the rice, corn, tea and hot peppers are all growing well," Paru thought. "I wish the gods would help me remember those verses from the Koran ... but they never do."

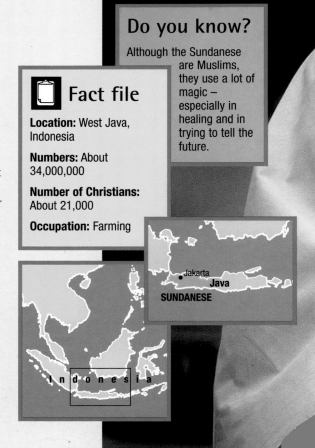

The early Dutch missionaries set up the Pasundan churches, and a lot of the 21,000 Sundanese Christians today belong to these churches. Many of them say they're Christians because their parents and grandparents were Christians. Not all of them really know what it means to have Jesus as their friend and savior, and so they're not really interested in telling their Muslim neighbors about Jesus.

Music and drama

Christians in other parts of Indonesia want to show the Sundanese that Christianity is not just a

Java, the home of the Sundanese, is the most important island of Indonesia. Jakarta, the capital of Indonesia, is on Java's northwestern coast. About 34 million Sundanese live in beautiful West Java, and millions of them, like Paru, have never heard about Jesus. Most Sundanese are Muslims, but long before they became Muslims they worshipped their own gods. When people from India brought Hinduism and Buddhism to Java in the fifth and sixth centuries AD, the Sundanese began to worship the gods of those religions as well. Even though they're Muslims now, many of them still worship the gods that they believe live in the mountains.

Christian villages

When the Dutch colonized Java in the nineteenth century, a few missionaries wanted to help the Sundanese. They set up clinics, schools and churches and tried to teach them about God's love, but the Dutch government didn't really want them there. The Sundanese didn't want them, either. And they certainly didn't want to hear about Christianity, because it was the religion of the Dutch, who had taken over their land and were telling them how they had to live.

In those days, Sundanese who did become Christians were often persecuted. So the missionaries built special villages for the new Christians. Some of these villages still exist, but they are no longer completely Christian.

Do you know?

Although the Sundanese are Muslims, they use a lot of magic – especially in healing and in trying to tell the future.

📋 Fact file

Location: West Java, Indonesia

Numbers: About 34,000,000

Number of Christians: About 21,000

Occupation: Farming

Jakarta
Java
SUNDANESE

Indonesia

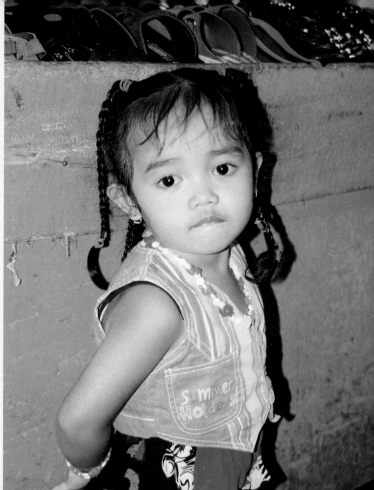

western religion. They use Sundanese drama and music to tell Bible stories so that the people will understand that God loves them, too.

One evening, two young people stopped Sita and her friends as they were walking along a busy street in Jakarta. "Come and watch this story," they invited them. "It's about why God in heaven sent his only Son to earth."

"What an amazing story," Sita told them afterwards, "and I think everyone could understand it because it was just like our Sundanese plays. The Christian's God must be really powerful to be able to bring his Son back to life again after he was killed. I'd like to know more about their God."

A few months later, Sita decided to follow Jesus. But her family was very angry. "What do you mean, you've become a Christian?" shouted her brother. "You can't be a Christian! We're Sundanese, and that means we're Muslims." Sita was sad because her family was so angry, but she knew she had to follow Jesus, the one true God.

Please pray for the Sundanese. More and more of the people, like Sita, are becoming Christians. But there are so many Sundanese and lots of them, like Paru, have never heard the good news about Jesus.

 ## To help you pray for the Sundanese

You can thank God for:

- Indonesian Christians who are telling the Sundanese about Jesus.
- every Christian in the Pasundan churches.
- Sundanese Christians like Sita, who follow Jesus even when it's very difficult.

You can ask God:

- to send Christians to the villages to tell children like Paru that Jesus is more powerful than all the gods in the mountains, and that Jesus promises to help everyone who trusts in him.
- to use the Christian drama and music programs to show the Sundanese that they can be Christians.
- that many Sundanese people will listen to the Christian radio programs and understand what it means to be a Christian.
- for many more people around the world to pray for the Sundanese.

A Modern Country but an Ancient Land

What's a Christian?

"What do you mean you've become a Christian?" Maria asked her brother Ibrahim. "Of course you're a Christian. You've always been a Christian, just like the rest of our family. We belong to a church, don't we? There have been Christians here in Damascus since New Testament times."

"Yes, that's true," Ibrahim said. "It even says in Acts 9 that Saul (Paul) came here to Damascus to arrest the Christians because he didn't want the faith to spread to other places. He knew how easily that could happen because travelers and traders came here from far and wide and would take the good news about Jesus with them. It's a good thing God spoke to him before he ever reached Damascus. And after Saul became a Christian, he himself took the good news about Jesus to lots of other places.

Fact file

Full name: Syrian Arab Republic

Area: 71,430 sq. mi.

Population: 16,124,618

Capital: Damascus

Language: Arabic

Religions: Islam (90.5%); Christianity (8%)

Chief exports: Oil; cotton; fruit; vegetables

"But Maria," Ibrahim continued, "when I went to study in Aleppo, I met Christians who were really excited about their faith. They told me that I could know Jesus as a special friend and they taught me to study the Bible for myself. It's an amazing book! Will you come to a Bible study group with me? My friends have a really good video, too, about the life of Jesus."

"I'll come," Maria said. "You're so excited about it … I wish I could know Jesus like you do."

An ancient land

Damascus, the capital of modern Syria, is an ancient city. It may even be the oldest city in the whole world! You can find Damascus in the very first book in the Bible, in Genesis chapters 14 and 15. You can also read there about the River Euphrates, which flows through Syria and has been dammed to provide hydroelectric power for the country.

Syria has been a secular country since

There have been Christians in Syria since New Testament times

1973, but three-quarters of the people are Sunni Muslims. There are other Muslim sects in the country, and the present rulers belong to a smaller Muslim group called the Alawites. For the last 50 years, the country has been involved in wars and conflicts with neighboring countries in the Middle East.

To help you pray for Syria

You can thank God for:

● the freedom Syrian Christians have to meet together to worship.

● the work of the Bible Society in providing Bibles and Christian books.

You can ask God:

● that those who follow Jesus will help others who only say they're Christians to really know and follow him, too.

● that many people will watch the *Jesus* video and understand God's love.

● to help Christians live so that other people will see their joyful, caring lives and want to know Jesus, too.

● that Christians will share the good news about Jesus with their Muslim friends when they have opportunities to do so.

● for wise government and peace in Syria and neighboring countries, especially Israel and Lebanon.

Bedouin family

Do you know?

Antioch, where the followers of Jesus were first called Christians (Acts 11:25), was in northern Syria. Paul set out from Antioch on several of his great missionary journeys.

Not just some old book

There are Orthodox and Armenian churches in almost every town in Syria. There are some Protestant churches too, but there aren't enough pastors and Christian workers to lead them. Although Christians make up only a small part of Syria's population, they have a lot of freedom. They can go to church whenever they want, and radio and television stations broadcast Christian programs at Christmas and Easter. They can buy Christian books and Bibles, and a lot of people watch the *Jesus* video in Arabic. Many Christians are highly respected in Syria and have good jobs as merchants, teachers, doctors and lawyers. Others work for the government and in the armed forces.

A lot of Christians in Syria are finding out that the Bible isn't just a big, old book of stories about things that happened a long time ago. As they read it, they realize that it's the word of the living God. The Bible has lots to say to people today. They're excited about it and many, like Ibrahim and Maria, are coming to really know Jesus for the first time.

Christians and Muslims

For 1,300 years, both Muslims and Christians have lived in Syria. "We live in the Christian part of Damascus, and that's where our friends are," Ibrahim explains. "We meet Muslims at work and at school, but we really don't understand each other, so it's very hard to talk about our faith.

"I have a few Muslim friends, and I try to show them who Jesus is by the way I live. I want them to see that Jesus has made my life pure and clean, and that he fills me with joy. Some of my Christian friends don't understand why I want my Muslim friends to know Jesus, and my Muslim friends are afraid they'll be persecuted if they become Christians. But I want all my family and friends to know Jesus, who makes our lives new when we trust in him."

Damascus

Tibetans

Following their God-king

A mysterious world

The Himalayan and Kun Lun Mountains surround the Tibetan plateau like a gigantic wall, and for hundreds of years few people ever visited it. Tibet was like a mysterious world. Now visitors can fly into Lhasa, the capital city, or travel through the country on roads built by the Chinese.

The Potala in Lhasa where the Dalai Lama lived and studied

Do you know?

Tsampa is the most important part of any Tibetan meal. Tibetans make *tsampa* by roasting barley, grinding it into flour, and then mixing it with salted tea and butter made from yak milk. All of the fat in yak milk helps the people stay healthy in the extremely cold climate in Tibet.

The Tibetan plateau, the highest and largest on earth, is often called "the roof of the world." It covers an area of 714,300 square miles and averages over 15,000 feet above sea level.

The Buddhist religious leaders used to also be the political leaders (this is called a theocracy). The officials and priests were looked upon as royalty, but most ordinary people were treated like slaves. They even had to stick out their tongues when they met important people to show they didn't have demons inside them! Some Tibetans still do this as a sign of respect.

The Dalai Lama

The Dalai Lama is the most important priest, or "lama," and the leader of the Tibetan people. Tibetans believe that the Dalai Lama is a god-king, and that when he dies his soul is "reborn" in a baby. So as soon as the Dalai Lama dies, the search begins for the next Dalai Lama – a

Fact file

Location: About 2,000,000 Tibetans live in central Tibet. Another 2,500,000 live in the western Chinese provinces of Qinghai, Sichuan and Gansu.
As many as 450,000 live in exile in India, Nepal, Bhutan and Sikkim, and some live in North America and Europe.

Religion: Tibetan Buddhism

Language: Tibetan, but most also speak the language of the country in which they live.

Tibetan mask

Tibetan nomad child

baby boy born within 18 months of his death.

Tenzin Gyatso (*Ten-zin Chi-at-zo*), the present Dalai Lama, was born in 1935 in a farmhouse hundreds of miles from Lhasa. Although he wasn't even two years old, he had to pass certain tests

to see if he was the new Dalai Lama. In one test, a number of objects were put in front of him. Some of them had belonged to the previous Dalai Lama. Everyone watched anxiously while Tenzin Gyatso pointed out exactly what had belonged to him. The new Dalai Lama had been found!

Thousands of five-year-old Tibetan boys used to enter monasteries to become monks and learn the Buddhist scriptures. Tenzin Gyatso, too, was only five years old when he was taken to Lhasa to be

To help you pray for the Tibetans

You can thank God for:

- the Tibetans who follow Jesus instead of a human god-king.
- the modern translation of the New Testament in Tibetan.
- the Christians who have helped Tibetan nomads when floods and other disasters have killed their flocks of yaks, sheep and goats.

You can ask God:

- for Chinese Christians and others to be able to travel freely throughout Tibet to tell people about God's love and care.
- that many Tibetans will listen to Christian radio programs, understand what they hear and follow Jesus.
- to show Tibetans that although the Dalai Lama is their leader and a very good man, he is only a man and not a god.
- to help many Tibetans discover that Jesus is the true King of kings and God over all.

Tibetans spinning prayer wheels outside a temple

Spinning yarn with a traditional wheel

enthroned in the Potala, the most important monastery in Tibet, and to begin his studies. Buddhist monks taught him everything they could about Buddhism. He wasn't allowed to leave the Potala except to visit another monastery. He must have been lonely without his family or other children to play with. Someone gave him a pair of binoculars, and he loved watching people out on the streets. He could see pilgrims twirling prayer wheels on their way to the temples to make offerings, prayer flags fluttering on the roofs, and officials arriving at the Potala on horseback.

The end of peace
In 1950, the Chinese army invaded Tibet and set up a Communist government. Monasteries, as well as the ancient Buddhist scriptures, were destroyed. The Chinese killed thousands of Tibetans. Thousands more fled across the high mountain passes to India and Nepal. In 1959, the Dalai Lama was forced to flee to Dharamsala, in

India, where he still lives. He has visited many countries around the world to ask for help to free Tibet from China's rule. He was awarded the Nobel Peace Prize in 1989 for his work promoting world peace.

The Tibetans are still devoted to their god-king, and want Tibet to be a free and independent country. Monks have led demonstrations against the

government, but the Chinese have stopped them. Lots of changes have taken place in Tibet. Priests don't have the power they once had. There are more Chinese in Lhasa now than Tibetans. Chinese has taken the place of Tibetan as the official language. Although more children are able to go to school now, a lot of their lessons are in Chinese.

Following the King of kings
There are only a few Tibetan Christians. For over a hundred years, missionaries have been telling Tibetans living in countries on the border with Tibet about Jesus. Tibetans living around the world are hearing about Jesus, the King of kings and God above all other gods.

Carnival and Calypso

A carnival

It's Mardi Gras, or Shrove Tuesday, and time for the carnival in Port-of-Spain, the capital of Trinidad! Thousands of men, women, boys and girls crowd the streets, and people are dancing to the beat of the steel drums, wearing beautiful costumes that sparkle and glitter in the sun.

Everyone taking part in the carnival has spent weeks preparing to play mas, *or masquerade. They've made elaborate costumes, practiced music and written funny calypso songs. And it's all over at midnight, because tomorrow is Ash Wednesday, the start of the Christian season of Lent.*

CARIBBEAN SEA

Trinidad

Venezuela

South America

CARIBBEAN SEA

Tobago

Port of Spain

Trinidad

Venezuela

Lots of festivals

People in Trinidad celebrate lots of festivals. In November they celebrate *Divali*, the Hindu festival of lights, when candles shine from hundreds of thousands of little clay pots while people spend the night feasting and dancing. Another Hindu festival, *Phagwa*, or New Year, takes place in March. During this festival, people celebrating on the streets throw red food dye at each other!

Muslims in Trinidad have festivals, too. On *Hosay* they remember the murder of two warrior brothers, Hosein and Hassan. They carry models of Hosein's tomb through the streets to the beat of drums and chanting, then they feast all evening and dance all night. The next day, they throw the "tombs" into the sea as a sign of burial.

Some of these traditions might seem a bit strange to us, but have you ever thought what someone from a faraway country might think if they saw you decorating a Christmas tree or blowing out candles on a birthday cake? Different cultures have special ways of having fun and celebrating what's important to them.

Trinidad and Tobago

Trinidad is one of two main islands making up the Republic of Trinidad and Tobago. Trinidad is the most southerly of all the Caribbean islands and is only about 4 miles from Venezuela. While some people are poor, the money from oil, natural gas, pitch and steel industries has given Trinidadians a higher standard of living than most people in countries near them.

People from all over the world

Although it was late at night, nine-year-old Earl was sitting outside his house with his father. He was too excited to sleep after the carnival. "I love festivals," he said. "Why do we have so many?"

"Because Trinidadians all come from different parts of the world," his father replied. "Most of us have our roots in Africa, India and Europe, but some come

To help you pray for Trinidad

You can thank God for:

- Christian radio and TV programs.
- Christians who are teaching children about Jesus in schools and in churches.
- Christian bookstores.

You can ask God:

- to help the different peoples of Trinidad live together in peace.
- that the Prime Minister and government will be wise and fair to everyone.
- that Christians will tell others the good news about Jesus.
- that the churches will help a lot more Trinidadians come to know Jesus.

Do you know?

Pitch Lake, in the south of Trinidad, is the biggest natural source of asphalt in the world. A local legend says that the lake was formed when a chief killed a sacred hummingbird. This made the gods so angry that they drowned his whole village in pitch.

from the Middle East, China and even South America. When people came to Trinidad from all those different places, they brought their cultures and religions – and festivals – with them."

"Why did they all come to Trinidad?" Earl asked.

"Oh, it all started a long time ago," his father said. "Christopher Columbus discovered this island in 1498. I've heard some people say that when he sailed near the southeast coast he saw three mountain peaks that reminded him of the Holy Trinity, so he named the island Trinidad.

"The island belonged to Spain after that, but there weren't many people

Playing *mas*

living here until the eighteenth century, when Catholic refugees from French colonies settled here. They planted sugar and cacao plantations and brought slaves from Africa to work for them. They tried to force the slaves to forget their African religions and become Catholics. In 1797, the British captured Trinidad and it became a British colony."

"What happened when the British came?" asked Earl.

"Well, the government finally did away with slavery in 1834, but the plantation owners still needed workers. This time they brought people from India, promising them that after they had worked on the plantations for five years they could have a free trip home. Many of these Indians decided to stay in Trinidad after five years, and they were given small plots of land for themselves. Some of them were Muslims, but most were Hindus. Both have kept their own religion and culture.

"Whether we came from Africa, India, Europe or somewhere else, we're all Trinidadians and we like to join in the different festivals. Do you remember singing those words in our national anthem, 'here every race and creed find an equal place'? That's a great thought, but unfortunately I don't think it's always true. Sometimes there are tensions between the people of different races."

As Earl listened to his father, he thought about the church he went to each Sunday with his family. He loved the singing and learning stories from the Bible. And he knew that the problems between people in Trinidad would make Jesus sad.

Even though more than half the people of Trinidad say they're Christians, most of them don't really follow Jesus. If Trinidadians of every race followed Jesus, the rejoicing in heaven would be better than any festival!

One Country on Two Continents

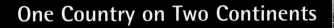

Istanbul is the only city in the world on two different continents. The smaller, western part of the city is in Europe, but the rest is in Asia. An important channel of water called the Bosphorus, which links the Black Sea to the Mediterranean Sea, separates the two parts of the city. Every day, thousands of people cross this waterway on their way to and from work. Some cross on the bridges that rise high above the water while others ride across on the busy ferryboats.

Bridge over the Bosphorus

Fact file

Area: 300,948 sq. mi.

Population: 66,590,940

Capital: Ankara

Language: Turkish

Religion: Islam

Chief exports: Textiles; leather clothing; iron; steel; fruit

A Turkish proverb
It's impossible to have a rose without thorns. (Even the nicest things always have a catch.)

A Turkish drink to make
Put 2 tablespoons of plain (or Greek) yogurt in a glass of cold water. Add a little salt and mix well.
This drink, called Ayran (*eye-ran*), is very refreshing. Turkish children often buy it at MacDonald's to drink with a hamburger.

There are only a few Turkish Christians, but their numbers are growing year by year

New friends

Gul and her little brother Ali were very excited. They were going to meet Debbie and Sue, friends of their older sister, Aysha, who lived in America. Aysha had shocked the family three years ago by telling them that she had decided to follow Jesus. Although her parents were upset when Aysha stopped following Islam and became a Christian, they saw that her faith had given her a new love and respect for them. A little later she had married an American Christian – and not the man her parents had chosen for her to marry. Gul and Ali could hardly imagine what Aysha's friends would be like.

Debbie and Sue were very friendly, and soon Ali was busy telling Sue all about his school and what he liked to do. Gul had recently decided to follow Jesus as well, and she was glad that she could talk with Debbie about being a Christian.

They all became good friends, and Debbie and Sue visited them often. Before long, Gul and Ali's parents became interested in the message

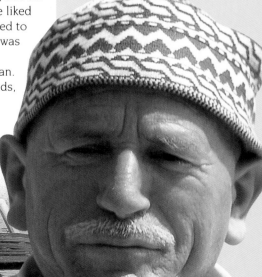

 ## To help you pray for Turkey

You can thank God for:

- the thousands of New Testaments that are sold or given away in Turkey each year.
- Turkish Christians who are telling their friends and families about Jesus.
- the Christians in Turkey who helped so many people after the earthquake.

You can ask God:

- to help church leaders teach people to understand the Bible.
- to provide a church in every one of Turkey's 81 provinces.
- to give strength to Turkish Christians who have been put in prison for believing in Jesus.
- to lead those taking correspondence courses to follow Jesus.

Devastation caused by the 1999 earthquake

You can speak Turkish

Hello is "Merhaba" (**mer**-hah-ba)
Goodbye is "Hoşçakal" (**hosh**-ja-kal)
Please is "Lütfen" (**lewt**-fen)
Thank you is "Tesekkür ederim" (tesh-e-**kewr** ed-e-rim)
Yes is "Evet" (eh-**vet**)
No is "Hayir" (hi-**yerh**)

of the Bible, too. They watched a video about the life of Jesus that really made them think about who Jesus was and why he came to die on the cross. Debbie and Sue gave them a New Testament. They read the Gospels, the stories of Jesus' life, and they began to understand more about God's love. Then they, too, decided to follow Jesus.

Earthquake!

In August 1999, a terrible earthquake destroyed many homes near Istanbul. Thousands of people died or were badly hurt, and everyone was very frightened. Christians from the small Protestant churches joined together to provide food and to help as many people as they could.

For several days, rescuers dug frantically in the rubble. At last they gave up hope of finding anyone else still alive. But as bulldozers started to clear the rubble, rescuers discovered Murat, a seven-year-old boy, trapped deep under a huge pile of bricks and concrete. He had been buried alive for nine days.

"It's a miracle," said the doctors who examined Murat. "It's so hot here in August, we don't know how anyone could live so long in this heat without water."

"But I did have water," Murat insisted. "Every evening, a nice man came to visit me and brought me bread and water." His family was puzzled. They had been sure Murat was dead and they knew no one could have visited him because he was buried so deep under the rubble.

Was this a miracle? Did an angel visit Murat? Does God have a special plan for Murat, who should have died but was wonderfully saved?

Telling others about Jesus

Because the 66 million Turks are almost all Muslims, it isn't easy for the few who follow Jesus to tell others about him. Although the law doesn't say that people can't become Christians, some Turkish Christians have been prevented from meeting together to worship God. Others have lost their jobs and some have even been put in prison because they believe in Jesus. Now many more families just like Gul's and Ali's are taking an interest in Christianity. Several thousand people are studying the Bible through correspondence courses, and Christians like Debbie and Sue are always ready to help those who want to learn more.

Christians have shown God's love to others as they helped those who were hungry, hurt and homeless as a result of the earthquake. Because of their kindness, more people are coming to know about Jesus' love for them.

United Arab Emirates

More Foreigners than Locals

Seven small states

At one time seven Arab sheikhs (chiefs) in the Arabian Gulf area each ruled their own independent states, which were called sheikhdoms or emirates. In 1971, the seven small sheikhdoms joined together to become the United Arab Emirates (or UAE for short). Each sheikh continues to have power in his own state, but they all meet together regularly to make decisions which affect the whole region. Abu Dhabi is the largest emirate and its capital city is also the capital of the UAE. Oil is found in five of the emirates, and the money from this has changed the country rapidly.

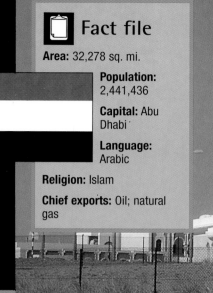

Old man grinding coffee

Simple villages in the desert have become modern cities. Harbors, once the haunt of pirates, smugglers and Arab *dhows* (trading boats) are now ports for huge oil tankers, and the airports handle millions of passengers a year.

Oil and sand

A popular pastime in the UAE is watching camel races and bullfights (in which bulls wrestle with each other). One bull usually shows quite quickly that it's stronger, and the other turns and runs – with its owner hanging on to its tether! Some sheikhs also hunt with falcons in the desert.

Most of the UAE is hot, dry desert, but a little rain falls in the eastern mountains. Farmers can grow vegetables, dates and limes where the land is irrigated. The government has spent some of the money from selling oil on removing the salt from sea water so that it can be used to irrigate crops, keep cattle and provide beautiful fountains and green parks in the cities.

There are presently about four foreign workers to every local person, but that's expected to change. Most people in the UAE can now have a good education, so nationals are beginning to replace foreigners in skilled occupations.

Bull fight – a typical Friday afternoon's entertainment

Christian hospitals

When the UAE was a poor country, Christian workers provided the only medical care available and saved many lives. Today modern hospitals and clinics are available to everyone, but the few remaining Christian medical centers are still popular because of the staff's love and care.

Oil has brought riches to the UAE, but not happiness or hope for the future

Oil refinery

To help you pray for the UAE

You can thank God for:

- the many guest workers who have come to know Jesus as their friend and savior while working in the UAE.
- the Christian hospitals and medical centers that continue to care for those who come to them.
- Christian radio and television broadcasts that can be received in the UAE.

You can ask God:

- to help Christian guest workers please him by the way they live.
- to show people in the UAE that wealth doesn't bring true happiness, but that Jesus offers forgiveness, joy and peace to all who trust in him.
- to help Christian doctors, nurses and midwives as they treat their patients and share his love.
- to bring children to know Jesus as their special friend.

Do you know?

Dubai is often called the "City of Gold" because it has more banks and jewelry shops, in proportion to the number of people who live there, than any other city in the world.

A proverb from UAE

"Too many captains sink the ship," which is just like our saying, "Too many cooks spoil the broth."

Veiled woman

Girls and boys at home

As in other Muslim countries, men can have more than one wife. So children in a family may have the same father but a different mother. When they grow up, many young men go to other countries to study, but only a few girls get that opportunity.

Sharifa adjusted her headscarf. She was now nine years old, and she had to wear it whenever she went out. "I'm not looking forward to having to wear the black cloak and veil when I'm thirteen," she confided to her friend one day.

"I'm not, either," her friend said. "Boys seem to have more fun. They can play soccer and go out with their friends. We don't get to do anything except play at home or go visiting with our mothers."

"At least we can go to school. I'd like to be a teacher some day like my sister," Sharifa said. "Did I tell you my father's arranging her marriage? She says she'd rather choose her own husband."

Christian guest workers

The discovery of oil has made the country rich, but that hasn't given the people happiness or hope for the future. Even the best Muslims can never be sure that God has forgiven their sins and accepted them.

Christians working in the UAE are allowed to meet and worship as long as they don't invite Muslims to their meetings. They could be sent back to their own countries or put in prison for talking about Jesus to a Muslim.

Birthday party at a Christian hospital

Where Christmas Day is Called "Family Day"

Taxicab evangelists

Ricardo slumped down on the back seat of the taxi. He had just been fired from his job, and he was miserable. He knew it was his own fault. But what could he do now? There weren't enough jobs for all the people looking for work. He never should have left his father's farm to work in the city. The taxi driver switched on the radio. "Whatever problem you have right now," the voice on the radio was saying, "God is ready to help you. He loves you and sent Jesus to die on the cross for you and take away your sins. Trust in him, and you'll discover he's a friend who is with you all the time." Ricardo sat up to listen.

The beach at Montevideo

Fact file

Area: 68,000 sq. mi.

Population: 3,337,058 (almost half live in Montevideo)

Capital: Montevideo

Language: Spanish

Religions: Roman Catholic; secular

Chief exports: Meat; leather; wool; textiles

"It's true," the taxi driver said as he saw Ricardo's interest. "Since I came to know Jesus as my savior and friend, my life has changed completely." The driver explained to Ricardo how his life, his family and his attitudes to things had changed, how God had answered his prayers and how he felt hope and peace with Jesus in his life. Ricardo agreed to think about it and read the Bible the driver gave him. "Maybe," he thought, "losing my job isn't the end of the world. Maybe there's hope after all."

In Montevideo, Uruguay's capital, more than 60 taxi drivers have become Christians. They meet together to pray and read the Bible, and every day they share the good news of Jesus with their passengers.

Tourists and cowboys

Uruguay, the smallest country in South America, is sandwiched between Brazil and Argentina. Tourists from around the world come to enjoy

Cowboy drinking *maté*

Montevideo

Uruguay's beautiful white sandy beaches and pleasant climate.

Away from the coast on the rolling grassy plains and low hills, cowboys raise cattle and sheep on huge farms called *estancias*. A lot of people, like Ricardo, leave the countryside because they think they'll be able to get better jobs and earn more money in the cities. But there aren't enough jobs in the cities for everyone.

An empty place

Most Uruguayans are descendants of settlers from Spain and Italy. Early in the twentieth century, many of them turned their backs on Roman Catholicism. Even

To help you pray for Uruguay

You can thank God for:

- Uruguayans who are listening to the good news about Jesus.
- the groups sharing the gospel in many different places.
- evangelistic teams from Brazil and Argentina telling people in Uruguay about Jesus.

You can ask God:

- that Christians will share their faith with others.
- that Christians working with young people will show them how to follow Jesus.
- to show the people that practicing spiritism and witchcraft can never make them happy.
- to use Christian books and radio broadcasts to help people follow Jesus.

South America

ATLANTIC OCEAN

Paraguay

Brazil

Argentina

Uruguay

Montevideo

ATLANTIC OCEAN

Many Uruguayans are discovering that there's an empty place in their lives when they don't believe in God

Christmas Day lost its name and became "Family Day." A lot of people who thought God didn't matter became agnostics.

Everyone in Uruguay goes to school, and many people go on to study at universities. Most people thought that a good education, a good job and a good pension were far more important than God. They're surprised when they find out this isn't true. There isn't enough work for everyone to have a good job, and there is more crime and violence.

About half of all Uruguayans say they're Catholics, but many of them never go to church. Instead, they're listening to Mormons and Jehovah's Witnesses who go from door to door talking about their beliefs, which are not true to the Bible. Others are listening to spiritists (who contact spirits), and children often wear charms, which they think will keep evil spirits from harming them. The people of Uruguay are discovering that there's an empty place in their lives when they don't believe in God.

God answers prayer

Twelve-year-old Gonzalo heard an evangelist speaking about Jesus and decided to follow him. He wanted to learn all he could about God, Jesus and the Bible, and for the next two years he went to a young people's club.

But Gonzalo's father belonged to a group that practiced a kind of witchcraft called Macumbas. One day he got angry with Gonzalo and told him he could never go to church again. Gonzalo decided he should obey his father, even though he didn't want to. The boys in the club prayed for Gonzalo. Three weeks later, his father changed his mind. Gonzalo came back to the club, and the boys thanked God for answering their prayers so quickly.

Books and Bibles

Carlos and his friends got permission to set up a bookstall in the public square, the busiest spot in town. People stopped to look at the Christian books and Bibles and Carlos and his friends were busy selling books and explaining the gospel. They were so pleased to be able to share the truth about Jesus with so many people who wouldn't otherwise have heard about him. The Christian Literature Crusade also has a specially equipped van to take books all around the country.

In almost every town, Christian churches are growing as Christians share their faith and talk to their friends about Jesus.

Uzbeks

Is Jesus More than the Christians' Prophet?

Who is Jesus?

Akmal and Timur were bored. The two eight-year-old boys lay in the shade of a leafy mulberry tree on a summer afternoon. "It's too hot to play soccer with Zahid and the others in the school yard," grumbled Akmal. "It's too far to go to the river for a swim and I don't have any money for the pool. There's nothing to do."

"Let's go over to my uncle's house and watch a video," suggested Timur. "Maybe he has some new ones. He's got air-conditioning, so at least we can stay cool."

"OK," said Akmal, "anything's better than sitting here doing nothing."

The two boys wandered down the hot, dusty street until they reached Timur's uncle's house. Timur's aunt was busy making bread, but she gave the thirsty boys some cold tea to drink. "You can watch a video with your cousins while I finish baking," she said.

"Hey, here's a new one called 'Iso' (Jesus). I wonder what it's about?" Timur put it in the VCR. They watched the video in silence for a few minutes.

"I don't like movies without gangsters and gunfights or karate," Akmal said doubtfully.

"Hey, look, that guy who was paralyzed can walk now!" Timur said.

"Yeah, and now that girl who was dead is alive again! Wouldn't it be great to be able to do that? I wonder who this guy Jesus is. Is he real? Does it say on the video case?" Akmal asked.

"No, not really ... oh, look! Why are they putting him on that cross? What did he do? Rewind it – I want to know why they're trying to kill him," Timur exclaimed.

"He just said he was king."

"What? Oh ... no! Why doesn't he do another miracle and just get down from there?" Akmal asked. "I can't believe they let him die in the movie. I thought he was a god or something who couldn't die. Wait ... there he is again! He didn't die! Oh, I knew he wouldn't!"

"But why did he die first?" Timur asked. "He did really die, didn't he? Why didn't he just escape? I'm glad he's alive, anyway."

"They just said he had to die to be punished for all the things everyone ever did wrong. You don't think that includes us, do you?"

"It says so ..." said Timur thoughtfully. "Do you think it's a true story? I wish it was. I'd like to meet Jesus and find out how he did those things. He seems like he'd be nice to talk to."

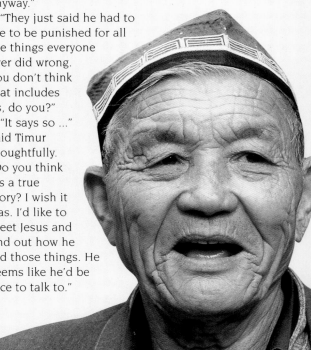

Uzbek family

[Map: showing Kazakhstan, Uzbekistan, Turkmenistan, Iran, Afghanistan, China, with Caspian Sea, Aral Sea, Tashkent, Samarkand labeled]

To help you pray for the Uzbeks

You can thank God for:

- all Uzbek Christians.

- the *Jesus* video in Uzbek.

You can ask God:

- for Uzbeks, both atheists and Muslims, to search for the forgiveness and peace that only Jesus can give.

- to take away any fear the Christians feel as they share Jesus' love and concern with their friends and families.

- that as Uzbek Christians read the New Testament, they will come to know Jesus better.

- to help the people producing Christian radio broadcasts.

- that Christians from other countries will share the good news about Jesus with the people in Uzbekistan.

That night Timur told his father about the video and asked if he knew who Jesus was. "Oh, he's the Christians' prophet," he replied, "but I don't know any more about him than that. If you're so interested in religion, go and ask your grandfather to tell you about our prophet Mohammed. We Uzbeks are Muslims, not Christians."

Timur decided he would go back to his uncle's the next day and watch the video again. He wanted to know more about Jesus.

In the vegetable market in Tashkent

Fact file
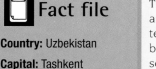

Country: Uzbekistan

Capital: Tashkent

Language: Uzbek

Population: 24,317,851 (18,500,000 are Uzbeks)

Religions: Islam; atheism

Chief exports: Cotton; textiles; gold; natural gas

No religions!
For almost 70 years, Uzbekistan was part of the former Soviet Union. The Communist government made it very difficult for the Uzbek Muslims and Russian and German Christians who lived there to practice their religions. They weren't allowed to teach their beliefs in schools, mosques or churches, and very few people had copies of the Koran or the Bible. Most young Uzbeks, like Timur, only knew about Islam from the little they heard at weddings, birth ceremonies and funerals.

Freedom once more
When the Soviet Union broke up in 1991, Uzbekistan once again became an independent country. Many Uzbeks have returned to their Muslim faith. But there are still lots of problems in Uzbekistan. The people hoped their new freedom would mean that they would have a better life. Instead, more than a million people have no jobs and there are many cotton growers who work hard in the hot sun all day for very little money.

There are more than 23 million Uzbeks, but only about 500 believe in Jesus. Some Christians from other countries have gone there to work, but they often have to share the good news about Jesus quietly.

Vagla

People of the Talking Drums

The fable of the drum

Once upon a time there was a Vagla man who kept getting lost while he was out hunting, and his son had to spend a lot of time looking for him. One day, when out searching for his father, the son reached a river where he heard drumming and singing. He listened carefully, wondering if his father was nearby.

A crocodile lying on the bank offered to take him out into the river to see who was drumming. As he sat on the crocodile's back, the boy looked down into the water and saw people dancing to the drums. "Have you seen my father?" the boy asked them.

"No, he's not here," they replied, "but we'll help you. You can have our drums, and you can beat them whenever your father is lost in the forest. Then he'll be able to find his way back to the village."

Traditional dancer

The boy never had to search for his father again. In fact, the drums sent such clear messages over long distances that the village elders began to use them for the whole village.

Communication

A Vagla chief told this fable to encourage young people in his tribe who were learning to read and write in their own language. He wanted them to understand that what they were doing would help the whole tribe – just as the talking drums do.

Vagla people can use drums to send messages because their language is musical. If someone says a word in a high-pitched tone, it means something different from saying it in a low-pitched one. This makes it possible to beat out messages in musical notes so that everyone can understand what is being "said" by the drums.

Wouldn't this be a great way to make God's message clear to the whole tribe!

The god Kiipo

The Vagla people live in northwest Ghana. There are only about 7,000 of them. They worship a god called Kiipo. The priest of Kiipo sacrifices sheep and cattle to this god at a special rock near the village of Sonyo. They hope that, because they do this, Kiipo will give them enough food and keep them safe from enemies and the evil spirits that they believe lurk in the bush. Every village has its own priest to make special sacrifices of chickens to these spirits to keep them from harming anyone.

Rooftop business

A Vagla village is made up of ten or more rectangular houses, each with a courtyard. The houses are

VAGLA

Ghana

Africa

Ghana

Accra

176

all joined together under one roof and this strong flat roof is used as a street. A lot of village life takes place up on the rooftop and Vagla men, wearing colorful cotton garments, meet there to talk business. They have to remember never to sit or stand still on the ladders leading up to the roof because

they believe the spirits also climb up and down between the yard and the rooftop.

Vagla Christians
Nearly all Vagla Christians are young men who still work with their fathers on family farms. Since they don't earn any money, they can't give much to

pay a pastor's wages. Because their houses are linked together, it's very obvious if someone wants to live or believe in a different way from everyone else. Relatives and village elders often try to force new Christians to take part in the ceremonies and sacrifices to Kiipo.

Translators have finished the Vagla New Testament and are working on the Old

A group of Christians

Testament. Several Vagla Christians have already been to Bible school and have become pastors and evangelists among their own people. Please pray that they will learn how to use fables, proverbs and even the talking drums to make God's message clear to the whole tribe.

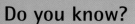

Children on their way to Sunday school

Do you know?

Christians are setting Bible songs to Vagla music. One person who works among the Vagla says that there's a song played on seven antelope horns that sounds like a traffic jam! Although their kind of music might sound like just a lot of noise to us, it's very special to the Vagla. And the Vagla might think the music you like to listen to sounds a bit strange, too!

To help you pray for the Vagla

You can thank God for:

- the New Testament that has been translated into Vagla and the work that is well underway on the translation of the Old Testament.

You can ask God:

- to keep young Vagla Christians faithful to him even when their families try to force them to worship Kiipo.

- that as they learn to read the New Testament, Vagla Christians will discover more about his love, power and the way they should live.

- to help Vagla Christians write stories, fables, songs and books which will explain the Christian message to their people.

- to show Vagla Christians just how important it is to teach their children to know Jesus.

- to demonstrate his power to the village elders and priests of Kiipo, so that they will know that he is more powerful than their god or the evil spirits.

- to help Vagla Christians share the good news about Jesus with their friends.

- that Vagla Christians who are helping with the translation of the Old Testament will be enthusiastic and thorough in their work and that the translation will soon be completed.

Children making their own toys

"Little Venice"

Oil and Indians

"My company's sending me to Venezuela for six months," Jim and Claire's father told them one evening. *"While I'm there, you can all come for a vacation!"* Jim and Claire were so excited, they tried to find out all they could about Venezuela.

Jim found an encyclopedia. *"It says here,"* he said, *"that Venezuela is the most northerly country in South America and has miles of sandy beaches. It also has mountains, plains, tropical jungles and more than 20 national parks."*

Bird of paradise flower

Caracas · Venezuela · Trinidad · Guyana · Colombia · Brazil

Rain forest

Claire was reading another book. "It also has some of the biggest oil fields in the world," she said. "They're at the north end of Lake Maracaibo. The Goaro Indians, who build their houses on stilts over the water, live nearby. When the first European explorers saw their villages they called the region Venezuela, 'little Venice,' because the Italian city of Venice is also built on water."

"That was a long time ago," Jim added. "It says here that most Venezuelans live in cities now. Some of them are very rich and live in huge houses with bars on the windows, alarm systems and guard dogs to protect them from thieves. But not everyone's rich. A lot of Venezuelans live in cramped houses made of metal, bits of wood and plastic. I wonder if all the children go to school, or just the ones from rich families?"

"This book says that schools are free," Claire said, "and that nearly all the children go to school. Some even start when they're only three years old. But a lot of children from poor families drop out because their families think it's more important for them to earn a little money than to study."

Missionary to the Indians

Five months later, Jim and Claire were in Caracas, the capital city of Venezuela. One day Jacinto, a Venezuelan missionary, came to visit the family. Jim and Claire had lots of questions for Jacinto. "How did you

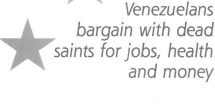

Some Venezuelans bargain with dead saints for jobs, health and money

become a missionary?" "Where are you working?" "What do you do?" they wanted to know.

Jacinto smiled. "I learned about Jesus and decided to follow him when I was in college. Then a friend took me to a camp where I met some missionaries working among Indians in this country. The government doesn't usually let missionaries from other countries live among them because they're afraid that they'll bring diseases and harm the Indians. But I could live with them, and I wanted to

![hand icon] **To help you pray for Venezuela**

You can thank God for:

● the *Jesus* video and its powerful message.

● Christians who go to Indian villages to share the good news about Jesus.

● Venezuelan Christians who go as missionaries to other countries.

You can ask God:

● that many people in Venezuela will decide to follow Jesus.

● that rich people who are Christians will help the poor and support missionaries.

● to help people understand that promises made to dead saints can't help them, but that Jesus is alive and is always ready to help anyone who trusts in him.

● to show people the foolishness and danger of trusting in charms.

Contrasting buildings in Caracas

tell these people more people about Jesus. So now I live in an Indian village in the rain forests in the southwest of the country. I'm just one of the many Venezuelan Christians there. We often use Christian recordings in the different Indian languages to tell people about God's love, and we've translated the New Testament into some of their languages. Some of the Indians are fierce and warlike, but others are peaceable and gentle. A lot of them know nothing of the world beyond their thatched houses, small vegetable plots and the wild pigs, monkeys and plumed birds that live in the forest."

Telling the good news

"That must be a lot different from life in the city," Jim said.

"That's right," Jacinto said. "From the time it was discovered by Christopher Columbus in 1498 until it became independent in 1830, Venezuela belonged to Spain. Because of this, almost everyone believes in God and Jesus. At Easter time people parade through the city streets carrying statues of Jesus on the cross and singing sad songs, but their religion doesn't seem to make a big difference in their lives. Getting a good job, staying healthy and having plenty of money are so important that a lot of people make promises to dead saints to bargain for such things. Others buy charms when they need help – but they rarely work! Not many people really understand who Jesus is, that he died and rose again and helps everyone who trusts in him.

"Some of the churches have started video clubs. There's one really good video, called the *Jesus* film, that shows the life of Jesus. It's a great way of sharing our faith with others and it's such a powerful story that lots of

Do you know?

In southeast Venezuela, the Caroni River rushes down more than 3,000 feet over Mount Auyantepui to form the Angel Falls, the highest waterfall in the world. The hydroelectric power generated by the Caroni River supplies three-quarters of Venezuela's electricity.

people use the prayer at the end of the video to tell Jesus that they want to follow him.

"Even though the evangelical churches in Venezuela are quite small, we're praying that many more people in our own country and around the world will hear the good news about Jesus. Some of us have become missionaries in other countries too, and we know our churches pray for us, asking God to bring lots more people to know Jesus as their friend."

"We'll pray, too!" promised Jim and Claire.

God is Faithful

Not afraid!

One by one, and as silently as possible, the montagnard Christians climbed the notched pole into Nai's bamboo and thatch house for the prayer meeting. They knew they would be punished if the agents of the Communist government caught them, but they weren't afraid.

Suddenly, two men burst into the house and grabbed Nai. They marched him away in the darkness, shouting, "You're under arrest. There is no God!" Like shadows, the other Christians slipped away home, wondering who had betrayed them.

Statue of Confucius in a temple in Hanoi

Although the laws of Vietnam say that the people are free to follow whatever religion they choose, the government still persecutes many Christians. Throughout the mountain region of Vietnam thousands of tribal people, or *montagnards*, are becoming Christians. Local government officials have burned their homes and churches and have put many people, even children, in prison. But they haven't been able to make them stop telling others about Jesus.

Vietnamese Christians who live in villages, towns and cities on the coastal plain are sharing the good news of Jesus, too. Pastors who have been put in prison have gone on sharing the good news about Jesus with all the other prisoners – and with their guards as well!

War

France ruled Vietnam from 1858 to 1954. Some Vietnamese people became very rich and lived in magnificent houses in the cities, but most people were poor. Even now, many people in the countryside live in houses made of bamboo and thatch, and some fishermen and their families live on small boats.

The Vietnamese wanted to be free, and in 1954 they defeated the French in a fierce battle. Vietnam was divided into two parts: the

Do you know?

Vietnam is a long, narrow country in southeast Asia. Look at the map and the picture to the right to see if you understand what the Vietnamese mean when they say it looks like a bamboo carrying pole with a basket of rice hanging from each end. The two areas that look like baskets are the Red River Delta in the north and the Mekong Delta in the south. These are the most fertile parts of the country, where they grow most of their rice.

Most westerners find it difficult to learn to speak Vietnamese. This is because there are six tones in the language and the same word can be said six different ways, each with a different meaning. So the word *ma* can mean but, mother, ghost, tomb, a young rice plant or a horse – all depending on the tone!

North, which was under Communist rule, and the "free" South.

The Communists wanted to control the South as well, and they sent guerrilla soldiers to force the people to follow them. America started to help the South, and the North fought

180

 To help you pray for Vietnam

You can thank God for:

- Christians who have followed Jesus faithfully even when they have been persecuted or put in prison.

- the many tribal people living in the mountain areas who are coming to know Jesus and are sharing his love with others.

You can ask God:

- that every tribal group in Vietnam will hear that when Jesus died on the cross, he was the perfect sacrifice for sins and that the sacrifices they make to the spirits will never take away their sins.

- to help boys and girls, as well as grown-ups, talk about Jesus with their friends and families.

- to make it possible for every Christian family to have a Bible.

- that the students who are allowed to study in Bible school will become faithful evangelists and pastors.

- for real peace and freedom so that all the people of Vietnam can worship him without fear of punishment.

Many Vietnamese Christians have suffered for their faith, but the church keeps growing

Carrying vegetables in traditional baskets

Tribal houses

Fact file

Area: 127,250 sq. mi. (slightly larger than Germany, but it's a long, narrow country)

Population: 79,831,650

Capital: Hanoi

Religions: Buddhism; animism (tribal); Christianity

Language: Vietnamese, but 88 languages are spoken

Chief exports: Oil; fish; rice

back. Many people died in this terrible war which ended in 1975 when the government of South Vietnam was overthrown. Once again, North and South Vietnam became one country.

Foreigners, including most missionaries, fled the country. Thousands of South Vietnamese, who were afraid the Communists would treat them badly, tried to escape. Some reached safety and have gone to live in many countries around the world.

Good News

Before the French came to Vietnam, missionaries had started to teach the Vietnamese about Jesus. There were Vietnamese and tribal Christians in towns and villages throughout the land. Their churches are called "Good News" churches. In 1994, the Vietnamese government gave permission for Bibles to be printed again and for a few Christians to be trained as pastors and evangelists.

Changes

After the war, Christian businessmen and aid organizations went to Vietnam to show the people they were not forgotten. Vietnamese Christians in other countries are going back to Vietnam to help those in need. It's a very beautiful country and is becoming popular with tourists once again.

Although many Christians have suffered for their faith under Communism, the church keeps on growing.

Wodaabe

Beautiful Nomads of the Sahel

Do you know?
The Wodaabe and their cattle, goats, sheep and camels often walk as much as 1,000 miles a year in their search for water and pasture in the Sahel.

Teach us about Jesus!

One Sunday morning in 1989, two young Wodaabe (woe-dah-bee) men walked into a church in Niger. The service had already started, but they walked right up to the front. Everyone wondered what would happen next. The men looked very poor. Had they come to ask for food? When they reached the front of the church, they turned around. "Will you show us how to follow the Christian way?" they asked. "We want you to teach us and our children about Jesus!"

The people in the church were so excited! Missionaries went with the two men back to their camp and taught the men, their wives and children about Jesus. Some, like the two men, decided to follow Jesus. Now they're telling others about Jesus because they want them to know that Jesus gives joy and hope – especially when life is hard.

Always on the move

And life is often very hard for the Wodaabe. They live in the Sahel, in Niger and Chad. The Wodaabe are nomads, traveling from place to place with their camels, cattle, sheep and goats. During the long dry season, the men often have to walk five hours a day to find water and pasture. When they move their camp, they pack all their belongings on the backs of their camels. "We're like birds in a bush," a village elder explained. "We never settle down, and we leave no trace of where we've been."

Their food is very simple. They eat porridge made from millet, but milk is the most important part of their diet. If the animals don't have enough food, they become weak and have no milk. Then the people become very hungry and sick. When there's no rain for several years, the cattle die and the people starve.

Wodaabe taboos

The Wodaabe have many taboos, or things they aren't allowed to do. Some of these might seem strange to us. Wodaabe means "the people of the taboo." How would you feel if you didn't have a name until you were 12 years old? Or if your mother was never allowed to talk to you or call you by name because you were the oldest child in your family?

Wodaabe men parade in an all-male beauty contest

We're taught to look people in the eyes when we talk to them, but the Wodaabe are forbidden to do this. These are just a few of the many taboos that control their lives.

 To help you pray for the Wodaabe

You can thank God for:

- each Wodaabe Christian.
- Wodaabe believers in Bible school who want to teach their people about Jesus.

You can ask God:

- that whole families will decide to follow Jesus so they can worship together and help each other as they live and move as a group.
- to help the Wodaabe realize that taboos don't have to control their lives.
- to bring more missionaries to the Wodaabe, and help them as they learn the Wodaabe Fulfulde language.
- to help Wodaabe Christians as they change parts of their culture that aren't pleasing to Jesus.
- that people will see the beauty of Jesus in the lives of believers and will want to follow him too.

 Fact file

Countries: Niger; Chad; Mali

Numbers: About 100,000

Language: Wodaabe Fulfulde

Religion: Folk Islam

Occupation: Nomadic herders

Beauty – inside and out

The Wodaabe think they're the most beautiful people on earth. Every year they hold special celebrations to show off their good looks. Like the other young men, Jebbi wanted to look really handsome on the day of the festival. So he rubbed yellow powder into his skin to make it look lighter. Then he tried to make his eyes and lips look bigger by drawing around them with a black substance called *kohl*. Since a high forehead is a sign of great beauty, he shaved the hair from the front of his head. Finally, he painted a line down his nose to make it look longer. He wanted to be sure he had done everything he could to make himself beautiful, so he hung some little bags of magic powder around his neck. After putting on his lovely hand-embroidered robe, turban, and copper and brass jewelry hung with beads and cowrie shells, he was ready to dance with the other men before their admiring audience.

Like all the Wodaabe, Jebbi wants to be beautiful on the outside. But while we only see what people are like on the outside, God looks at our hearts. He wants us to ask Jesus for forgiveness for all the wrong things we've done. Only then can our hearts be clean and pure and beautiful to him.

Following the nomads

How can you teach people to follow Jesus if they're always moving from place to place? More than 100 Wodaabe people have decided to follow Jesus, and they want others to know him, too. A few have become evangelists, and they move from camp to camp telling people about Jesus. Others are at Bible

school, learning more about Jesus and how to teach their people. Missionaries and evangelists are praying that whole families will come to know Jesus so that they can learn about Jesus together and encourage one another, especially when life is difficult.

Xhosa

Red-Blanket People of the Transkei

Jill, a missionary in South Africa, made friends with many Xhosa (koh'-suh) children. Here are a few stories she told about some of those she met.

God changes a whole family

Zawa and Sikhono were brothers from a big family in Johannesburg. One day a friend took them to a special meeting for children. At this meeting, they heard for the first time that God loves them. They decided to follow Jesus, and a few weeks later they went to a children's camp to learn more about Jesus.

Shops in a squatter area

They had lots of fun at the camp, but they liked the Bible talks the best. They had never realized how special they were to God. When they went home, they talked constantly about all the fun they'd had and all the exciting things they'd learned. Their alcoholic father and tired, overworked mother could hardly believe all that Zawa and Sikhono told them about the way God is always ready to help people who

trust in him.

A few months later, Jill showed a video of the camp at Zawa's and Sikhono's school. When it was over, their father jumped up to say he'd started to go to church because of what his sons had told him. He said he was so happy with God in his life that he didn't want to drink alcohol any more and was giving his wife enough money

to care for the family. Their mother told everyone that Jesus had changed her sons and her husband so much that she, too, had become a Christian. God used two brothers to bring the entire family to follow Jesus, and to change their lives completely!

"Leave me alone, Satan!"

Daniel, a Xhosa boy who lives in the city of Pretoria, decided to follow Jesus at an evangelistic meeting in a big tent. When Jill met him a few days later, he didn't look very happy.

"What's wrong?" she asked him.

"I'm very angry with Satan," he

Do you know?

To speak the Xhosa language, you need to make click sounds by pulling your tongue sharply away from the roof of your mouth or from the teeth at the side of your mouth.

- Botswana
- Namibia
- XHOSA
- Johannesburg
- South Africa
- Lesotho
- XHOSA
- Cape Town

Fact file

Country: South Africa

Numbers: About 7,500,000

Religions: Christianity; African traditional religions

Languages: Xhosa; English; Afrikaans

said. "I was just in a store, and Satan told me to steal like I used to."

"Did you?"

"No! But I can't believe he's bothering me like that," he replied. Daniel was very wise, because he realized that Satan was his enemy. He also knew that God would help him to be stronger than Satan.

A bad boy

Bhekinkosi was one of the naughtiest boys in Gugulethu, a poor part of Cape Town. Sometimes he even jumped on the back of moving vans for free rides, but since he was crippled in one leg and couldn't run very fast, angry drivers often caught and beat him. But when he went to a Christian meeting, Bhekinkosi was very serious when he realized how bad he had been. He wanted to be good. Tears were rolling down his face when he prayed, "Lord Jesus, it is I, Bhekinkosi. I'm a bad boy. Please make my heart clean and come and live in me forever."

Life in a township

Most of the seven million Xhosa people live in the Eastern and Western Cape provinces of South Africa. Some of them have been to university and have become teachers, lawyers, businessmen and government officials. Many others are poor and have never been to school. Lots of them live in townships on the edges of big cities where they work as servants or in factories. Others work in the gold or diamond mines, but some have no work at all.

Village life

Life is quite different in Xhosa villages. Families live in beautiful round huts with a fireplace in the center and mud benches built against the walls. Village children work hard. They often have to walk for miles to get water, firewood and food, and little boys know how to look after big herds of cattle. Village women wear black turbans and red blankets, which they dye themselves. They always wear the red blankets when they worship their ancestors. Even though more than half of the Xhosa people say they

are Christians, some of them still practice their old traditions as well.

Jill loved to listen to the Xhosa people singing. Even small village schools have choirs. "I'll always remember dancing and singing with some Xhosa Christians on the mountainside at night," she said. "They sang, 'This Jesus of mine, he has power.' I pray that God's power will work in the lives of many Xhosa people."

 ## To help you pray for the Xhosa

You can thank God for:

- every Xhosa who has come to know Jesus as their savior and friend.

- the modern translation of the Bible in Xhosa.

- Xhosa Christians who are part of the new government in South Africa.

- getting rid of the terrible law that separated people of different colors and races in South Africa.

You can ask God:

- to help Xhosa Christians who run Bible camps and Sunday schools, that lots of Xhosa children will be excited as they learn that Jesus loves and cares for them.

- to encourage Xhosa Christians to write Bible songs in their own language.

- that Xhosa Christians will always be ready to share Jesus' love with others.

Along the Silk Road

Go in but never come out ...

The Takli-Makan (tah-klah mah-kahn) Desert is one of the loneliest and most desolate places on earth. Fierce winds often howl across its huge sand dunes and rocky outcrops, whipping up whirling clouds of sand. In winter it's freezing cold and in summer it's scorching hot and there's almost no water to be found. It's no wonder it's called "the go in but never come out" desert, for that is what its name means. Yet it's an area rich in minerals such as coal, gas, oil, gold and gems, and a number of companies are developing the outer edges of the desert to mine these resources.

Do you know?

The great Chinese inventions of silk, gunpowder, paper making and printing were all carried along the ancient Silk Road, through Xinjiang, to the west.
Nestorian Christians traveled east along this route in the fifth century AD and Buddhism and Islam came to China along this road.

On the way to market

Fact file

Xinjiang is a self-governing region of China

Area: 127,400 sq. mi.

Population: 16,610,000 (60% of the population belong to the nine Muslim peoples of the region. These include Uyghurs, Kazakhs, Kyrgyz, Hui and Tajiks.)

Main city: Urumchi

Products: Silk; cotton; fruit; oil; gas

This huge desert, which is almost as big as Germany, is in Xinjiang (*sin-chi-ang*) in northwest China. But not all Xinjiang is desert. Xinjiang is surrounded by spectacular mountain ranges. Water from these mountains feeds the broad pasture lands for sheep and herds of cattle and horses. There are fertile oases, too, where fruit and vegetables grow in abundance.

Muslims and Christians

Let's visit a Uyghur family in the south of Xinjiang. The family gives us a warm welcome to their flat-roofed home built inside a courtyard. Soon we're nibbling sunflower seeds and drinking tea. As we talk, they tell us, "More than half the people living in Xinjiang are Muslims, and the Uyghur are the largest of the nine Muslim groups living here. The

Communist government tried to get rid of all religions, but many Muslims in Xinjiang remained faithful to their beliefs and continued to pray five times a day. The government has a different attitude now and has even given money to rebuild mosques, open an Islamic college and print Muslim books. We're very grateful to Allah."

We ask if there are any Christians in Xinjiang. "Oh, yes, my grandmother told me that about 100 years ago some Uyghurs did become Christians. Most of them were killed or fled to other countries during a time of persecution and violence. I don't think there are any Uyghur Christians now, though. Of course, there are a lot of Christians among the Han Chinese who have been sent here by the government to try to control Xinjiang. Sometimes they try

Russia

Kazakhstan

Mongolia

CELESTIAL MOUNTAINS
● Urumchi
Xingjiang
TAKLI-MAKAN DESERT

China

India

Veiled Uyghur women

![hand icon] **To help you pray for Xinjiang**

You can thank God for:

- Christians who have gone to work in Xinjiang so they can share the good news of Jesus' love with the people living there.

- the few Uyghurs who have started to follow Jesus.

You can ask God:

- to break down the barriers of fear, hatred and suspicion between the Muslim peoples of Xinjiang and the Han Chinese.

- that Chinese Christians working in Xinjiang will have courage to share his love with their Muslim neighbors.

- to help Christians who have come from other countries to learn the languages of the local peoples so that they can share with them who Jesus is and why he died.

- that his Holy Spirit will help each Uyghur Christian to read the New Testament, and understand what it means to be a follower of Jesus.

- that many people will tune in to the Christian radio broadcasts in Uyghur and other languages spoken in Xinjiang.

to tell us about the love of someone called Jesus who, they say, is God's Son. But why should we listen to them? After all, they've been sent here to control us!"

A Sunday market

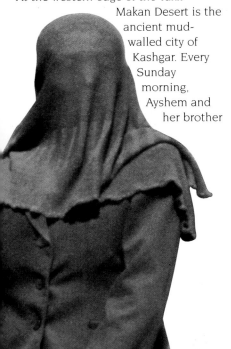

At the western edge of the Takli-Makan Desert is the ancient mud-walled city of Kashgar. Every Sunday morning, Ayshem and her brother Aziz load their flat donkey-cart with fruit and vegetables to take to the market in Kashgar. People come from far and wide, on bicycles, motorcycles, tractors and donkey-carts to sell their produce and buy things to take home.

As soon as they arrive at the friendly, busy, noisy market place, Ayshem and Aziz set out their vegetables on the ground. There's plenty to buy: fruit and vegetables, flowers, knives, Atlas silk cloth, blankets, nan bread, chickens, horses and even camels. Everyone wants a bargain!

Leaving her brother to sell their vegetables, Ayshem wanders off to meet her friends. She's wearing a colorful, knee-length dress, long trousers and embroidered cap. Her long black hair is neatly plaited. She's glad she doesn't have to wear a heavy brown veil like some of the women. The open-air theater is their favorite place in the market. They watch skilled acrobats, dancers and conjurers perform. When Aziz's turn comes to join his friends, he goes to watch the horses as they race along a track.

Young men studying the Koran

The Silk Road

Marco Polo, the famous thirteenth-century traveler, passed through Xinjiang along the Silk Road, an ancient trade route that connected Europe and the Middle East with China. Two friars went with him to teach the people the Christian faith. Only a few people have gone to Xinjiang to tell the people about the love of God. Today there are Christians working in Xinjiang, as well as Christian tourists traveling the Silk Road.

Yanomamo

The Children of the Moon

Fierce ...

The Yanomamo live deep in the rain forests of South America, in a region called Amazonia on the borders of northwestern Brazil and southern Venezuela. One of their legends says that long ago one of the first living creatures on earth shot the moon with an arrow. The blood of the moon fell to the earth and turned into the first people – the Yanomamo, "Children of the Moon."

Since they were born as a result of this battle with the moon, they call themselves the Fierce People.

The Yanomamo live up to this name. Villages are always fighting other villages, and people are always fighting each other, too. When they're raiding another village, the Yanomamo men cover themselves with charcoal and poison the tips of their arrows.

Yanomamo hunters

Fact file

Countries: Southern Venezuela; northwest Brazil

Numbers: About 23,000; there are probably 15,000 in Venezuela

Religion: Animism

Occupations: Farming; hunting

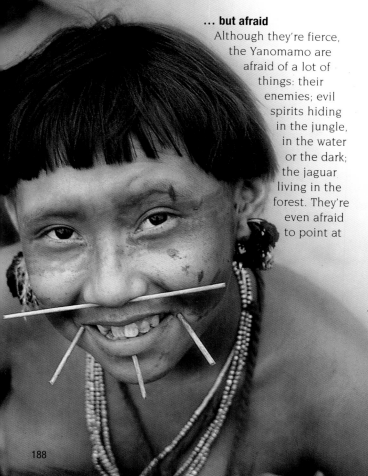

... but afraid

Although they're fierce, the Yanomamo are afraid of a lot of things: their enemies; evil spirits hiding in the jungle, in the water or the dark; the jaguar living in the forest. They're even afraid to point at the moon in case their fingers rot and fall off.

The medicine man asks the spirits to guard them and to give them help when anyone is sick. He also asks the spirits to hurt their enemies.

Not worth much

Since she learned to walk, Little Girl (she doesn't have a name) went out with her mother to get firewood in a small basket on her back. She was always tired and her legs hurt, but no one noticed. Some girl babies are killed as soon as they're born. Little girls aren't worth much to the Yanomamo.

One day, when she was only four years old, a man from another village asked Little Girl's father if he could have her to be his wife. In exchange, he gave her father a dog. Now Little Girl has to look after the men in her new family, gather the firewood, cook and work in the gardens. She has to work hard, and she's often hungry.

Living in one big house

A Yanomamo village is really like one big circular house with a big courtyard in the middle, and is called a *shabano*. Each family collects trees, vines and thatch from the jungle to help build the *shabano* and cover the roof of their own section. The outside wall of the *shabano* separates the village from the jungle, but there aren't any inside walls. If a Yanomamo person sees that someone

 ## To help you pray for the Yanomamo

You can thank God for:

- the New Testament in Yanomamo.

- those who are teaching the Yanomamo health care, reading and writing.

- church leaders, evangelists and Sunday school teachers.

You can ask God:

- that Yanomamo Christians will tell others about Jesus.

- to show the Yanomamo that when they believe in Jesus they don't have to be afraid of the spirits.

- to help Yanomamo Christians speak out against fighting and the terrible way women and girls are treated.

- that the Yanomamo will understand that God created them to be good, not fierce.

You can speak Yanomamo

Where are you going? is "Wedi hami wa huu?" (we-di ha-mi wa **huu**)

Did you arrive? is "Wa walokei kufawa?" (wa **wa**-lo-ke ku-fa-wa)

Are you healthy? is "Wa demi tawa?" (wa **de**-mi ta-wa)

else doesn't want to be disturbed, he acts like a "ghost" (like he's not really there!) to give the other person privacy. People get in and out of the village through little holes left in the outside wall.

Outside the village, the Yanomamo cut down the jungle to make fields for their manioc, plantains, bananas, gourds and sweet potatoes. The men hunt wild pigs, tapir, armadillo and monkeys in the jungle for meat while the women work in the fields.

Help for the Yanomamo
Until the 1940s the Yanomamo didn't have much contact with the outside world, but when they did, a lot of them died from catching "white man's" diseases. More than 1,000 Yanomamo died in the

1980s when mercury, which was used by illegal miners to find gold, poisoned their rivers. Since then, both Brazil and Venezuela have set aside huge areas of the rain forest especially for the Yanomamo so that other people can't hurt them.

When the New Tribes Mission came in 1950 to tell the Yanomamo about Jesus, they found many people who were sick. The missionaries helped them, prayed with them and learned all they could

about them. They also wrote down the difficult Yanomamo language, and now there's a Yanomamo New Testament. At first, only a few Yanomamo people seemed interested in hearing about God, the Great Spirit, who loves them. But God is changing lives, and now there are about 300 Yanomamo Christians in Venezuela and more than 100 in Brazil. Some Yanomamo

Christians are being trained to teach the people in their villages to read and write, and they'll also be part of the government's program to help the Yanomamo. Other Yanomamo, like Maloco, want to tell others about Jesus. He was only eight years old when he decided to follow Jesus. "Don't laugh at me because I'm small," he said. "I want to tell everybody about Jesus."

In a *shabano*

Yao-Mien

Children of the Dragon-dog

A tribal legend

A strange creature, half-dragon, half-dog, returned from his long journey across the seas. He had killed the enemy of the emperor of China, and now he had come to claim the promised reward, the emperor's beautiful daughter. They had six fine sons and six lovely daughters who, the legend says, were the first ancestors of the Yao.

Mountain village

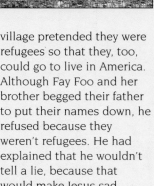

Working in a paddy field

Fact file

The name "Yao" refers to 12 different tribal groups. Each group has its own name. They speak different languages, wear different kinds of clothes and build different kinds of houses.

Countries where there are Yao peoples:
China (700,000)
North Thailand (40,000)
Laos (50,000)
Vietnam (240,000)
USA (25,000)

Mountain homes

"Yao" really refers to a number of different tribal groups, each with its own name, that live high up in the mountains of northern Thailand, Laos, Vietnam and southern China. One of these groups is the Yao-Mien.

Let's visit one of their villages in north Thailand. Most of the houses are built from wood, but the poorer families live in houses with bamboo walls, grass roofs and dirt floors. The villagers keep pigs and chickens. We might even see a water buffalo plowing a rice paddy field. The Yao-Mien grow mountain rice and other crops like maize, soya beans and peanuts in fields on the hillsides. The government doesn't allow them to grow opium anymore (although a few people still smoke it).

Sadly, some teenagers have given in to peer pressure from their Thai school friends to take drugs.

A heavenly home

Fay Foo comes to meet us. She is wearing beautifully embroidered clothes and a black turban with a red, fluffy collar around her neck. About ten years ago, refugees from the country of Laos came to stay in their village. Thai officials said that any refugee who wanted to live in America should go to the nearby refugee center. Everyone in the village was excited, and about 80 families from her village pretended they were refugees so that they, too, could go to live in America. Although Fay Foo and her brother begged their father to put their names down, he refused because they weren't refugees. He had explained that he wouldn't tell a lie, because that would make Jesus sad.

"When we followed the spirits, we thought the most important things in life were money, our fields and our feasts," he said. "When we first left the spirits and did Christian things, the change was only on the outside. Later, we realized that Jesus wanted a change deep

 ## To help you pray for the Yao-Mien

You can thank God for:

- the *Jesus* film.
- the Old Testament translation team.

You can ask God:

- that many people will listen to the Christian radio programs.
- that people will learn to follow Jesus at the new center in Thailand.
- that those who have studied at Bible school will help people understand the Bible.
- for many people to share the good news about Jesus with the Yao-Mien people.
- that Christians will help and encourage Yao people wherever they live.

A Yao-Mien story

Welcoming visitors is very important in Yao-Mien culture. This little story describes the reward of being kind even to a visitor who is unwelcome.

One day, a big snake came to visit two sisters. The older sister refused to invite the snake into the house. She wouldn't give it a seat to sit on, water to wash in, a bed to lie on, or food to eat. The younger sister, however, welcomed the snake and gave it everything it needed. During the night, she discovered the snake was really a handsome prince in disguise.

You can guess the rest of the story!

inside our hearts." He reminded them that Jesus had promised them a home in heaven that was a thousand times more wonderful than America.

It was true – there was a difference between the Christians and the animists in Fay Foo's village. The Christians no longer worshipped the spirits when they were sick. Instead, they prayed to God in Jesus' name. They were always ready to help others and pray for them. Many of the Christians who had never been to school had learned to read so that they could sing songs from the hymnbook and read the New Testament.

Fay Foo is excited that the *Jesus* film is being translated into the Yao-Mien language. She's sure that it will bring many of her people to follow Jesus. She's excited, too, that most of the Old Testament has been translated into her language. Soon the Yao-Mien will have the whole Bible in their language.

Reaching out

The Yao-Mien Christians have saved money to buy a large plot of land in northern Thailand. They plan to build a conference center there, a radio-recording studio and a hostel for the children who have to leave their village homes high up in the mountains to study at high schools in town. The Christians want the hostel to be a happy place where the children will learn to love Jesus and to share his love with their friends.

The Yao-Mien living in other countries are able to listen to Christian radio broadcasts, and some have become Christians and are learning more about Jesus. Some Yao-Mien in America are praying about becoming missionaries to their own people in South East Asia.

Land of the Queen of Sheba

An ancient land

Do you remember the Bible story of the Queen of Sheba? In the Old Testament, in the book of 1 Kings 10:1–13, you can read about how she and King Solomon gave each other amazingly expensive gifts. The Queen of Sheba probably came from what is now the Arabian land of Yemen, and the great cities of her kingdom are buried beneath the desert sands. More than 1,500 years after the Queen of Sheba lived, Yemen became a Muslim country.

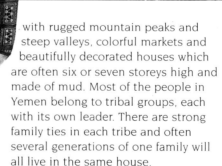

Curved daggers form part of the traditional dress of Yemen

Do you know?

In many parts of Yemen, the mountainsides are terraced to make extra fields where crops can be grown. Some of these terraced fields are more than a thousand years old.

The palace on the rock of Wadi Dhahr

Yemen, at the southern tip of the Arabian Peninsula, was once thought to be one of the most mysterious countries in the world since few people were ever allowed to visit it. It is a beautiful place, with rugged mountain peaks and steep valleys, colorful markets and beautifully decorated houses which are often six or seven storeys high and made of mud. Most of the people in Yemen belong to tribal groups, each with its own leader. There are strong family ties in each tribe and often several generations of one family will all live in the same house.

The country's most important export used to be frankincense, but now it is oil.

Dinner guests

Wearing his white turban and *zanna* (ankle-length cotton tunic), Gadeed watched closely as his father greeted his guests. The Europeans were interested in everything: the mud-walled pen where the goats were tethered, the room storing grain from the harvest, even his sister making bread.

Gadeed also watched as his sister kneaded the dough and slapped it against the sides of the mud oven. A fire blazed at the bottom of the oven, and, unless she was very careful, the flat bread could easily slip off the side into the fire. Later, sitting together on the floor, the men ate chicken, rice and vegetables. Gadeed carefully poured the coffee. After the meal, his father would show the guests his new water pump and vineyard.

To help you pray for Yemen

You can thank God for:

- the few Yemeni Christians.
- Christians from other countries who live and work in Yemen.
- the Christian radio broadcasts that are beamed into Yemen.

You can ask God:

- to safeguard the letters that listeners send to the Christian broadcasting company from being opened by Yemeni officials and that the Christian literature sent back to them arrives safely.
- to bring whole families to know and love him so that they can help one another to follow Jesus.
- that as Yemenis read the Koran they will notice what it says about Jesus and will want to find out more about him.
- to use Bibles in Arabic, which are quietly given to Yemenis who ask, to help them understand that the true way to know God is through trusting in Jesus alone.

First, however, Gadeed's father placed a copy of the Koran on a special stand and then read aloud several passages about Isa (the Muslim name for Jesus). Gadeed was sorry when his father put the Koran away and the guests talked about other things: gold, silk and carpets in the *souk* (market), decorated glass windows and curved daggers.

Suddenly a booming noise from the nearby mosque made the guests jump. Through a loudspeaker, a voice was calling people to prayer. The guests looked around at their Muslim hosts and wished they could tell the veiled women and fierce-looking men that Jesus really is the Son of God, who offers them complete forgiveness and a new life.

North and South

For many years, North and South Yemen were separate countries. South Yemen was Communist, while North Yemen, made up of warring tribes, was strongly Muslim. Then, in 1990, the two countries became one, with Sana'a as its capital. The president wants to unite his 18 million people, but there are many problems and differences between the people.

For a long time, Christians have tried to talk to people in Yemen about Jesus. It's hard because Muslims are proud of their religion and all Yemenis are expected to be Muslims. Because families are very close, it would be unthinkable for one member of the

family to choose another religion. Such a person is considered a traitor who deserves to die. There are a few Yemeni Christians. Unfortunately, most Muslims think all foreigners are Christians. So when they see the terrible things people do on foreign TV shows, they have a bad impression of what Christians are like.

Yemenis are Muslims, and they think a person who chooses another religion is a traitor

Zimbabwe

Promises and Poverty

Forgiven!

Stephen Lungi couldn't believe his ears. The preacher said, "Some people are so mixed up inside, they'll even kick paraffin stoves!" How did the preacher know that he'd been so mad when his stove wouldn't light that morning that he'd kicked it right across the floor?

Stephen and his friends had gone to the meeting to make trouble. Instead, he was surprised to find that Jesus was real, and that he had to ask him to forgive his sins and change his heart. And what a change there had to be!

When Stephen was a little boy, his mother had left. He stayed with his grandmother, but she was so poor he'd had to scavenge for food. He hated his mother for what she had done to him. But when God forgave him, Stephen knew that he had to forgive his mother as well. One day Stephen did meet his mother again, and he told her how God had helped him to forgive her. She was so sorry for what she'd done, and Stephen helped her to trust in Jesus.

Helping others

Like Stephen and his mother, a lot of Zimbabweans are finding that Jesus is the friend who is always ready to help them. Some have become strong Christians through the work of organizations like Scripture Union, who meet in schools and run camps for young people. Others are learning to follow Jesus in their churches and through Christian friends.

Do you know?

Almost half the population of Zimbabwe is under 15 years of age, and about 600,000 children are orphans. Many of their parents have died from AIDS.

Fact file

Area: 150,804 sq. mi.

Population: 11,669,029

Capital: Harare

Official language: English

Religions: Christianity; traditional religions

Chief exports: Tobacco; gold; nickel; steel; iron alloys

Christians in Zimbabwe are praying for a new beginning in their country

When Macmillan went to agricultural college, his friends laughed at him. "You're wasting your father's money," they told him. They don't laugh at him any more, because Macmillan's crops always grow better. But Macmillan has forgiven them for teasing him, and he's helping them to improve their farms. "God loves them as much he loves me," he says, "so I can show them his love by helping them."

194

You can thank God for:

- every Christian in Zimbabwe.
- Christians who help the poor and care for those who are sick, unemployed or orphans.

You can ask God:

- that he will be with missionaries, evangelists and church workers as they tell others the good news about Jesus.
- that Christians will reach out to the many orphans, giving them love, care and hope in Jesus.
- to give Christians hope and courage to trust him even when they are sick, homeless or have no money.
- to use Christian books, leaflets, radio and TV programs to help Zimbabweans learn more about Jesus.
- for wise leaders who will do what's best for their country and the people.

Africa

Zimbabwe

Victoria Falls

Lioness

Zambia

LAKE KARIBA

Harare

Zimbabwe

Botswana

Mozambique

South Africa

The smoke that thunders

Some parts of Zimbabwe are quite spectacular. The Zambezi River in the west, which forms the border with Zambia, cascades over the Victoria Falls. There's so much spray and noise that local people call the Falls "the smoke that thunders." Further east, the Zambezi has been dammed to form Lake Kariba. It's one of the largest man-made lakes in the world and provides enough hydroelectric power for both Zambia and Zimbabwe. Zimbabwe's national parks are full of elephants, lions, cheetahs, hyenas and rhinos.

Promises not kept

But Zimbabwe has many problems, and fewer people go there now as tourists. White people ruled Zimbabwe for almost the entire twentieth century. They became wealthy from mining gold and nickel, and some of them owned huge farms. They employed Africans to work in the mines and on the farms. In 1980, after years of fighting, the country gained independence and Africans became the new leaders. The new government promised the people land of their own to farm. The government has divided up some of the big farms, where crops like tobacco used to be grown for sale, and given Africans plots of lands. But the plots are small, and a lot of farmers barely manage to grow enough food for their families to eat. Then, in the year 2000, groups of thugs forced some of the remaining white farmers from their land and destroyed their homes. There are huge areas of land that aren't being used because no one helps poor farmers to settle or learn

how to use the land properly. In the towns, too, there is a lot of unemployment and young people find it very hard to get work. Another big problem in Zimbabwe is AIDS, which kills many people – and their children become orphans.

Jesus is our friend

Despite all of these problems, there are Zimbabweans like Stephen and Macmillan who have come to know Jesus and are helping others. They know that Jesus really is alive and ready to help them when they are poor, sick, lonely and afraid. And Christians in Zimbabwe are praying for a new beginning in their country that will bring hope to their people. They want a government that will rule wisely so their country will be a place where everyone has enough and where people can forgive each other for wrong things done in the past.

Zulus

Mighty Warriors of South Africa

Life is changing

The Zulus are famous for their great armies of well-disciplined, highly trained men. They call these armies impis. The Zulu impi is the only African army that has ever defeated the British army. The Zulus still have a king and a royal family, but the glory of their past is now only a memory. The Zulu way of life is changing, and they don't hold their great feasts and ceremonies very often anymore. A lot of Zulu men have left their families and homesteads in the countryside and gone to South Africa's mines and cities to earn a living. Whole families, too, sometimes go to live in townships on the edge of the cities.

Many Zulus call themselves Christians, but a lot of them still worship their ancestors and practice witchcraft. Sadly, even some churches mix up spirit worship with the Christian message.

Most mothers carry their babies on their backs. This little girl learns about rhythm as her mother moves to the music in a church service.

South Africa

ZULUS
Natal
Lesotho
• Durban

Africa

Fact file

Country: South Africa

Numbers: About 8,500,000

Religions: Christianity; African traditional religions

Language: Zulu, also English and Afrikaans

Zulu stories

A lady called Jill Johnstone met many children all over the world who didn't know Jesus. She wrote the book *You Can Change the World* because she knew that God would use the prayers of children like you to change the world. She was right! Here are some stories about Zulus she met in South Africa during a week of meetings, held in a big tent, to tell Zulu people about Jesus.

A brave singer

It was cold in the mission tent in Natal, South Africa. Thandiwe, a young Zulu girl, came up to the platform to sing. She was wearing her father's jacket, which nearly touched the floor, with the sleeves rolled up. But she sang bravely into the microphone, her small face shining with happiness.

Jill looked around at all the children singing with such excitement and was so glad to be here as a missionary in Africa. Ever since she was four years old, Jill had wanted to tell African children about Jesus.

After Thandiwe and the other children sang that night, God did some wonderful things! Before long, over 30 Zulu children loved Jesus so much that they started telling everyone they met about him.

Risking his life for Jesus

Beaumont was on his way to the store, thinking about what he would steal this time. Maybe some food? Or a knife? Or something to play with? Then he noticed a big tent he hadn't seen before. He heard some music and a lot of voices coming from inside,

To help you pray for the Zulus

You can thank God for:

- Christian camps where children can learn about him.
- every Zulu Christian who is sharing the good news of Jesus' love with their friends, families and people they meet.

You can ask God:

- to help Zulu pastors and church workers to teach the Bible clearly and to show people how to obey God.
- to show Christians ways in which they can help Zulu boys and girls who have never been to school and find it hard to get jobs.
- to help Christians as they reach out to poor and lonely people, to those who can't get jobs and to people who have been hurt in violent crimes.
- to help Christians of all races in South Africa to love, respect and care for one another, and to work together for the good of their country.
- to help the Zulu leaders guide their people in God's ways and bring peace to South Africa.

Zulu *impis*

Do you know?

Good manners are very important to the Zulus ... and having good manners for a Zulu means more than saying "please" and "thank you!" At mealtimes in the homesteads, the people usually sit on grass mats. A woman must kneel to serve a man, making sure that her head is always lower than his, and the man must accept the food with both hands.

so he went in to see what was going on. When he came out again, his life had changed! The man speaking in the tent said that stealing was a sin, that it was wrong. But he also said that Jesus had died to take away the sin of everyone in the world, and that Jesus would give anyone who trusted in him a clean fresh start. Beaumont was so excited to hear that Jesus would also be with him all the time to help him. Beaumont became a Christian, and for four years he told everyone he met about Jesus. He told them outside shops, on buses and while visiting people in their homes. Some bullies got really angry with him. They hated him because he helped so many people to follow God's way. So one day they beat him up and Beaumont died, a martyr for Jesus. We can thank God for Beaumont and his life. Before he went to heaven to be with Jesus forever, he helped lots of other people to know Jesus so that they would go to heaven one day, too.

Killing a chicken

Mrs. Kadebe, who lived near the big tent, was sacrificing a chicken to God when Jill visited her. Mrs. Kadebe told her she was a Christian. "But Jesus died so that we don't have to make sacrifices," Jill told her. "God loved the world so much that he gave his only Son, Jesus, to die on the cross so that our sins can be forgiven. Jesus was God's one and only perfect sacrifice for sin."

Mrs. Kadebe couldn't believe it. Was it really true that she just had to believe that Jesus died for her and ask him to forgive her for all the bad things she'd done? She didn't have to kill chickens or follow any other rituals from other religions? Was that really all there was to it? Mrs. Kadebe didn't sleep for nights as she thought about all she had heard. At last she understood that Jesus died so she could be forgiven and not have to be afraid of evil spirits anymore. She became a great evangelist and traveled to many towns to tell others about God's love and the sacrifice he had made for each one of them.

Animism

A world of spirits

All around the world, there are millions of people we call animists. Groups of people who are animists usually feel very weak and helpless against all the powers of nature that surround them.

Making an offering at a shrine

They don't understand these powers, and they're afraid because they believe that disasters like drought, famine, sickness, fires, earthquakes, storms and floods are really the work of evil spirits.

Animists believe there are spirits living in everything they see around them, as well as in places like caves, mountaintops or at a fork in a path. Some of these spirits are friendly, but others are evil and are always making bad things happen. The people are afraid of these evil spirits, and they make special offerings and sacrifices to them so they won't hurt them and their families. They'll make other offerings and sacrifices to get what they want from the spirits – perhaps sacrificing a chicken to get a good harvest or success when they go out hunting. Others wear special bracelets or charms (called fetishes) which, they think, have magical powers to protect them from harm.

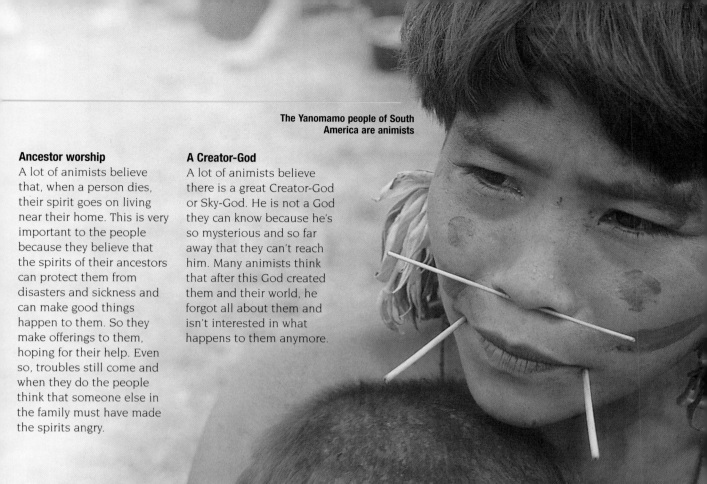

The Yanomamo people of South America are animists

Ancestor worship

A lot of animists believe that, when a person dies, their spirit goes on living near their home. This is very important to the people because they believe that the spirits of their ancestors can protect them from disasters and sickness and can make good things happen to them. So they make offerings to them, hoping for their help. Even so, troubles still come and when they do the people think that someone else in the family must have made the spirits angry.

A Creator-God

A lot of animists believe there is a great Creator-God or Sky-God. He is not a God they can know because he's so mysterious and so far away that they can't reach him. Many animists think that after this God created them and their world, he forgot all about them and isn't interested in what happens to them anymore.

Priests and others

As in any religion, animists have people with special roles. Some of them are known as shamans, medicine men or witch doctors, who have a special knowledge of the spirit world.

Their work is to help their people understand omens and signs and tell them what they must do to keep on the right side of the spirits. Others are priests who look after their shrines and help to organize important festivals and activities.

Some animist peoples

Some of the people we've read about in these books, such as the Bijago, Dogon, Dayak and Yanomamo, are animists. They each have their own ways of reaching out to the spirits and have their own special beliefs and ceremonies. Because animists are afraid of the world of unseen spirits, it's not easy for them to leave their beliefs and turn to another faith. Some who do decide to follow another religion often cling to the power of the spirits and so try to mix the two together. But those who have decided to follow Jesus have discovered that he can set them free from the fear and power of the spirits. Only Jesus is more powerful than any spirit or power.

Making a roadside offering

Buddhism

The beginning of Buddhism

Prince Siddharta Gautama lived in India about 2,500 years ago. His wealthy parents didn't want him to see anything that might make him sad. He lived in luxury, got married and had a son, but he felt his life had no meaning.

Young Gautama went on four journeys and saw a man who was sick, a frail old man, the funeral of a dead man and a holy man. It made him sad that people get old, sick and die. He left his parents, wife and child and wandered throughout India for six years, trying to understand the meaning of suffering, life and death.

The Eightfold Path

Gautama spent the rest of his life wandering around and teaching the people who came to him. His followers called him the Buddha, the "enlightened one."

He taught them that only by following the Noble Eightfold Path could they eventually be free from pain and suffering, death and rebirth. They must be kind; not harm any living thing; live in a right way; tell the truth; not think of self; think about others; understand suffering; and meditate. People who follow his teachings are called Buddhists.

Young monk spinning a prayer wheel

Gautama had been taught that everyone dies many times and has thousands of lives. This is called reincarnation. How a person lives in this life affects his next life. If a person has done a lot of good deeds, he or she may be reborn as a wealthy or wise person. People who do bad things will probably be poor and suffer a lot in their next life. Gautama finally decided to seek the answers to his questions through meditation. After a while, he felt that at last he understood the meaning of suffering and the way to be free from it and from endless rebirths. This is called nirvana, or nothingness – the end of the cycle of birth, death and rebirth.

Gaining merit

To reach nirvana, Buddhists try to earn merit by doing good things. Some become monks for a few weeks to gain merit, others for their entire lives. Monks live and dress very simply, usually in a yellow or red robe, and they meditate and teach the laws of the Buddha. Ordinary people try to get merit by giving food to the monks and making offerings in the temples.

Buddhism spread to other Asian countries like Thailand, Burma, Sri Lanka, Tibet, Mongolia, China, Vietnam and Korea. In all these countries there are thousands of Buddhist temples, each with at least one statue of the Buddha. People come seeking merit every day, leaving offerings of flowers, candles or incense in front of the Buddha. They also meditate and pray.

In countries like Tibet, prayer flags flutter from the roofs. People spin small prayer wheels as they walk or sit, and outside the temples are much bigger prayer wheels that people spin as they pass by. On the flags and in the prayer wheels is a mantra, or holy saying, which the people believe carries their prayer to the farthest part of the universe.

Prayer flags on a Buddhist temple in Nepal

The Dalai Lama

The Dalai Lama, one of Buddhism's greatest leaders and teachers, is reported to have said that Buddhism and Christianity are the same. But they are completely different. Buddhists hope to reach nirvana by their own efforts. Jesus gives new life now – and eternal life – to all who believe in him.

Christianity

Jesus Christ

There are more than 2,000,000,000 people in the world today who call themselves Christians.

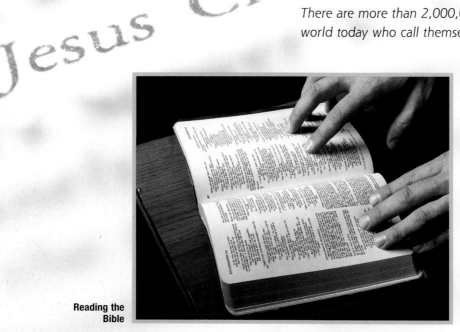

Reading the Bible

Jesus, sent from God

Jesus was born in Bethlehem about 2,000 years ago. God told Mary, his mother, that this baby was God's very own Son, the Messiah (or Savior).

When he was about 30 years old, Jesus chose 12 men to travel with him around the countryside. For three years, wherever they went, Jesus healed the sick and taught people about God's love and the way he wanted them to live. Peter, one of these 12 disciples,

What Christians believe

When God made man and woman, he made them perfect. He wanted them to be his friends and promised to look after them. But because people chose to do what they wanted instead of the good things God wanted, sin came into God's perfect world. Sin isn't just telling lies or stealing. We all want to do things our own way, thinking that God doesn't matter. That's sin, too.

Our sin is like a huge wall that stops us from reaching God. But God loves us very much and wants us to be his friends. So that's why he sent his Son, Jesus, who had never done any wrong, to earth. When Jesus died on the cross, God took all our sins and put them on Jesus. Jesus destroyed that huge wall, so the way to God is open to everyone who trusts in Jesus.

Orthodox church in Eastern Europe

realized that Jesus was the Messiah the Jews had been expecting for many years.

A lot of people loved Jesus, but the Roman rulers thought he was planning a revolt and the Jewish leaders thought he was breaking Jewish laws. They arrested him and accused him of saying things against God!

Jesus was crucified on a big wooden cross. But that wasn't the end. Three days later, Jesus rose from the dead. Over the next 40 days, many people saw him. They believed that Jesus had been raised from the dead by the power of God. Then Jesus returned to his Father in heaven, where he lives forever. Before he went, he promised to send the Holy Spirit to be with his people always.

Christians meeting in a South African township

Churches
There are many kinds of Christian churches (including Orthodox, Roman Catholic, Protestant and evangelical). Some Christians worship God in huge cathedrals, while others meet in very simple buildings, a room or a hut. But the real church is not the buildings but all the people who have asked Jesus to forgive them and who try to follow his teachings.

The Bible
The first part of the Bible is called the Old Testament. Many parts of it talk about the Messiah God would send to help his people. Both Christians and Jews read the Old Testament. The four Gospels in the New Testament tell us the story of Jesus' life and his teachings.

Christians know that Jesus is alive today and that he will come back to earth again. They're glad that even though they can't see him, they know he's near and always ready to help them, in hard times as well as good times. They also know that life doesn't end when we die, because Jesus has promised that anyone who believes in him will live forever.

Hinduism

An ancient religion

Hinduism grew out of the way people lived and worshipped in India more than 3,500 years ago. They passed on their beliefs in stories, hymns, poems and prayers. Many of these have been recorded in holy books.

About 80% of the people who live in India are Hindus. India is such a huge country that Hindus who live in different parts of the country worship in different ways and keep different festivals. Temples in the north of India are quite different from those in the south.

Everywhere you go in India you'll see temples and shrines where people worship their gods and goddesses. You'll also see shrines in offices, stores and houses.

A Hindu Sadhu

There are thousands of Hindu gods, but they're all different forms of one supreme god. Hindus can choose which gods or goddesses they want to worship. Some of the most popular are Vishnu, the protector of the world; Lakshmi, the goddess of wealth and beauty; the fun-loving Krishna who's often thought of as an older brother; and Ganesh, the elephant-headed god of good fortune. Hindus offer their gods food, money and prayers and ask for their help in everything they do.

High caste Indian bride

Caste

Every Hindu is born into a group called a caste. A person can't do anything to change caste. Some castes are considered better than others. At the top is the priestly caste, then rulers and soldiers, then merchants and farmers. The people in the lowest castes are usually the servants of the higher castes. The "Untouchables" don't belong to any caste and usually do the jobs nobody else wants to do. Higher caste Hindus don't usually mix with people from the lower castes because they consider them impure.

Life after this life

Hindus believe that when people die, they come back to life again as another person or even an animal. This is reincarnation. They believe in karma, which means that the way people behaved in their past life affects their place in this life, and what they do in this life will decide their place in the next. If they keep the rules of their caste, they believe they'll have a better rebirth. Rebirths may go on forever, as people can never be sure they've done everything the right way. Some Hindus will give up everything – home, family and possessions – to spend their lives in meditation and prayer. They want to become so holy that when they die, they won't be reborn.

Pilgrimage

Going on a pilgrimage to a holy place is an important part of Hindu life. Thousands of pilgrims visit Varanasi, Allahabad and Haridwar each year, some of the many holy places on the River Ganges. A Hindu may go to worship a particular god or goddess or to say thank you for something good that has happened. Most pilgrims will bathe in the river as they pray and worship to purify themselves from bad deeds.

A Nepali man celebrating the Hindu festival of *holi* when color is splashed over the body and thrown over family and friends

Festivals

Each year there are lots of festivals to celebrate the special days of certain gods and goddesses and events like New Year or harvest. Most of these festivals are lots of fun. Although they have many gods, not one of them has power over sin and death to give us eternal life. Only Jesus can do that.

A Hindu goddess

Islam

The prophet Mohammed founded Islam, the religion of Muslims. He was born 1,400 years ago in Mecca, Saudi Arabia. He believed the archangel Gabriel gave him messages from Allah, the Muslim God, which were put together as the Koran, the Muslim's holy book. The Koran describes the way Muslims should live.

There are more than a billion Muslims in our world today. There are two main sects, Sunni Muslims (90%) and Shi'ite Muslims.

The minaret of a mosque. The call to prayer is made from the upper balcony

Prayers

Muslims worship in mosques, which are often beautifully decorated, but they have no pictures or statues because Mohammed thought people might worship them instead of Allah. Five times every day, the call to prayer "There is no God but Allah, and Mohammed is his prophet" comes from the minaret, the tall tower by the side of the mosque.

Muslims can pray wherever they are, but they have to face towards Mecca, the Muslim's holy city. On Fridays, the Muslim holy day, they pray in the mosques at noon. The men wear a cap and the women a headscarf or veil to show their respect to Allah, and

Muslim men bow down and face Mecca to pray

The Five Pillars of Islam

There are five important duties for every Muslim, called the "Five Pillars of Islam." First, they pray five times every day and declare their faith by repeating the call to prayer. Every year in the month of Ramadan, Muslims fast during the day and only eat and drink between sunset and sunrise. They are to give money to charity. Finally, all Muslims are expected to go to Mecca on a pilgrimage (Hajj), at least once.

they wash before they pray. They kneel on a special mat and use a string of beads to help them remember the 99 names of Allah in the Koran.

Children
As soon as a baby is born, it's washed and the call to prayer is whispered in its right ear and then in its left, and a little honey or sugar is put on its tongue to make sure it will have a happy life. When they're about seven years old, Muslim children learn to read the Koran in Arabic. They also learn how to pray and how to behave in the mosque. At home they learn what foods they can eat and how to cook them, and how they should behave and dress.

Dress
Muslims are usually modest in their clothing. Neither men nor women would ever wear shorts or tight clothes. Women often wear ankle-length trousers covered by a skirt and a long-sleeved top, or dress, and cover their heads. In some countries women cover themselves in long veils whenever they leave their homes.

Muslims and the Bible
Mohammed taught that there is only one God, Allah. Christians also believe in one God, but Muslims find it hard to understand how God the Father, God the Son and God the Holy Spirit can be one God.

Muslims have a great respect for the Bible and think of Abraham, Moses, David and Jesus as prophets. They're often willing to read the stories about Jesus in the New Testament, which they call the *Injil*. We can tell Muslims about the wonderful things Jesus said and did, and how we can be close to God through him.

Judaism

Judaism, the religion of the Jewish people, is based on the first five books of the Old Testament (the Torah, or teachings).

The Jews believe that God is the creator of everything, that people are created in the image of God, and that the Jews are God's chosen people.

A *dreidel* or spinning top, used in a game played at the festival of Chanukah

GIMEL

Jews use the 9-branched menorah in celebrating Chanukah

The Hebrew Bible (our Old Testament) is the Jews' holy book. Hebrew is read from right to left

The beginning

God chose Abraham and his family to be his people. He told Abraham to leave his own country (Genesis 12:1–3) and promised him that he would bless him and all the peoples of the world through him.

A chosen nation

Hundreds of years passed, and Abraham's descendants became slaves in Egypt. God chose Moses to lead them out of Egypt to the Promised Land. (You can read the story in Exodus chapters 1–19.) God told Moses that if they obeyed him, they would be his special people. He wanted them to worship him alone and so be different from all the other nations who worshipped lots of gods.

God wanted them to be holy, like himself, so he gave them a set of rules called the Ten Commandments. God promised to bless and help them if they were obedient. If they did not keep God's rules, they would be punished.

Throughout their long history, the Jewish people have seen that everything that has happened to them has been the work of God. He has given them his love and care, guided, helped and punished them. Wherever they have lived and whatever they have suffered – and they have suffered a lot – they have remained Jews.

Orthodox Jew praying at the Western Wall in Jerusalem

Wine cup, container for spices and candle used at the *Havdalah* ceremony at the close of the Sabbath

The promised Messiah

The Jews have looked for God's promised Deliverer, or Messiah, to lead them back to their own land and to bring peace and justice on earth. A lot of Jews are still waiting for him to come, but others don't believe in a Messiah at all. Christians, whose beliefs and knowledge of God are based on the Old Testament, are sure that Jesus is the Messiah promised by God.

Worship

The first prayer a Jewish child learns comes from Deuteronomy 6: "Hear, O Israel: the Lord our God is one Lord; and you shall love the Lord your God with all your heart, and with all your soul, and with all your might." They say it every morning and evening.

The Jewish people have lots of festivals during the year that remind them of their history, but every week they keep the Sabbath. The Sabbath starts at sunset on Friday and ends at sunset on Saturday and is very special to Jewish families.

It's their holy day, a day of rest. The family usually goes to a service in the synagogue on Friday evening and again on Saturday morning.

There's always a special Sabbath meal on Friday evenings. Before they eat, the mother lights two candles and blesses God, then the father takes a cup of wine and says a blessing for his family. Everyone eats a piece of bread with salt to remind them of the way God provided his people with manna for food on the way to the Promised Land.

All around the world

There are about 14 million Jews living in countries all around the world. Only 4 million live in Israel, but Jews come from many places to pray at the Western Wall of Herod's Temple in Jerusalem. This is their Holy Land.

209

What Next?

Get to know Jesus

God has a special purpose for your life and has already planned what he wants you to do. Maybe you're thinking, "I'm not sure if I really know Jesus. So how can I know what he wants me to do?" Jesus knows all about you and wants you to ask him to be your friend! He loves you and died for you because that was the only way to take away all the wrong things that get between God and us. Tell him that you're sorry for all the bad things you've done and that you want to live his way and do what he wants you to do.

Spend time getting to know Jesus. Talk with him and listen to what he says and learn to obey him. Read the Bible and know what it says. God's Holy Spirit will help you to pray and tell other people about Jesus. You can be sure that he will help you and will start showing you his plan for your life.

Make friends

- If missionaries come to your church, listen to what they say. Ask them questions and find out how you and your church or Sunday school can help them. If the missionaries have children, make friends with them and write to them.

- There might be people in your church or school who have recently come from another country and might feel very lonely. Be a friend and help them to feel at home.

Pray

Remember that God wants us to share with him in his work through our prayers. Sometimes it's hard for us to keep on praying, but here are a few ideas to help you.

- Choose seven different topics, countries, people groups or individuals. Write them on separate pages in a notebook and pray for one each day of the week.

- When you know a prayer has been answered, write that in your notebook, too.

- Get a world map. Mark on it the places you pray for and add pictures of the people you pray for.

- It helps to pray with someone else – a friend, your family or in Sunday school.

Read

- Get books from your local library about the countries you've read about. Find out how most people make their living; what the government is like; if Christians are accepted in that country or are persecuted. An encyclopedia will answer some of these questions for you.

- There are some exciting missionary biographies that have been written for children. They will help you to understand what it's like to work for Jesus.

Look

- Watch the news and travel programs on TV.

- Look through magazines for pictures of the countries and people you have been learning about.

- Go to the web sites of mission agencies working in the countries you have been learning about. They have lots of interesting information and sometimes they have special pages for children. Countries often have web sites, too. (Remember to ask your parents first.)

Taste

- Ask your parents if you can try food from different countries.

Give

Missions often have special projects. Find out about them and give some of your money to help that project. Your Sunday school and friends might want to help support a project and your teachers will have ideas to help you raise money.

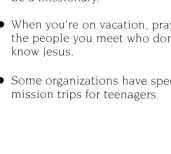

Go!

- Some missionary societies have summer camps for children (for example, WEC International in Britain) where you can have a lot of fun, meet missionaries and learn about their work.

- You or your whole family might even be able to visit missionary friends to find out what it's like to be a missionary.

- When you're on vacation, pray for the people you meet who don't know Jesus.

- Some organizations have special mission trips for teenagers.

Addresses

To Help You Find Out More ...

... on this page are some addresses and web sites of Christian agencies in North America and Britain who may be able to help you. There's also a list of some of the countries they may be able to tell you about. Some agencies, like Gospel Recordings and Wycliffe Bible Translators, have specialized work in many countries all around the world.

If you want to find out more about a people group, first make sure you know which country they live in. Then look for agencies that may have information about that country. If you write to an agency, decide what you want to ask about before you write.

Why not visit the web sites of some of these mission agencies (with your parents' permission) and discover more of what God is doing around the world. Some agencies have lots of interesting and exciting information on their web sites with special pages for children. Agencies marked * have some materials that have been specially prepared for children (general information, activity packs, videos, web pages, pictures, worksheets or books).

... Finding out is fun!

Some North American Mission Agencies

ABWE*
(Association of Baptists for World Evangelism)
USA: P.O. Box 8585, Harrisburg, PA 17105
CANADA: 160 Adelaide Street South, Suite 205, London, Ontario N5Z 3LI
Web: www.abwe.org
(Bangladesh, Central America and the Caribbean, China, Colombia, Japan, Mongolia, Papua New Guinea, Peru, Romania, Spain, Thailand, Uruguay)

American Bible Society
1865 Broadway, New York, NY 10023
Web: www.biblesociety.org/bs-usa.htm
(Worldwide production and distribution of Scriptures)

AmeriTribes*
P.O. Box 27346, Tucson, AZ 85726-7346
Web: www.ameritribes.org
(Native American tribes in USA and Mexico)

Campus Crusade for Christ International*
100 Lake Hart Drive, Orlando, FL 32832
Web: www.ccci.org
(*Jesus* film)

Christian and Missionary Alliance
P.O. Box 35000, Colorado Springs, CO 80935-3500
Web: www.cmalliance.org
(Colombia, Cuba, Guatemala, Guinea, Haiti, Indonesia, Israel, Lebanon, Mongolia, Peru, Russia, Spain, Syria, Thailand, Uruguay, Venezuela, Vietnam)

Christian Literature Crusade
701 Pennsylvania Ave., Fort Washington, PA 19034
Web: www.clcusa.org
(Literature work in 55 countries including Trinidad and Uruguay)

European Christian Mission
110 Juanita Drive, South Zanesville, OH 43701
Web: www.ecmi.org
(Albania, Greece, Romania, Spain)

Gospel for Asia
1932 Walnut Plaza, Carrollton, TX 75006
Web: www.gfa.org
(Bhutan, China, India, Nepal, Russia, Sri Lanka, Thailand, Vietnam)

Gospel Missionary Union*
10000 N. Oak Trafficway, Kansas City, MO 64155
Web: www.gmu.org
(Mali, Morocco, Greece, Russia, Kyrgyzstan, Spain)

Gospel Recordings/Global Recordings Network
122 Glendale Boulevard, Los Angeles, CA 90026
Web: www.gospelrecordings.com
(Recording, producing and distributing audio recordings for evangelism worldwide)

Mission Aviation Fellowship*
P.O. Box 3202, Redlands, CA 92374
Web: www.maf.org/
(Congo, Haiti, Indonesia, Lesotho, Mali, Papua New Guinea, Russia, Venezuela, Zimbabwe)

New Tribes Mission*
1000 E. First Street, Sanford, FL 32771
Web: www.ntm.org/
(Work among people groups in Colombia, Greenland, Guinea, Indonesia, Mongolia, Papua New Guinea, Thailand, Venezuela and in many other countries)

OMF International
10 W. Dry Creek Circle, Littleton, CO 80120
Web: www.omf.org/
(Thailand, Indonesia, Japan)

OMS International
941 Fry Road, Greenwood, IN 46142
Web: www.omsinternational
(Colombia, Haiti, Indonesia, Japan, Russia)

Operation Mobilization, Inc.
P.O. Box 444, Tyrone, GA 30290
Web: www.usa.om.org
(Afghanistan, Bangladesh, India, Kazakhstan, Romania, Russia, Turkey, Uzbekistan. OM works in 85 countries and has two mission ships.)

Rainbows of Hope
P.O. Box 517, Fort Mill, SC 29716
Web:www.wec-int.org/rainbows
(Street children and children in crisis around the world)

TEAM*
(The Evangelical Alliance Mission)
P.O. Box 969, Wheaton, IL 60189
Web: www.teamworld.org/
(Chad, Colombia, Indonesia, Japan, Nepal, Russia, Spain, Trinidad and Tobago, Venezuela, Zimbabwe)

United World Mission
P.O. Box 668767, Charlotte, NC 28270
Web: www.uwm.org
(Bulgaria, China, Cuba, Ethiopia, Greece, Guatemala, India, Mali, Morocco, Nepal, Peru, Romania, Russia, Spain, Uruguay, Uzbekistan, Venezuela, Vietnam)

WEC International*
P.O. Box 1707, Fort Washington, PA 19034
Web: www.wec-int.org
(Albania, Bulgaria, Chad, Greece, East Asia, Guinea, Guinea-Bissau, India, Japan, Spain, Venezuela and other countries in this book)

World Team
1431 Stuckert Rd., Warrington, PA 18976
Web: www.worldteam.org/
(Cuba, Haiti, Indonesia, Peru, Russia, Spain, Trinidad and Tobago, as well as other countries)

Wycliffe Bible Translators
P.O. Box 2727, Huntington Beach, CA 92647
Web: www.wycliffe.org
(Worldwide, helping people put the Bible into their own language for the first time.)

Some Mission Agencies in Britain

Action Partners Ministries
Bawtry Hall, Bawtry, Doncaster, DN10 6JH
Web: www.actionpartners.org.uk
(Chad, Congo, Egypt and North Africa)

Africa Inland Mission International*
2 Vorley Road, Archway, London N19 5HE
Web: www.aim-eur.org
(Chad, Congo, Lesotho, Madagascar, Namibia)

Albanian Evangelical Mission
29 Bridge Street, Penybryn, Wrexham, LL13 7HP
Web: www.albanianmission.demon.co.uk
(Albania)

Arab World Ministries*
P.O. Box 51, Loughborough, LE11 OZQ
Web: www.awm.com
(Middle East and North Africa including Egypt, Lebanon and Syria)

BMS World Mission*
P.O. Box 49, 129 Broadway, Didcot, Oxon. OX11 8XA
Web: www.bms.org.uk
(Albania, Bangladesh, Guinea, India, Nepal, Sri Lanka, Trinidad and Tobago)

British & Foreign Bible Society
Stonehill Green, Westlea, Swindon, Wilts. SN5 7DG
Web: www.biblesociety.org
(Production and distribution of Scriptures worldwide)

Church Mission Society*
Partnership House, 157 Waterloo Road, London SE1 8UU
Web: www.cms-uk.org
(Working in 40 countries in Africa, Asia and Europe)

Church's Ministry Among Jewish People
30c Clarence Road, St. Albans, AL1 4JJ
Web: www.cmj.org.uk

Christian Literature Crusade
Shawton House, 792 Hagley Road West, Oldbury, B68 0PJ
Web: www.clc.org.uk
(Literature ministry in 55 countries)

Christian Witness to Israel
166 Main Road, Sundridge, Sevenoaks, Kent, TN14 6EL
Web:www.cwi.org.uk
(Israel, and among Jewish people in other countries)

Crosslinks*
251 Lewisham Way, London SE4 1XF
Web:www.crosslinks.org
(Ethiopia, Greece, India, North Africa, SE Asia, Spain, Zimbabwe)

European Christian Mission (Britain)
50 Billing Road, Northampton, NN1 5DB
Web: www.ecmi.org
(Albania, Greece, Romania, Spain)

FEBA Radio
Ivy Arch Road, Worthing, West Sussex, BN14 8BX
Web: www.feba.org.uk
(Christian radio broadcasts to more than 30 countries)

Interserve
325 Kennington Road, London S11 4QH
Web: www.interserve.org
(Middle East, North Africa, India, West Asia, Mongolia, East Asia)

Language Recordings, UK
P.O. Box 197, High Wycombe, HP14 3YY
Web: www.gospelrecordings.com
(Recording, producing and distributing audio recordings worldwide)

Latin Link UK
175 Tower Bridge Road, London SE1 2AB
Web: www.latinlink.org
(Colombia, Peru and other South American countries)

Middle East Christian Outreach
22 Culverdon Park Road, Tunbridge Wells, Kent TN4 9RA
Web: www.gospelcom.net/meco
(Egypt, Lebanon, Syria, Turkey, Yemen)

Mission Aviation Fellowship*
Castle Hill Avenue, Folkestone, CT20 2TN
Web: www.maf-uk.org
(Chad, Congo, Haiti, Indonesia, Lesotho, Madagascar, Mali, Mongolia, Papua New Guinea, Venezuela, Zimbabwe)

New Tribes Mission
North Cotes, Grimsby, DN36 5XU
Web: www.ntm.org.uk
(Colombia, Greenland, Guinea, Indonesia, Mongolia, Papua New Guinea, Russia, Thailand, Venezuela)

Operation Mobilisation (OM)
The Quinta, Weston Rhyn, Oswestry, SY10 7LT
Web: www.uk.om.org
(Afghanistan, Bangladesh, India, Kazakhstan, Romania, Russia, Turkey, Uzbekistan. OM works in 85 countries and has two mission ships.)

OMF International*
Station Approach, Borough Green, Sevenoaks TN15 8BG
Web: www.omf.org.uk
(East Asia, Indonesia, Japan, Thailand)

OMS International*
1 Sandileigh Avenue, Didsbury, Manchester, M20 3LN
Web: www.omsinternational.org/uk
(China, Colombia, Haiti, India, Indonesia, Japan, Russia, Spain)

People International, UK
P.O. Box 310, Tunbridge Wells, TN4 8ZJ
(Afghanistan, Kazakhstan, Kyrgyzstan, Turkey, Uzbekistan)

Red Sea Mission Team
P.O. Box 19929, London N3 1WW
Web: www.rsmt.u-net.com
(Djibouti, Mali, Middle East)

SIM UK*
(Society for International Ministries)
Wetheringsett Manor, Wetheringsett, Stowmarket, IP14 5QX
Web: www.sim.co.uk
(Working in 43 countries in Africa, S. America and Asia)

South American Mission Society*
Allen Gardiner House, 12 Fox Hill, Birmingham, B29 4AG
Web: www.samsgb.org
(Peru, Spain, Uruguay)

Tearfund*
100 Church Road, Teddington, Middx. TW11 8QE
Web: www.tearfund.org/youth
(Working in 90 countries around the world including Bangladesh, Cuba, Haiti, Mali)

The Leprosy Mission*
Goldhay Way, Orton Goldhay, Peterborough, PE2 5GZ
Web: www.leprosymission.org/

UFM Worldwide*
47a Fleet Street, Swindon, SN1 1RE
Web: www.ufm.org.uk
(Eastern Europe, Java [Indonesia], Mongolia, Papua New Guinea, Spain)

WEC International*
Bulstrode, Oxford Road, Gerrards Cross, Bucks. SL9 8SZ
Web. www.wec-int.org
(Albania, Bulgaria, Chad, Greece, East Asia, Guinea, Guinea-Bissau, India, Japan, Spain, Venezuela and other countries in this book)

Wycliffe Bible Translators*
Horsleys Green, High Wycombe, Bucks. HP14 3XL
Web: www.wycliffe.org.uk
(Worldwide, helping people put the Bible into their own language for the first time.)

Youth With a Mission
Highfield Oval, Ambrose Lane, Harpenden, Herts. AL5 4BX
Web: www.ywam-england.com
(Albania, Thailand, China, India, Kazakhstan and other Central Asian countries, Middle East, North Africa, Russia)

If you have any difficulty in obtaining the information you need, please contact: Children's Resources, WEC International, who will try to help you.

Word List

agnostic: a person who believes that we can't know anything about God or even if he exists.

Allah: the Muslim God.

alpaca: a South American animal that looks like the llama and is related to the camel; usually raised for its fine wool.

altar: 1. the communion table in a church; 2. a flat-topped block of stone for making sacrifices and offerings to God (in Old Testament times) or to gods.

ancestor: anyone from whom you are descended. Your parents, grandparents and great-grandparents are all your ancestors.

animism: see p. 198.

Armenian Church: historic Armenia (including Georgia, eastern Turkey, Syria and northern Iraq and Iran) was the first country in the world to make Christianity its official religion (in the third century). There are still Armenian churches in most of these places.

Ash Wednesday: the first day of Lent (the 40 days before Easter). Some churches put ash on the foreheads of worshippers as a sign that they're sorry for their sin.

atheist: a person who believes that there's no God.

Bible school: a college where people study the Bible. Churches often hold Bible schools for a week or several weeks.

Buddhism: see p. 200.

cacao: the tree and its seed from which cocoa and chocolate are made.

calypso: a West Indian song with an African rhythm. The singer often makes up the words as he or she sings.

caste: a group into which a Hindu person is born. The most important caste is the priestly caste; then leaders and soldiers and traders and storekeepers. There are other lower castes and "outcastes" (untouchables) who have to do things like sweep and wash clothes; they're often servants of the higher castes.

Catholic: the word "catholic" means "universal," and there are Catholic churches all around the world. Like other Christians, Catholics believe that Jesus is the Son of God and the Bible is the word of God. But they also believe that other traditions are important and worship Mary as the Mother of God. They believe that Jesus gave the apostle Peter special authority, which was handed down to the bishops of Rome. The Pope is the Bishop of Rome, the head of the Roman Catholic Church.

charm: something worn to bring good luck.

civil war: a war between groups of people inside the same country.

colony/colonize: an area taken over, settled and ruled by another country. People who colonize a country often bring foreign cultures, religions and values to the people already living there.

Communism: a political movement. The original idea was for a society in which there would be neither very rich nor very poor people but where everyone was equal. This became the form of government in countries like Russia where the state controlled everything.

continent: one of the seven big land masses in the world. The continents are Africa, Antarctica, Asia, Australia, Europe, North America and South America.

correspondence course: a course (on any subject) in which a teacher mails lessons and questions to students, who return their answers in the same way.

coup: a sudden, and often violent, takeover of a government by a small group of people.

cremation: burning the body to ashes after death.

cult: a religious group that has its own objects of worship and its own ceremonies.

culture: the customs, traditions and way of life of a people.

customs: opinions or beliefs passed on from one generation to the next; the usual ways of doing things.

democracy: a system of government in which the adult population of a country elects ordinary people to govern them.

descendant: a person who is descended from another. You are a descendant of your parents, grandparents and great-grandparents.

dialect: the way people in a particular part of a country speak their language. This includes the words they use and the way they pronounce them.

dictator: a ruler who has total power over all that is done in his country.

drought: a long period of time without rain so there is a shortage of water.

drug cartel: a group of people who control the sale and price of illegal drugs.

embassy: the place where an ambassador (someone representing the government of his own country) lives and works in another country.

emigrate: to leave one's own country and live in another.

evangelical: a person who believes that the Bible is God's word and that the four Gospels tell us about Jesus' birth and sinless life, that he died for our sins so God could forgive us, and rose again from the dead. Evangelical Christians believe that only by having faith in Jesus can we be forgiven for our sins and go to heaven. We cannot earn our way to God by doing good things.

evangelical (church): a church that teaches that Jesus died for us and is alive forever, and that it's important for us to know and follow the Bible, which is God's word.

evangelist: a person who tells others the good news of Jesus' love.

evil spirits: a being that can't be seen but that makes bad things happen.

exile: a person sent away from his or her own country and forced to live in another country.

export: anything people in one country grow or make to sell to another country.

famine: a time when food is scarce so that people (and animals) sometimes die from starvation.

to fast: to not eat for a while, often for religious reasons.

fetish: an object that's worshipped.

guerrillas/guerrilla war: members of a rebel army (against the government) who fight a war by ambush or surprise attacks. They may work on their own or in small groups.

Hajj: the Muslim pilgrimage to Mecca, their holy city in Saudi Arabia. All Muslims are expected to go on this pilgrimage at least once in their lifetime.

Hebrew: the language in which the Old Testament was originally written, a modern version of which is spoken in Israel today.

heretic: a person who believes things that are different from the accepted teachings of his or her church.

Hinduism: see p. 204.

Holy Trinity: God the Father, God the Son and God the Holy Spirit together are called the Holy Trinity, three persons in one God. The Father, Son and Holy Spirit are all equally God; they are all eternal and never change. They all took part in the work of creation. Jesus is the Son of God who came to earth to live and die to save us from our sins. After Jesus returned to heaven, God sent the Holy Spirit to work in the lives of Christians and be with them always.

icon: a sacred painting of Jesus, his mother Mary, or a saint.

idol: a statue or image of something which is worshipped as a god.

Islam: see p. 206.

Jain: a member of a small Indian religion. They must not hurt or kill any living thing and are strict vegetarians.

Jehovah's Witnesses: a cult founded in America in 1872. They believe the whole Bible is from Jehovah (God) and tells them exactly what they must believe and do. They don't believe that Jesus is the Son of God. They believe that God's kingdom is the only kingdom, so sometimes they refuse to obey certain laws of the countries in which they live such as serving in the armed forces. They believe that the end of the world is near and that there will be a great battle, called Armageddon, between God and Satan before a new kingdom belonging to Jesus will be set up.

Jesus **film:** shows the life of Jesus from Luke's Gospel. It's been translated into many languages and millions of people have seen it. It's available on video and is used in many churches and homes all around the world to help people understand who Jesus is. A lot of people have come to know him through watching this film. In these books you can read about some of the countries like Iraq, Mongolia and Syria and people groups like the Buryats, Garifuna and Uzbeks who have the film in their own language.

jinns: spirits with power to appear in human or animal form.

Judaism: see p. 208.

Koran: (or Qur'an) the Muslim's holy book.

legend: a story passed down from one generation to the next about something that happened a long time ago. The story may or may not be true.

Lent: 40 days, from Ash Wednesday to Easter Eve, of fasting and repenting for sin. Many branches of the Christian Church observe Lent. Some people skip one meal a day during Lent, or give up something they really enjoy, like chocolate, and give the money they would have spent to charity.

linguist: a person who studies languages.

looting: stealing things from houses or stores during a riot or battle or other disaster.

malaria: an illness spread by mosquitoes in which a person has very high fevers and chills.

mango: the delicious, yellowish-orange colored fruit of the mango tree. While it's still green, the fruit is often used to make pickles.

manioc: a plant grown in many tropical countries. The thick roots, a bit like potatoes, are used for food.

March for Jesus: a yearly march in which Christians tell others about Jesus, praise God, sing and pray. Since it began in 1987, more than 50 million people in 117 countries have taken part in the marches.

martyr: a person who is killed because of his beliefs.

masquerade: to wear a mask or costume and pretend you're someone else. The same word is used for a party where everyone is in disguise.

Mass: the service of Holy Communion (in the Roman Catholic Church).

medicine man: in animism, this is a person who has powers of healing. This may be through contact with the spirits or through their knowledge of plants and other natural things that can help healing. (See also: witch doctor; Shamanism.)

meditation: thinking deeply about things, often religious matters.

merit, earning: doing something good that will bring a reward in the future. Buddhists believe that if they earn merit they will be reborn into a better life when they die.

Messianic Jews: Jews who are Christians. They believe Jesus is the Messiah sent by God and have accepted him as their Savior.

millet: a very tall cereal plant with small seeds that are very nutritious. (If you have a pet bird you may feed it millet!)

minaret: a tall, slender tower connected to a mosque.

215

Word List (continued)

missionary: a person who goes to another place to teach others about his or her faith.

Mohammed: the founder of Islam (see p. 206).

monastery: a building or buildings where monks live, work and study their religion in peace and quiet.

monk: a man belonging to a religious group living in a monastery.

Mormon: a member of a large cult often called the Church of Jesus Christ of Latter-day Saints. Their teaching is based on the Book of Mormon and other writings and uses the Bible as well.

mosque: the Muslim place of worship.

Muslim: a follower of Islam (see p. 206).

noble: a person of high rank by birth such as a duke or duchess.

nomad: a member of a tribe that moves from place to place to find food and pasture for their animals.

offering: something given as a gift and a sign of devotion.

omen: something that happens and is taken as a sign that something else will happen. Some omens mean good things will happen, but others mean bad things will happen.

Orthodox churches: a branch of the Christian Church found in many countries, but mainly in Eastern Europe, Greece and Russia. They base their beliefs on the Bible, the Creed (a statement of faith) and traditions. They have many pictures of saints in their churches. There are no organs or musical instruments, but the services are always sung. Often the only seats in the churches are around the walls, so people stand during the services or move around to pray in front of icons.

papaya (pawpaw): a palm-like tree originally from Central America, now grown in many tropical countries. Its edible fruit is oval, yellow or orange, and can weigh from a few ounces to several pounds.

pastor: a minister in charge of a church.

peasant: a person who lives and works on the land, often as a hired worker.

Pentecost: the day when Christians celebrate the coming of the Holy Spirit (Acts 2). It's sometimes called Whitsun or Whitsunday and takes place on the seventh Sunday after Easter.

persecution: attacking, killing or driving people from their homes because they have different political or religious beliefs.

pilgrimage: a journey to worship at a holy place. People who go on pilgrimages are called pilgrims.

plantain: a kind of large banana that has to be cooked before it can be eaten.

plantation: a large farm or area of land that's planted with trees or crops such as tea, coffee, cotton or sugar. A lot of people are hired to work on plantations.

plateau: an area of high, level ground. It's sometimes called a "tableland."

poncho: a garment, something like a cape, worn in some South American countries. It's made from a piece of cloth with a slit in the middle so it can be put on over the head.

poverty: when someone is very poor and doesn't have enough money to live on.

prayer beads: a string of beads used to help a person repeat prayers. Buddhists and Muslims use them, and in the Christian Church Roman Catholics call it a rosary.

prayer wheels: a tube-shaped box with a prayer written in it. Small ones are held in the hand, but bigger ones are attached to a spindle. It's thought that, as the wheel spins around, the prayer goes out into the universe. They are used by Tibetan Buddhists.

Protestants: members or followers of Christian churches that broke away from the Roman Catholic churches during the Reformation in the sixteenth century.

raid: a sudden attack on another group of people.

Ramadan: a month of fasting during which Muslims don't eat or drink from sunrise to sunset.

to ration: to divide something so that everyone has the same amount; to restrict how much of something someone can have (for example, food during a famine).

rebel: a person who refuses to obey those in authority and fights against them.

refugee/refugee camp: a person who has been forced to flee from his or her home or country because of war, famine or beliefs. Refugees often go to refugee camps where they are looked after until they can go back to their own homes or can settle in another country.

revolt/revolution: a rebellion which overthrows a government.

Russian Revolution: during World War I, a lot of peasants had to join Russia's badly-equipped army. Those who stayed to work on the land were extremely poor. Factory workers were also very poor, and in 1917 they led the revolution against the government and the tsar (king) who stepped down from power. The workers elected councils, helped by a political party called the Bolsheviks who later changed their name to Communists. They seized power and set up "government by the workers." The government took over everything – farms, banks, factories, industries and railways.

Sabbath: the seventh day of the Jewish week, from sunset on Friday to sunset on Saturday. It's the Jews' holy day and day of rest.

sacred: something that's holy and precious to the followers of a religion.

sacrifice: killing an animal as an offering to a god or goddess.

Sahel: sometimes called "the shore of the desert," it's the hot, dry, semi-desert area on the southern edge of the Sahara Desert.

saint: a holy person.

savior: a person who saves another from harm or difficulty. Jesus is our Savior because he died to save us from our sins.

sect: a group of people who have turned their backs on some of the main beliefs of a religion and have formed their own beliefs.

secular: not sacred or holy, but dealing with the ordinary things of this world.

settler: someone who goes to live in a new country, often in an area that hasn't been developed.

Shamanism: a form of animism mainly found in Siberia but also in other parts of Asia and among American Indian peoples. The word "shaman" means "one who knows," and a shaman keeps in touch with the spirits so that he can guide his people to do what the spirits want them to do. (See also: witch doctor; medicine man.)

sheikh: the chief of an Arabian tribe or village.

Shi'ite Muslims: (also called Shi'as) believe that their leaders must be descendants of Ali, Mohammed's cousin and son-in-law.

shrine: a building or place where sacred things are kept.

Sikh: a member of a north Indian religion founded about 500 years ago by a man called Guru Nanak. Sikhs believe in one God and that all people are equally important. Sikh men do not cut their hair but keep it in place with a comb and wear turbans on their heads. Their place of worship is called a *Gurdwara*, and their holy book is the *Guru Granth Sahib*.

slum: an overcrowded and often dirty area of a city. Most people living in slums are often too poor to live anywhere else.

sorghum: a kind of grass grown in dry parts of the world. Its grain (seed) is used to make a kind of bread.

spirit: a supernatural being; ghosts and fairies are spirits.

spiritist: a person who believes that it's possible to make contact with spirits, often with the spirit of a dead person.

Sunni Muslims: Most Muslims belong to the Sunni branch of Islam and closely follow the teachings of the prophet Mohammed. They elect their leaders.

superstition: an idea or action based on a belief in ghosts, lucky and unlucky signs and supernatural happenings.

taboo: something that's forbidden or not acceptable, for religious or social reasons.

tapir: a pig-like animal related to the rhinoceros.

temple: a building used for worship.

terraced fields: level fields made on a hillside, with the outer edge of each field kept in place by a wall. Terraced fields go up a hillside like a series of large steps.

thatch: straw or reeds used to make a roof.

tradition: opinions, ways of doing things or beliefs that have been passed on from one generation to the next.

traditional religion: a religion or way of worship that has been handed down from one generation to another within a tribe or people group.

translate/translation: to put the words of one language into the words of another language so that both mean the same. The person who does this is called a translator. A Bible translation is a Bible put into the words of another language. Bibles translated into hundreds of different languages, then, all say the same thing.

tribe: people belonging to the same race or group and ruled by a chief.

United Nations: a worldwide organization of about 180 countries who want to work together for world peace. It began in 1945 at the end of World War II. It tries to settle quarrels between countries or within a country; to develop friendships between nations; and to help overcome some of the world's problems, like poverty.

visa: an official stamp in a passport that gives someone permission to go in or leave a particular country.

voodoo: a religious system in the West Indies that practices witchcraft.

west, the: can mean the western part of a country or region. We also use it when we talk about the well-to-do countries of western Europe, Great Britain and the United States.

witch doctor: in animism, a person who has contact with the spirits and can understand signs and omens. (See also: medicine man; Shamanism.)

yak: a long-haired Tibetan ox.

Acknowledgements

A great many people and mission agencies have helped in the production of *Window on the World* and I want to thank each of them for the part they have played.

First of all, my thanks to everyone who has prayed for this project. Among them are my own precious grandchildren and their parents as well as friends, colleagues and acquaintances all around the world. They have prayed because they know God hears and answers prayer and are convinced that children have a special part to play in praying for the world in which they live.

Mission agencies and Christian workers all around the world have graciously answered my questions, provided information, stories and pictures, and have checked the results. Their letters have often been a great source of inspiration. Tara Smith, who has edited the material, has been a constant encouragement.

Others have encouraged me as they have told me how much their families, children's groups and churches appreciated the first edition. It gave them a glimpse of a world in need and helped even small children to pray for the world.

The greatest encourager of all is God himself. Time and time again he has given fresh vision, new joy, answers to my prayers and verses from the Bible that have spoken to my heart. And as I have worked, I have discovered that he has answered many of the prayers included in the first edition.

My thanks to each one and may we encourage one another to change our world through prayer.

Daphne Spraggett

Picture Acknowledgements

Acknowledgements are given for each spread. Where there is more than one source on a spread the credits are given clockwise from left.

Front Cover
1, 3, 4 & 7 Photodisc, 2 Sarah Errington/Hutchison Picture Library, 5 International Mission Board, 6 Getty Images

Back Cover
All Photodisc

Introduction, pp 8–9
Photodisc
pp 10–11
1 & 2 International Mission Board, 3 Tim Dowley/Three's Company

Afghanistan
1 & 4 Roy Spraggett, 2 & 3 Alex Macnaughton/Impact

Albania
1 Justin Williams/Impact, 2 Material World/Impact, 3 & 4 Howard Sayer/Impact

Azeri
1–3 Caroline Penn/Impact, 4 Danny Isenring

Balinese
1 David Palmer/Impact, 2–4 Dominic Sansoni/Impact,

Baloch
1 Caroline Penn/Impact, 3–5 Roy Spraggett

Bangladesh
1, 2 & 4 Piers Cavendish/Impact, 3 International Mission Board

Beja
All Sarah Errington/Hutchison Picture Library

Bhutan
1, 2 & 4 Alain Le Garsmeur/Impact, 3, N. M. Sture, 5 Material World/Impact

Bijago
All Norman Cuthbert

Bulgaria
1 & 2 Christophe Bluntzer/Impact, 3 Bruce Stephens/Impact, 4 Janet Wishnetsky/Impact, 5 International Mission Board

Buryat
1–4 Judy Starr, 5 Roy Spraggett

Chad
1, 3 & 4 Pauline Wager, 2 International Mission Board

Children of the Streets
1 & 4 Roy Spraggett, 2 & 5 Rainbows of Hope, 3 Wendy Dezan

China
1 & 3–6 Photodisc, 2 Roy Spraggett

Colombia
1 Alexis Wallerstein/Impact, 2 & 4 David Reed/Impact, 3 Robert Gibbs/Impact, 5 Charles Coates

Cuba
1 Tim Dowley/Three's Company, 2 Larry Jerden/United Bible Societies, 3 José López/United Bible Societies/Bible Commission of Cuba, 4 WEC Press

Dai Lu
1, 2 & 4 Mark Henley/Impact, 3 Photodisc, 5 Bruce Stephens/Impact

Dayak
1–3 Robert Francis/Hutchison Picture Library, 4 Michael Macintyre/Hutchison Picture Library

Djibouti
1 Hutchison Picture Library, 2 Trevor Page/Hutchison Picture Library, 3 Timothy Beddow/Hutchison Picture Library, 4 Christina Dodwell/Hutchison Picture Library, 5 Red Sea Team International

Dogon
1 Photodisc, 2 & 3 A. Lorgnier/Cedri/Impact, 4 Joanne Ellington

Druzes
1 & 2 Gail Berrieman, 3 Alan Kedhane/Impact, 4 Roy Spraggett

Egypt
1, 3, 4 & 6 Tim Dowley/Three's Company, 2 David Rudford/United Bible Societies, 5 International Mission Board

Ethiopia
1 & 4 Alice Mason/Impact, 2 Women Material World/Impact, 3 International Mission Board, 5 Material World/Impact

Falashas
1 & 2 Mark Cator/Impact, 3 Jean Cowley/Church's Ministry Among Jewish People

Fiji
1 James Barlow/Impact, 2 & 3 Caroline Penn/Impact, 4 Bhim Singh

Garifuna
All Piers Cavendish/Impact

Gonds
All Stephen Pern/Hutchison Picture Library

Greece
3 & 4 Photodisc, 1, 2 & 6 James McKee, 5 Tim Dowley/Three's Company

Greenland
1 Liv Rognsvåg, 2–4 Eivind Rognsvåg

Guinea-Bissau
1 L. Gaynor, 2–4 Trevor Page/Hutchison Picture Library

Gypsies
1 David Gallant/Impact, 2 & 4 John Cole/Impact, 6 Mark Cator/Impact, 3 & 5 Christian Outreach to Travellers Salisbury Diocese

Haiti
1, 3 & 4 Material World/Impact, 2 Christopher Pillitz/Impact

Hazara
All Andrew McGavin

Herero
1 & 4 Africa Inland Mission, 2 Paul Freestone/Impact, 3 Rhonda Klevansky/Impact

Hui
All Roy Spraggett

Iceland
1, 2 & 6 Piers Cavendish/Impact, 3 V. E. Bowern, 4 & 5 Heather Knight

India
1 Simon Shepheard/Impact, 2 & 6 Material World/Impact, 3 Daniel White/Impact, 4 & 5 Tim Dowley/Three's Company

Indonesia
All Pat Fore

Iraq
1, 2 & 4 Caroline Penn/Impact, 3 Impact

Israel
1 & 3 Roy Spraggett, 2, 4 & 5 Tim Dowley, Three's Company, 6 WEC Press

Japan
1–5 Photodisc, 6 Christophe Bluntzer/Impact

Jolas
All John Hamilton

Kal-Tamashaq
All L. Glover

Kazakhstan
1 & 2 Jin Rice/Impact, 3 Roy Spraggett, 4 Janet Wishnetsky/Impact, 5 Roy Spraggett

Kurds
All Roy Spraggett

Kyrgyz
All Roy Spraggett

Lesotho
1, 3 & 5 Marjorie Froise/Baptists Today, 2 Jorn Stjerneklar/Impact, 4 Steve Van t'Slot

Lobi
1, 2 & 4 Jo Parnell, 3 Crispin Hughes/Hutchison Picture Library

Madagascar
1 & 2 Michael Frith, 3 Alain le Garsmeur/Impact, 4 & 5 International Mission Board

Maldives
1 Frontiers, 2–5 Dominic Sansoni/Impact

Mandinka
All Hildegard Damm

Minangkabau
All Pat Store

Missionary Kids
All Jean Barnicoat

Mongolia
All Roy Spraggett

Navajo
1 Heather Knight, 2 & 4 AmeriTribes, 3 & 7 Robin Laurance/Impact, 5 & 6 Sheila Fairmaner

New Zealand
1 David Slimings/Impact, 2 & 6 Simon Grosset/Impact, 3 & 5 S. Fairmaner, 4 Mike McQueen, 7 Louvet/Visa/Cedri/Impact

Newars
1, 5, 6 & 7 Roy Spraggett, 2 & 3 V. E. Bowern, 4 Photodisc

North Korea
All A. Bradshaw/Visions/Impact

Oman
1 J. Rowe, 2 & 4 Alan Keohane/Impact, 3 Robin Laurance/Impact, 5 John Shelley/Impact

Papua New Guinea
1 & 5 Caroline Penn/Impact, 2 Liz Thompson/Impact, 3 Lynn Wood, 4 Grace Fabian

Pygmies
All Brian Woodford

Qatar
1–3 Hutchison Picture Library, 4 Bernard Gerard/Hutchison Picture Library

Quechua
1–3 & 5 A. Donnelly, 4 Charles Coates/Impact

Refugees
1 K. Diagne/UNHCR, 2 R. Chalasani/UNHCR, 3 H. Timmermans/UNHCR, 4 M. Kobayashi/UNHCR

Republic of Guinea
1–3 A. de Bruin, 4 H. Bohl

Riffi Berbers
All Mike Creswell

Romania
1 John Cole/Impact, 2–5 Janet Wishnetsky/Impact

Russia
1 Roy Spraggett, 2 Uba Taylor/Hutchison Picture Library, 3, 4 & 5 Heather Knight

Samoa
All WEC Press

San
1 Marjorie Froise/Baptists Today, 2, 3 & 5 David Reed/Impact, 4 V. E. Bowern

Saudi Arabia
1 & 3 Robin Laurance/Impact, 2 Gail McGowan

Spain
1 Tim Dowley/Three's Company, 2 Antonio Gig Binder/Impact, 3 & 4 Peter Stephenson, 5 Roy Spraggett

Sri Lanka
All Roy Spraggett

Sundanese
All Roy Spraggett

Syria
All Alan Keohane/Impact

Tibetans
1 Ian Collinge, 2–6 Roy Spraggett

Trinidad
1 Christophe Bluntzer/Impact, 2 & 4 Mitch de Faria/Impact, 3 & 5 T. Fung

Turkey
1 Roy Spraggett, 2–6 International Mission Board

United Arab Emirates
All Stella Morfey

Uruguay
1 & 2 Robert Gibbs/Impact, 3 & 4 Nick Haslam/Hutchison Picture Library

Uzbeks
All Roy Spraggett

Vagla
All Terry Lobb

Venezuela
1, 3 & 5 Martin Josten, 2 Panayiotis Sofroniou/Impact, 4 Peter Sofroniou/Impact

Vietnam
All Roy Spraggett

Wodaabe
1 Hutchison Picture Library, 2 & 4 Leslie Woodhead/Hutchison Picture Library, 3 Vision Africa

Xhosa
1, 2 & 4 Marjorie Froise/Baptists Today, 3 Nancy Durrell McKenna/Hutchison Picture Library

Xinjiang
All Roy Spraggett

Yanomamo
All Símun í Túni

Yao-Mien
1 J. Hitchings/Impact, 2 Piers Cavendish/Impact, 3 & 4 Alain Evrard/Impact

Yemen
1 Michael Good/Impact, 2–6 Roy Spraggett

Zimbabwe
1 & 4 David Reed/Impact, 2 Roger Perry/Impact, 3 S. & D. Stearns

Zulus
1 & 4 Marjorie Froise/Baptists Today, 2 Rives/Visa/Cedri/Impact, 3 T. E. Clark/Hutchison Picture Library

World Religions

Animism
1 & 5 Photodisc, 2 Digital Vision, 3 Howard Sayers, 4 Símun í Túni

Buddhism
1–3 Photodisc, 4 Roy Spraggett, 5 N.M. Sture

Christianity
1–3 & 5 Photodisc, 4 Marjorie Froise/Baptists Today

Hinduism
1–3 & 5 Photodisc, 4, 6 & 7 Roy Spraggett

Islam
All Photodisc

Judaism
1, 2 , 4 & 5 Photodisc, 3 Tim Dowley/Three's Company

NB Every effort has been made to acknowledge sources accurately. If any inaccuracies have occurred please let us know.

Index

To keep things simple, this index gives just one page number for each two-page spread. For example, 'Afghanistan 12' really means you will find information on Afghanistan on pages 12 to 13.

The index includes names of organizations in the main part of the book, but for these you should also look in the list of addresses starting on page 213.